Narrative as Performance

Narrative as Performance

THE BAUDELAIREAN EXPERIMENT

Marie Maclean

ROUTLEDGE · London and New York

First published in 1988 by
Routledge
11 New Fetter Lane, London EC4P 4EE

Published in the USA by
Routledge
in association with Routledge, Chapman & Hall, Inc.
29 West 35th Street, New York NY 10001

Typeset by Keyset Composition, Colchester, Essex
Printed in Great Britain by Richard Clay Ltd, Bungay, Suffolk

BRITISH LIBRARY CATALOGUING IN PUBLICATION DATA
Maclean, Marie
    Narrative as performance: the Baudelairean experiment.
    1. Narration (Rhetoric)
    I. Title
    809'.923   PN212

ISBN 0 415 00663 5
     0 415 00664 3 Pbk

LIBRARY OF CONGRESS CATALOGING IN PUBLICATION DATA

Maclean, Marie.
    Narrative as performance.
    Bibliography: p.
    Includes index.
    1. Baudelaire, Charles, 1821–1867 – Technique.
2. Narration (Rhetoric) 3. Reader-response criticism.
4. Experimental poetry – History and criticism.
I. Title.
PQ2191.Z5M216   1988   841'.8   87-28214

ISBN 0 415 00663 5
     0 415 00664 3 (pbk.)

For Hector, who cares

Contents

Acknowledgements

My thanks are due to colleagues, friends, and family for their help in the preparation of this book. I owe an especial debt of gratitude to Ross Chambers, who first encouraged my specialization, both in Baudelairean studies and in the field of narrative, and who has been unfailingly generous with both enthusiasm and constructive advice. His scholarship is equalled only by his willingness to help others. Another patient reader and percipient critic has been Ian Reid; indeed I must thank not only him but the whole narrative research group which he leads at Deakin University. My husband has been a constant source of feedback and untiring in both scholarly and emotional support. His interest in performance has been an invaluable stimulant to my own work.

Colleagues and students at Monash University have provided comment, friendship, and advice. Particularly I should thank Wallace Kirsop, not only for his help in questions of bibliography and index but also for his permission, as editor of *Australian Journal of French Studies*, to reprint part of Chapter 4. Rosemary Sorensen has provided research assistance well beyond the call of duty, and I cannot praise Marie-Rose Auguste enough for her patience in processing and typing the manuscript. I should have been lost without her expertise and friendship, as well as those of Gail Ward and Ginette Rivalland. Monash University has provided practical support in the form of a research grant, and a period of study leave in which to complete the work.

Finally, I should like to record my appreciation for the friendly and knowledgeable encouragement I have received from Janice Price of Methuen.

Monash University, Melbourne

Foreword

This study has arisen out of a long experience of using narrative poetics in the practical work of analysis and interpretation. Starting with a structuralist perspective, I learnt to appreciate the formal aspects of narratology, as I used the approaches of the 1960s and 1970s to develop my own perceptions and those of my students. Dissatisfied at length with an analysis centred on the text as object, I realized that narrative could not be satisfactorily explored except as the site of an interaction, just as a body or a mind can only be fully appreciated when seen in interplay with those of another. Deconstruction has helped us to appreciate the shifting, changing play of meaning in the ever quoting, ever quotable, ultimately ungraspable web of language. But something more is needed in the study of textual dynamics.

The context of performance seemed to provide the best clue to the play of forces involved. Performance at its most general and most basic level is a carrying out, a putting into action or into shape. Both movement and interaction are involved. Even the physical performance of, say, clockwork connotes two things beyond the putting into action of the machinery; the first is variability, since the notion of performance implies grading against previous form, and the second is judgement, since someone is needed to provide appreciation. Performance always implies submitting to the gaze and measurement of others.

Whether it is of a mechanical, linguistic, or sexual nature, performance is not subjected to the criterion of truth or falsehood, but judged on success or failure. Its standards are those of desire or lack rather than of fact. Thus, for a performance to be successful, it is not enough for it to have purpose; it must have energy and effect. Where linguistic performance, for instance, differs from competence is that meaning and grammaticality are in themselves not enough; also needed are the choices and combinations required to produce personal interaction. Linguistic performance implies an active and variable relationship between sender and receiver, as well as between the collective social and cultural forces controlling the language and the individuals putting it into practice. The same is true of sexual permance which involves the erotic assumptions of our society as much ѕ our own sexual competence, but which always relies on a personal interplay assuming both variability in the performance itself and in the mutual judgement of the participants.

Thus, where performance differs from action or structure is that every performance is unique. Every performance is subject to variation. Not only can the performers vary, as can the participants in the interaction, but also the context in which it is set and the different expectations and capacities influencing the production and the reception. Because of this quality of uniqueness, because too its only measurement is the satisfaction it gives, a study of performance provides a way of approaching the basically dialogic nature of narrative.

The narrative performance, even at its most minimal as in the recounting of short events in everyday life, always involves interaction between teller and hearer. Like the dramatic performance, narrative always exceeds the elements which compose it. We can measure the component signs but, no matter how exhaustive our semiotics, a performance will always be more than its parts. Just as a mechanical or linguistic performance needs purpose, energy, and effect beyond the basic signs or parts involved, the narrative must include not only the tale itself but the factors of teller, 'tellability', and audience response. It is clear, I hope, that just as narrative is not merely prose fiction, but a much more basic form of human verbal behaviour, so performance is not merely theatrical but extends into many different spheres of action.

Through a narrative text *I* meet *you* in a struggle which may be co-operative or may be combative, a struggle for knowledge, for power, for pleasure, for possession. The meeting is manifest in the course of the narrative performance in which the performer, whether human or textual, undertakes to control the audience by words or signs alone, while they, the partners in the act, use their power as hearers to dictate the terms of the control. If you tell me a story, I can refuse to listen, but if I become a listener, even a forced listener, I can also always remind you that words, in the last resort, can only mean what my mind allows them to mean. I, too, am constantly performing. The many facets of this interplay of 'I' and 'you', whether they assume the role of teller or of reader, are the subject of this study. They can vary from the supposedly predictable reactions of the unlettered to that 'battle of hypnotists in a closed room' (Sartre) which is the pleasure of the intellectual.

Narrative performance thus involves an intimate relationship which, like all such relationships, is at once a co-operation and a contest, an exercise in harmony and a mutual display of power. It is both 'act' and interaction, and implies a contract, a recognition of obligation and expectation, thus acknowledging the rules which govern the interplay. The two parties to the agreement, the narrative performers and the narrative audience, must be seen in their relationship to the text and to each other. Any performance also necessitates a very special attention to space, which both defines and shapes it, and which provides an arena both of display and of judgement.

This study will examine in detail all these aspects of narrative performance. The choice has been made to follow the examples of Barthes on Balzac and Marin on La Fontaine, and to use a small, unified, and available corpus of texts by one author as demonstration pieces. The experimental narratives of Baudelaire, highly worked and reduced to an elegant minimum by that self-conscious performer and master of the private stage, have been used to display my theories in performance. The book closes with Baudelaire's own acerbic comment on the relationship between theory and performance, that necessary and sometimes painful application of our critical enterprises.

1 · *The dynamics of narrative*

Telling as performance: oral narrative

We all know what we mean by a well-told tale, distinguishing automatically between the tale and the telling. What is implicit in this distinction is that telling involves a performance. A traditional performance relies on an agreed relationship of the seer and the seen, of the hearer and the heard, a relationship both of inclusion and of exclusion. The teller includes certain hearers within the space of the telling, admits them to a position of privilege or duty from which others, for a variety of reasons, are excluded. However, this admission to a space is not one-sided: the teller also enters a privileged space which we may call the arena of play (Caillois 1962) or at least the arena of reception. The teller is governed by the rules of his or her own territory, but audiences are equally governed by the rules of theirs, rules which may of course change drastically according to context. The situation of tellers may vary from territorial liberty, as when a mat laid on a street corner creates an instant telling place, to territorial restriction, as when a tale may be told only in a temple sanctuary. In the same way, audiences may vary in their reactions between such extremes as physical and verbal abuse of the teller on the one hand and submission to actual indignity on the other, such as the demand that they be naked or covered in ashes; and each will depend on the received view of particular performances and the local conditions and context of telling.

A long study of narrative has convinced me, as it has already convinced so many distinguished theorists of the genre (Propp, Todorov, Brémond, Prince, Greimas), that the basic problems of narrative can, in the first instance, be better understood in relation to oral narration. However, my focus is different from theirs. This study will put the major emphasis on the teller–hearer nexus inherent in all narrative. For this reason, telling in relation to the audience will be privileged rather than telling in relation to the tale. The latter has already been extensively studied, with particular clarity in the work of *nour* Chatman (1978). However, traditional models, both those of narratives themselves and the models of critical approaches, have not accounted sufficiently for the fact that enactment demands interaction, that a tale is altered in *each* telling. The variables introduced by the context of each particular hearer, interacting with both the context of the teller and that of the telling, are in shifting interplay with the repeated factors of the text (Smith 1978). Oral telling, for instance, involves a stock of motifs (Thompson 1955–8), formulas, and rhetorical traditions which are drawn upon to produce a performance text, to borrow a term from the theatre.[1] The textual stability, such as it is, is provided as much by the demands of the audience as by the memory of the teller.

NARRATIVE ENERGY

The energy involved *in* performance, the energies unleashed *by* performance can perhaps best be appreciated at the most fundamental level in oral narrative. Later in this study we will endeavour to map the transformations as the *énonciation* (the textual utterance of the speaking subject) shifts into the more sophisticated written mode. Whether spoken or written, performance involves energy, and energy is neither husbanded nor spent without consequences.

Narrative, like communication, involves negentropy, a marshalling of the resources of language against the seemingly random dispersion of our experience. Telling, because of its negentropic force, is one of the earliest creative formal skills we acquire. Two-year-olds alone in bed have been recorded constructing and relating narratives which already contain the three basics of critical situation, complication, and resolution (Crago 1981).[2] Acting as audience for one's own performance is as crucial as the mirror stage in the process of recognition of the self as other. But the negentropic energy of telling is matched by that of reception. The earliest form of reception is energy channelled into the demand that stories should conform to an exact formula. This is not the passivity of reception of which such audiences are often accused, but is an active refusal of waste, of dispersion, a demonstration of the forces of conservation against the 'heat-death' of the narrative.

The situation in another context is reversed. A performer may be encouraged to break the rules of society, of decorum, of the narrative, in an outpouring of anarchic energy matched by that of the hearers (Bakhtin 1968). Here the transgressive power of the performance cracks the rigid framework of ideologies and preconceptions to allow a release of energy which can then be channelled negentropically in renewed creativity, as is shown in Harold Scheub's 'Oral narrative process and the use of models' (1975).

So the teller must constantly balance redundancy, or the many varied forms of repetition of the message, against entropy, or the danger that the new may be dispersed as random before it can be recognized. The aggregative and conservative form of the oral tale is seen as a defence against anarchy. A balance between the pull of the old and the shock of the new must be maintained, and this balance partly results from feedback as the teller adjusts the tale according to the response of the audience. Thus, the teller is as much in the control of the hearer as the hearer is in that of the teller (Labov 1972; Eco 1979). The teller must also find a delicate balance between providing not enough information and providing too much. There must always be 'gaps' or 'blanks' in the narrative sequence which trigger the hearers' imagination and the structuring power of their minds. These conditions apply in traditional as well as in written narrative. An excellent study of the energetic forces of the traditional narrative is Walter Ong's 'Some psychodynamics of orality' (1982: 31–77).

Just as the traditional conditions of narrative display redundancy (I must repeat myself so that you get the message, but not in such a way that you switch off); entropy (although my use of the seemingly random is in fact governed by the ordering capacity of my listeners); and feedback (there is nothing with such constructive immediacy or which concentrates the mind so well as an accurately thrown ripe tomato); so too, and perhaps most importantly, these conditions display what is meant by 'noise'. Noise in this sense is an amalgam of all the factors interfering with communication (Fiske 1982). We tend to think of these factors as mechanical: actual noise, bad printing, radio interference. We forget that most 'noise' which disturbs communication is actually in the minds of the hearers/receivers and includes such factors as their ignorance, incompetence, or unwillingness as well as, for example, their physical discomfort. When I was lecturing about communication I was told: 'The noise which is interfering with your message is the fact that I am thinking about *Star Wars*.' In the teller–hearer relationship, therefore, just as redundancy is possibly the teller's most useful tool, so 'noise', the hearer's emotional, ideological, physical, linguistic tendency towards non-co-operation, seems at first the greatest enemy. Yet at the same time it can be an invaluable stimulus, constantly setting the challenge of winning the battle for control. The best study of this phenomenon is Michel Serres's *The Parasite* (1982). Serres insists that noise, the interferer in the channel, the 'grit in the oyster' as he calls it, is an invaluable creative force.[3] Thus in performance, the dual input of performers and audience is always necessary, even if the audience input assumes a seemingly negative and disruptive character (see Chapter 8).

Narrative energy, therefore, like all energy, works in a delicate balance. Semantic, syntactic, and phonetic redundancy works together with audience feedback to ensure stability, to preserve the basic fabric of the text from the forces of randomness, of loss of energy, of dispersion. But the very factors of preservation, of reproduction and of negentropy can become conservatism and eventually stasis. The disruptive input of anarchy, of violence, of noise, stimulates the mutation and the new growth of narrative forms and their evolution within the wider interplay of social forces.

CHOICE AND RESTRICTION OF AUDIENCE

Another performance factor seen in its clearest form in traditional societies, linked with and yet distinct from that of feedback, is related to the changes in telling which are provoked by social factors such as the selection and limitation of the audience. New paradigmatic choices in both form and expression are necessary in the light of changing circumstance. While everyone knows that Vladimir Propp studied the syntagmatic chain of the narrative and its performance, very few realize how much study he devoted to paradigmatic transformations in the light of changed audience context (1972).

Restriction works just as effectively as change of circumstance. In some cases it is the audience which is restricted, certain sacred tales being told only to the old high-ranking males of the society, certain initiation stories only to boys at puberty. In other cases, stories may be told to an unrestricted audience but only by a teller whose family 'owns' the rights to the tale. Again, certain stories may be unrestricted as to tellers and audience, but limited geographically (to be told in aetiological relation to a certain natural feature), synchronically (to be told at harvest time or at the winter solstice), or historically (to be told when a victory is gained in battle) (Finnegan 1977; Maranda 1972). These conditions of context regarding the teller, the tale, and the hearer have been translated in the case of written cultures into more subtle variations of utterance and reception, variations of code and discourse, variations of ideology and fashion. All performances, as I have said, are context-dependent, and the seeming independence and 'subject identity' of the modern writer mask the fact that he or she is just as moulded by social forces and just as dependent on audience vagaries as any anonymous oral teller with mat and collection bowl.

One of the most undervalued features of narrative – apropos of this question of restricted codes and restricted audiences – has been the exploitation of identity and difference in the matter of gender. In many narrative situations, such as all-female work gatherings or gossip sessions, lying in childbirth, or laying out the dead, men have been the excluded audience. In many more narrative situations women have been the excluded audience; work, war, hunting, drinking, and religion have traditionally been segregated activities. So how does like talk to like? How does one gender parody the narratives of the other? How can one gender appropriate or deterritorialize (Certeau 1980; Deleuze and Guattari 1975) the discourse of the other? Then one must also ask how tellers, male or female, react to the gender of the audience.

To take one example of possible reactions: a quick sketch of the story of the 'Pregnant man'. There are hundreds of versions of it, and it dates back to the ninth century.

A village priest, a petty tyrant, preaches morality to his flock. One day his overburdened servants play a trick on him. They stick a cockroach up his arse when he's asleep, and it starts to move around. The priest wakes up and thinks he's pregnant. Terrified, he decides he's got to have an abortion. Then he has to go to the women of the parish (and he's been giving them hell about their sex lives in confession) to get the right mixture to do the job. Finally he succeeds in aborting the cockroach, a worthy son of a worthy father.

The performance of this tale will obviously vary tremendously according to the gender of teller and hearers. A woman telling it to women might stress the humiliation of the strong before the weak, the inversion of the patriarchal relationship. A woman telling it to a mixed audience might perhaps emphasize the rights of sexuality. A man to a mixed audience could use it to evoke laughter at the expense of authority. A man to a male audience could indulge in black humour at the degrading aspects of pregnancy. Each time the telling will vary according to the relationships, the needs, the reactions, and the gender of teller and audience (Maclean 1987; cf. Lanser 1981: 61).

Another possibility is that a telling will vary if a member of the excluded audience is known to be listening. How will a woman's tale be told if a man is known to be snooping at the window: with what knowing glances, what *sous-entendus*, what half-hidden ironies? We need more study of the markers which enable us to use a restricted code ironically. Another dimension to narrative may be perceived if one tries to imagine the terms in which the excluded but successful eavesdropper will retell the story to his masculine cronies. And so we find ourselves on the shifting ground of quotation and requotation, of the code twice used, the tale twice told (Bakhtin 1973; Booth 1974).

Oral narrative studies have laid great emphasis on the value of narrative in reinforcing community structures, on the almost hypnotic reactions of audiences with strong empathetic links. I recently witnessed this in the reading of a story by a popular author to a hall full of SF fans, and there are of course far more frightening manifestations by the ideologically or religiously committed. But another dimension of the teller–hearer relationship is almost totally occluded in discussions of narrative, and yet it obviously occurs among the unlettered as among the lettered; it is as follows: what is the attitude of the hearer to the teller, what is the feedback if the hearing has been enforced? After all, a great many of the narratives we hear, if not the majority, we hear in spite of ourselves, because custom, religion, our education, our sense of self-preservation demand it.

Hearers are often seen as having the whip-hand in the narrative relationship because they can terminate it, but not all narratives are told over a collecting-bowl, or even over a cup of tea. Many narrators, such as the tellers of educational stories, exercise not only narrative authority, but actual authority. Many hearers (*pace* William Labov) are not in a position to say 'So what?' (1972: 366). They have to go on listening. They have to accept the communication. One of the most interesting facets of narrative reception, and one I intend to explore, is what takes place in an enforced reader relationship. Is the communication, and the authority which mediates and ideologically enforces it, accepted, or does it produce repression? If, as so frequently happens, it produces repression, or indeed resistance, we must then ask ourselves in what form it will return either to haunt the receivers, or, in the second case, to revenge itself in satirical vein and pay back the original tellers. The retelling of colonial stories by the colonized is a case in point.

In white Australian folklore, for instance, Captain Cook figures as the wise humane founder of the colony and Ned Kelly as the 'wild colonial boy', the doomed but gallant outlaw. Aboriginal stories have been collected which completely reverse these roles, seeing Captain Cook as the figure of evil, the negative father figure, while Ned Kelly becomes the trickster-helper figure, even, in one very strange version, saving the sheep which Captain Cook is endeavouring to steal away.

THE MULTIPLE VOICES OF THE TELLING AND ITS MULTIPLE RECEPTION

While many stories in traditional societies are not only sanctioned but enforced by the rules and conventions of the culture, it must be remembered that the most lasting authority is that of the performance itself. Performance generally works on a base of shared expectations, whereby power is granted to others, to the hearers as well as the teller in this case, in the expectation of certain results. Oral performance is not just an act *of* saying something, it is produced by all the different acts involved *in* saying something.[4] *What* is said is less important than the *saying*, an interaction which, as we have seen, involves purpose, energy, and effect as well as the 'message' conveyed.

The narrative flexibility of the traditional teller can be most clearly seen in the relationship of the speaking subject (the *sujet de l'énonciation*), the saying, to that of the spoken subject (the *sujet de l'énoncé*), what is said (Benveniste 1971, 1974).[5] One must remember that through the speaking subject is heard not just the voice of the teller but the voices of language,[6] of narrative tradition, of ideology, of the whole social context. In the spoken subject we have the whole range of voices of the tale itself and its various actors. Different voices speak in what is said, sometimes in the form of dialogue, sometimes in the form of quotation in, for example, the formulaic utterances of oral narrative (Bakhtin 1981: 50).

Unlike the writer, restricted by choice of voice and of person in the narrator, the teller/performer can truly be a microcosm of the creating divinity, in his or her work of 'subcreation' as Tolkien calls it. She (let us call her she in tribute to woman's role as teller of oral tales) has the privilege of speaking *at the same time* in the omniscient voice of the authoritative narrator through which the text imposes itself, and *also* in her own physical voice and body, the I present and performing the text, an I whose context and territory include the text itself and the licence to perform it. This double narrative voice, both intimate and imposing, splits in turn into the multiple voices of the 'dramatis personae',[7] as Propp aptly called the narrative performers, later to be christened *actants* by Greimas (Propp 1968; Greimas 1983). So tellers are at once external to the tale and internal to it. If one likens a telling to the model of Greek drama, as I will do later, the teller can be in turn leader of the chorus, chorus, protagonist, and antagonist. In this way we see a concrete demonstration of the text at once speaking through the performing I and being spoken through the actantial voices, at once *énonciation* and *énoncé*.

Linked with the multiple voices of the telling is a multiplication of the focuses of reception in the audience. Only the very young and the very naïve judge the tale purely as tale, receive it purely as *énoncé*. Most of the audience are receiving the message as tale, while also receiving and judging the variations in style, in voice, in rhetorical *savoir-faire*, provided by the performance. The performance, in other words, functions as metatext to the hearers, and the audience's attention moves, in a form of dialogue, between the tale and the telling. Their judgement is an active one, constantly providing feedback on the demands of variability versus invariability, on the delights of surprise as opposed to the pleasures of the formulaic. As with all performances, the audience's expectations of outcome may be fulfilled or unfulfilled (Brémond 1973), to their approbation or chagrin. As Propp has shown, every function in the traditional tale may be negative, contradictory, or positive, so the sequences are both fixed and infinitely flexible (1968: 92–117).

What must be remembered, however, is that the very restrictions of code and context in oral narrative prompt a critical reception which is focused more on the performance as a total dramatic text than on the tale which is the pretext of the performance. Already at this level there exists within the same people what Peter Rabinowitz (1980) would call an authorial audience (and I would rather call the audience of the *énonciation*) as well as a narrative audience (which I would rather call the audience of the *énoncé*) (see Chapter 4).

Drama and narrative: relation and reflection

Oral narrative may be seen as the begetter of both written narrative and staged drama, although it remained of course a living form co-existing with its progeny. I take written narrative and drama both to be forms of *narrative* performance and hence distinguish drama from other forms of theatrical performance without a narrative component (although it is very hard to find one, since an abstract dance sequence, for example, often has an implicit narrative structure, just as a lyric poem does). The roots of drama in ritual and the relationship of both to myth must be assumed as a background too vast to be discussed here. Oral narrative as an active performance was constrained both by the memory capacity of the teller and the attention span of the hearers. It developed in response to the demands of a verbomotor life style which valued interaction rather than information: a society in which 'the sounded word was power' (Ong 1982: 31–77; see also Goody and Watt 1968: 27–68).

With the advent of the written word, narrative became increasingly separate from the immediate concerns of the life-world and could develop in new ways, progressing from the written manuscript, which was performed by being read aloud and hence still provided a shared experience, to the eventual use of the printed book as a form of solitary individual enjoyment. As Walter Ong tellingly puts it, 'Sight isolates,

sound incorporates' (1982: 72). With the advent of writing, narrati
performance was able gradually to divide into a genre which depends
on sight alone (on the power of reading symbolic signs) and a genre
which maintains its dependence on sound (although within a visual
framework).

> Outside drama, in narrative as such, the original voice of the oral
> narrator took on various new forms when it became the silent voice
> of the writer, as the distancing effected by writing invited various
> fictionalizations of the decontextualized reader and writer (Ong,
> 1977, pp. 53–81).

(Ong 1982: 148)

Writing enabled narrative to emancipate itself from the limitations of
spatial presentation and from the time limits oral performance placed
on absorption. Bakhtin (1981) explores the effects of this generic
emancipation on the development of the novel. Drama gradually,
however, freed itself of the narrative voice, as 'the narrator buried
himself completely in the text, disappeared beneath the voices of his
characters' (Ong 1982: 148).

Drama opted to follow the empathetic participatory direction of oral
narrative. Its continuation of the traditional audience involvement
and of role differentiation by means of physical performance meant
retaining the emphasis on the situational aspects of narrative. It relied
on the unifying sense of sound and on immediate aural and visual
contact between performers and audience and between members of the
audience among themselves. Indeed, all the senses are involved in this
experience. Drama in performance also uses audience power directly.
In a drama space, audience feedback has a direct impact on actual
performance, which becomes a whole living thing, using the reciprocal
energy of both speakers and hearers.

In written narrative, signs become both more specialized and more
controllable. Time, for instance, when reduced to textual space, can be
infinitely manipulated both by author and by reader. A book is totally
in the reader's power – it can be opened at any page, one may read the
end before the beginning – but this power of flexibility may also extend
to the text, forcing or persuading the reader to accept chronological
mayhem. More importantly, a book has by its nature to be a succession
of signs which the audience can influence and incorporate only retro-
spectively. Feedback in written texts means in essence *re*reading. The
reader can only experience *après coup* the synchronism or syncretism of
a written text, whereas the theatre audience experiences simultaneity
with multiple signs functioning together, just as verbal redundancy can
be translated into multi-sensory messages.

THE *ÉNONCIATION* OF THE WRITTEN TEXT AND THE DRAMATIC TEXT

Most vital is the radical change which occurs in the relationship between the *énonciation*, the telling or saying of the text by the speaking subject, and the *énoncé*, what is told, the spoken elements of the tale, when the performance elements of oral telling are transformed into a series of choices about the conditions of written utterance. In written texts, a radical change of signifiers occurs as the motivated signs of the oral *énonciation*, intonation, gesture, phrasing, phonetic redundancy, facial and bodily expression, are turned perforce into the arbitrary signs of the 'stable' text.

This becomes even more marked when the written text becomes printed, and public reading becomes private reading. The printed text is a representation of the act of telling itself, and so the actual narration becomes part of the fictional world. The teller is embodied in the narrator, whether implicit or explicit, and the original live audience is embodied in the narratees present in the text and the narrative audience, a fictional construct. The narrator may relate his or her own fictional world or may produce yet another possible world in the course of the narration. The printed text is a fabrication which only becomes itself an act when read, that is when interacting with an actual audience.

In printed fiction, the text relates directly to its reader, so that each reading produces a type of individual performance in which text and reader co-operate (Smith 1978: 5–7). Here the text must, as it were, perform, which is the function of the *énonciation*, and be performed, which is the result of reading. The increasing development of self-reflexivity in the written text may be seen as supplying performance direction in which the *énonciation* adds to its functions those of *metteur-en-scène*.

The written dramatic text, on the other hand, should go through a double process of *énonciation* and an equivalent complication of the *énoncé*. A dramatic text, the written text itself, is reduced to a state of almost pure *énoncé*, an *énoncé* looking for its *énonciation*, with the latter suggested merely by such factors as context, symbolism, and irony (stage directions barely count as they are not binding on theatrical interpretation). Thus the isolated reading of a script demands in effect that the reader produce a private performance, but without the nar-ratorial framework which is there to provide guidance in the case of printed fiction. The omission of the second stage, the performance text, results in an incomplete understanding of the script as play. What should occur is that the original written script be read and interpreted by director and actors, together with their supporting team, and, from this initial reading performance, a second text, the performance text, is elaborated (Elam 1980: 44–9). This new *énonciation* is the combined creation of the original script, the director, the actors, and the space available for the second, public performance. Thus the *énonciation* has multiple performers, is multi-sensory, and combines the verbal and the physical, as well as motivated signs and arbitrary signs. The final *énoncé*, the words and signs actually exchanged on stage, is also a composite of the original textual *énoncé* and the additions of the performance text.[8] The *énonciation* and the *énoncé* are so closely interrelated that they are really only distinguishable in terms of speech-act theory (see Chapter 4). The audience receives the two as a whole, contributes to the performance by feedback, and finally interprets the complete event in the light of such traditions as genre, and such social contexts as fashion and ideology.

In both cases, in the written narrative text and in the multiple text of the theatre, the audience forms an essential creative part of the performance, but, as we have seen, in very different ways. Nevertheless, since the original roots of both forms are in the same tradition, that of oral narrative performance, the resemblance between them remains very great, and the homology which it is possible to establish between them is a very powerful tool in the investigation of the functioning of narrative in general and more particularly of written prose fiction (cf. Hamburger 1973: 194–218).

DRAMATIC MODELS IN NARRATIVE: THE PRIVATE STAGE

To some extent all written narratives are, to use Musset's term, 'a theatre in an armchair'. Dramatic models, and indeed theatrical models, are constantly used within written narrative. We are seldom allowed to forget the intimate relationship which exists between narrative and drama. Such models are self-referential in so far as they are a way of portraying within the text the homology between related genres and the fact that one can reflect the other.

The first model, which stresses the dynamics of performance and the syntagmatic chain of the narrative, is quite simply the use of dialogue. With dialogue there is a radical change in the sequence of exposition, a mobilization of continuity in space and time. The immense variability of narrative time changes to the artificial chronological stability of performance time, and this produces a different spatio-temporal orientation in the reader (Stanzel 1984: 64–5). While the dialogue continues, relationships in space are concentrated into those between the actors (or, indeed, between the *actants*: after all, a man may talk to a tree), the territories marked out by their movements, voices, and discourse. Some texts, as we will see, are all dialogue, not just the first-person monologue of narrator to narratee that we find in many novels, but an I–you relationship at the level of the *énoncé*, of the *spoken* subjects who now speak in their turn. Here, as in drama, the narrating instance is completely hidden behind its textual creations (Chapter 4 looks closely at this phenomenon). In other words, dialogue must be seen as an ongoing performance within a performance. This is particularly clearly marked as self-reflexive when one of the actors tells another a story. In this way, a microcosm of the narrative performance is produced within the dialogue itself. Such effects are analysed by Ross Chambers in *Story and Situation* (1984).

Whereas the dialogue model is linked to effects of *sequence* and helps to carry the action along, the second model is linked to effects of *embedding* (Todorov 1977). Embedding can itself of course include sequences, so let us look first at the relatively static: the narrative importance of tableau scenes.

This device, eminently theatrical, stresses the iconic value of the portrayal of selected moments (Elam 1980). The framed spectacle has a particular iconic and deictic function. It serves not only the obvious purposes of enhancement and illustration, but by acting as the frozen moment *within* the sequence it functions as microcosm to the macrocosm of the text. Its particular relation to performance, that of a framed spectacle, is itself a model of a relationship of inclusion/exclusion, which defines both what it includes and what it excludes. That is why a particular form of private stage and of tableau, much used in narrative, is the view through a lighted window. On this internalized stage we see *en abyme* not just the actors within the frame but the spectator as voyeur. The inverse can also apply where the spectator looks through the frame of the window, her gaze leaving the scene of intimacy to look out on the (safely) enclosed spectacle of the world beyond. So the internalized spectacle leads to a new appraisal of narrative itself as spectacle, with the *énonciation* providing the *mise-en-scène*.

Perhaps the most striking example of the mirroring effects whereby written narrative and drama reflect one another occurs when what we find embedded in the narrative is not just a tableau moment but an entire performance. The variety is endless. In *Don Quixote* alone, for example, we find theatrical performances, narrative competitions, wedding rituals, and fairground mumming, enacted personal histories, and epic poetry. Each embedded performance has its self-reflexive elements, each tells us something of the nature of narrative, each helps to produce the text, *our Don Quixote*.

Of all the different performance models to be found in narrative, the theatrical or dramatic model is perhaps the most striking. As I have tried to indicate and will show in exact concrete example, the theatrical model highlights the complementarity of written narrative and drama and their common roots in oral performance. In such a model we are shown the play within the play, while we as audience find ourselves reflected in another audience. Major novels of all periods have used embedded dramatic models over the centuries, from *The Golden Ass* to *David Copperfield*, or across Europe from *Mansfield Park* to *Madame Bovary*, to *Wilhelm Meister*, to *Anna Karenina*. Bakhtin (1981) discusses this 'chronotope of the theater' as part of the multi-layeredness of the novel. A parallel phenomenon in drama is the use of embedded narratives, of which the most studied has been the classical messenger scene. Even more revelatory of an awareness of a link between the two genres is the dramatic use of an actual narrator figure. The varied use made of the stage narrator runs all the way from the Greek leader of the chorus through Shakespearean narrators, such as those of the romances, to the singers and commentators of Brecht, or the reporter figure of Thornton Wilder (cf. Farcy 1986). These narrators may be single or multiple, either part of, or divorced from, the action of the play.[9] Each type of the embedded model, that of drama in narrative or that of narrative in drama, reflects the homology between the two forms of narrative performance.

Performance models and narrative theory

The ways in which the written text has converted telling into fixed forms of narrative, and the teller into the narrating instance, have been extensively studied. There is no intention here to undertake a review of the immense critical literature of narratology. The reader is referred instead to Shlomith Rimmon-Kenan's excellent survey of the field, *Narrative Fiction: Contemporary Poetics* (1983). A terminological problem which reflects a major critical difficulty should, however, be mentioned. This is the shifting nature of the word 'narrative' itself in critical literature. The word is used most often to imply fictional prose narrative, just as *le récit* tends to be used almost exclusively by French critics. And yet the basic model of narrative, an event, sometimes a very minimal event, related in the form of a tale, belongs not to literature but to everyday life. The Russian studies of *skaz*, or vernacular extra-literary narration (Eichenbaum 1978; Bakhtin 1973, 1981), and William Labov's epoch-making *Language in the Inner City* (1972) have provided a valuable corrective to the exclusively literary views on narration. Narrative is an essential principle of verbal organization, important not only for its communicative value as performance, but also as an essential factor in the development of memory and a vital ingredient in the successful communication of ideas and in the learning process. The study of narrative models in history, philosophy, and even science is yielding remarkable and sometimes controversial results (Norris 1985).

The preceding discussion of narrative performance has already revealed the deficiencies in critical terminology, even without moving into other disciplines. Oral narrative, for instance, includes both the unskilled everyday tale or *skaz*, and the narrative in traditional society, most often performed by a skilled or semi-skilled performer, such as anecdotes or *Sagen*, wonder-tales or *Märchen*, myths or epics (Dundes 1965). When discussing written narrative, further critical problems attend the initial division into: (a) narrative performed by several role-players, which becomes drama, and in which the narrator figure tends to disappear behind the characters; and (b) narrative destined to be performed by one teller in the form of reading aloud or singing. As this latter form becomes internalized, and printing permits the spread of private reading, the narrator-teller is either subsumed into the *énonciation* or absorbed into the tale in various ways. Further sub-headings can then divide written narrative into fiction and non-fiction and into verse and prose – all this without even poking the hornets' nest of narrative genre and sub-genre. My own examples, like those of my predecessors, are mostly taken from prose fiction, but I use 'narrative' in the wider sense of the term (cf. Greimas 1970). However, the three complementary waves of narrative poetics have been almost exclusively concerned with the literary narrative.

These waves may be roughly divided into those concerned with narrative *structure*, those concerned with narrative *authority*, and those concerned with narrative *interaction*. No clear-cut distinction is possible between these areas, but one can distinguish the 'objective' descriptions of the tale and its telling, which belong to the first, from the emphasis on textual strategy and the relation between the teller and the telling characteristic of the second, whereas the third shifts the emphasis to the relationship between teller and hearer or between *énonciation* and interpretation. My interest is rather in showing how different aspects of narrative are revealed by the use of different performance models. Shoshana Felman, in *The Literary Speech Act* (1983: 29), suggests that performance in literature occurs in three connotative categories, the erotic, the theatrical, and the linguistic. To these I would add at least two more, the physical or energetic, and the ludic, in the sense that a game is a struggle for power.

Studies of narrative structure have had a strong relationship with the theatrical model, perhaps because this enterprise is so firmly grounded in the study of oral narrative. Studies of narrative authority on the other hand are closer to the ludic model, with the text seen as a strategic battleground between narrator and narratee, and self-reflexivity the main weapon in making sure the rules of the textual game are observed. The text is here seen as a trap or else as a game of snakes and ladders in which the inscribed reader moves constantly backwards in order to move forwards, responding to the dictates of the board. The erotic model, the interplay between partners in the narrative act, with constant shifts in dominance and in the manipulation of desire, is most present in studies of narrative interaction. Interpretation here is seen as the ever-renewed and ever-deferred moment of satisfaction. I will briefly discuss these models before moving on to recent developments in the energetic and linguistic fields.

THE THEATRICAL MODEL: THE TALE AND THE TELLING

The theatrical model is perhaps the most used in narrative studies, sometimes consciously, sometimes unconsciously. This bears witness to the phenomenon I have just been discussing, the age-old relationship between drama and prose narrative whereby each is the *alter ego* of the other. The theatrical aspects of narrative recur in the very metalanguage of narratology. An explanation of this is suggested by Rainer Warning (1979). He claims that:

> the theatrical model can be considered as the situational constitution of the fictional discourse in general. On the one hand, we have an internal situation of enunciation with speaker(s) and receiver(s): on the other hand, an external situation of reception which is peculiar inasmuch as, contrary to the usual situation of enunciation, the receiver finds himself deprived of a relationship with a real speaker. This real speaker, the author, has disappeared within the fiction itself, he has been dispersed among the roles of the fictional characters including, in the narrative genres, the role of narrator.
>
> (cit. Pavis 1982)

In all the 'grammars', 'taxonomies', and 'morphologies' of narratology, the metalinguistic signs are those which represent pointing, showing, displaying, acting, speaking, framing, décor, and *mise-en-*

scène. The strength of the actantial model also lies in its dramatic roots. Greimas's *actants* and their narrative dynamics are the direct descedents of Propp's 'dramatis personae' and the functions they perform, not to mention Souriau's *functions* in his 'dramatic calculus'. Greimas has refined and developed these models to produce a universal grammar of narrative, independent of medium, and has thus gone far beyond his predecessors, but actantial theory still derives its strength from being an interactive 'performance' system. An account of the energy inherent in actantial models, the controlled development of power (Greimas's transformation of Propp's narrative syntagm into the energetic syntagm *vouloir, savoir, pouvoir* (1983)) is perhaps the main lack in Rimmon-Kenan's study.

I have already indicated how dialogue and tableau scenes are basically dramatic in nature. The theatrical model also helps in giving an account of the essentially iconic nature of much narrative representation. While popular wisdom suggests that a picture is worth a thousand words, it is also true that words present us with a thousand pictures. The iconic verbal sign stands for a visual object, which is itself *pars pro toto* in the basically metonymic functioning of prose narrative (see Jakobson 1960). In analysing such effects, we should remember that metonymy is also the main constituent figure of the theatre and of performance in general. This is not only the case with actual objects of décor but with the necessarily partial (synecdochic)[10] representation of words or actions. 'Metonymy is the figure which shows on stage what for various reasons can not be shown, the concrete present standing for a real absent present which is much greater: the stage object thus indicates the place of the unrepresentable' (Ubersfeld 1981: 158). In narrative, as on stage, one action must represent a whole series of actions, the words spoken stand for words unspoken, what we are allowed to see becomes metonymic of the unseen.

In Chapter 5, I hope to show also that theatrical models of space can contribute significantly to the discussion of narrative space. Such a comparison helps us to understand the shift in relationships between space and time which occur when the simultaneity of space must be represented by a necessarily sequential process in time. Bakhtin's study of the *chronotope* (1981: 84–258) looks at this problem and stresses the role of the theatrical chronotope in the development of the novel. Yet another use of space is translated, as Barthes perceived, into questions of narrative focus and perspective:

> The theatre is precisely that practice which calculates the place of things *as they are observed*: if I set the spectacle here, the spectator will see this; if I put it elsewhere, he will not, and I can avail myself of this

masking effect and play on the illusion it provides. . . . The scene, the picture, the shot, the cut-out rectangle, here we have the very *condition* that allows us to conceive theatre, painting, cinema, literature. . . .

(1977: 69–70)

Thus in the analysis of focalization initiated by Gérard Genette (1972) and formalized by Mieke Bal (1977), we have a reminder of the relayed power of selection implicit both in the focused gaze and in *lighting*. The focus highlights certain aspects (the focalized) and leaves others in the shade, but that focus and the focalizer are relaying the selective principles at work in the text, just as the spot moves in accordance with the skill of the technician and the plan of the director.

A vital aspect of the theatrical model is the one which takes into account the role of the audience. Studies of the audience present in the text (Prince 1980b; Genette 1983) and implied in the text (Iser 1974) are related to his model, and Chapter 4 deals with the different categories of the narrative audience. However, the specifically theatrical model assumes such importance in any discussion of audiences that I have devoted a separate section to it in this chapter (pp. 33–41: The reader as spectator). Gérard-Denis Farcy (1986) suggests that theatre and cinema studies could benefit by the extension of narratology into their domains. I think a prerequisite to such a communal enterprise is the recognition by narratology itself of the relationship between those fraternal enemies, narrative and theatre.

THE LUDIC MODEL: THE TELLER AND THE TELLING

Another aspect of the narratological endeavour moves the interest from the relationship between the teller and the tale to that between the teller and the telling. A very necessary complement to the studies of the voices in the text has been the analysis of the listener in the text, the sometimes elusive narratee (Prince 1980b; Genette 1983) and the different reactions implied by the different positions of authority in the narrative voice. Even such simple questions as 'Do I confide in you?' (first person) 'inform you?' (third person) or 'command you?' (second person) can uncover enormous variations in textual strategy. Fictional narrative is a game, but a game for high stakes, in which nothing less than the power of the text over the players is involved.

How does a text maintain its authority, how does it keep a firm grasp on interpretation? The rules of the game involve control, at first seen as the control of the telling by the teller. Narrative may be seen as a delicate interplay of power in which the narratee submits to the control of a narrator, while the narrator must scheme to overcome the power of the narratee. Each experiences an invasion of his or her territory by the other. The narrator has the advantage that a map of the territory (a *self-reflexive* segment) can be included in the text. This is a means by which the narrator can control the advance of the other, turn it into desired paths, and ultimately even persuade him or her to cede territory.

To take the most obvious example of self-reflexivity, stories of all types and ages come replete with embedded instances of the power of the tale, of the word, of the sign. How many fates have been averted, how many lives have been changed, by telling a story, singing a song, knowing the word of command? Each victory of the sign within the tale is a signpost to the territory, a direction in its turn to submit to the power of the teller.

The maintenance of narrative control, of narrative authority, is easier in a face-to-face situation where direct feedback enables the teller to gauge the audience reaction and the degree of 'noise' and thus to assess gains or losses of control. Studies in textual directiveness, with their emphasis on the manipulation of the *énonciation* and the role of the speaking subject, tend to focus on self-reflexivity and particularly on the *mise-en-abyme* (Ricardou 1978; Dällenbach 1977). The *mise-en-abyme* is an embedded segment which reflects either syntagmatically or para-digmatically the structure of a greater whole, just as a mirror within a room reflects the room as a whole. Chapter 3 briefly examines the different ways in which *mise-en-abyme* suggests textual authority and proposes guidance to both narrative audience and real audience.

The difference between these two approaches, the one which analyses the text as a thing-in-itself, and the one which shows it at once as game and as means of control, is roughly comparable to the funda-mentally different approaches of Stanislavsky and Brecht in the theatre. With the former, the actors were encouraged to construct a perfect illusion of living reality, insulated necessarily from the audience. What went on beyond the footlights was not their proper concern and, when it intruded, could only harm their performance. Brecht, on the other hand, put the accent on the relation between performance and audience, using self-reflexive segments of every sort – songs, slides, posters – to remind both the actors and the audience that it *was* a performance, in other words to focus on the telling. Brecht also distinguished between the narratee constructed by the text, the peasants in *The Caucasian Chalk Circle* for instance, and the actual audience.

Such a distinction seems essential. It is a performance-orientated distinction between the narratee who is a function *of* the text and the reader called for *by* the text, which Genette calls the virtual reader. In this respect, the seminal work of Wolfgang Iser in *The Implied Reader* (1974) has done much to clarify the situation. But here too the problematics of the 'stable' text are seen in part as a constantly frustrated attempt to achieve proprietorial control. The advent of the named author, the titled and genre-labelled text, the imprimatur of printing and publication, have all tended to turn the previously fluid relationships of narrative performance into a static relationship of possession. Even Iser sees the reader very much as a puppet whose strings are pulled by the text. Naomi Schor acutely observes that this sense of proprietorship, of owning the text and controlling the rules of the game, has merely passed from the author to the critic in recent years.[11] The most recent studies respond to her demand (1980) that narrative be seen not as a matter of ownership but of negotiation, and concentrate on the interplay between telling and hearing.

THE EROTIC MODEL: THE TELLER AND THE HEARER

Control of people's minds is not a simple thing. Just as a teller endeavours to use audience feedback to control audience reaction by modifying the performance, so the text endeavours to construct its own reader. However, while narrators and narratees are and remain textual constructs, there is never any guarantee that the virtual reader/audience will obey the promptings of the text. Audience feedback, without which no live production is complete, is transformed in the case of the printed book and becomes the individual interpretation of the written text.[12] Both are always context-related and are constantly subject to variation. There is no one 'true' proprietorial interpretation.

The performance–audience relationship for fiction has become more private, erotic rather than theatrical, but is still subject to the dictates of fashion, of ideology, to the rules of the game. The variability of even completely congruous interpretations shows that individual readers can apply as many differing criteria as the partners in other performances. The *point* of a narrative may change as much according to its audience as according to its teller, as was seen in the case of gendered telling and hearing.

The best recent studies of the dynamics of narrative performance, on which I rely heavily in the demonstrations of the practices of individual texts which follow, are those of Ross Chambers in *Story and Situation: Narrative Seduction and the Power of Fiction* (1984). They deal with that necessary and yet always ambiguous relationship with the narratee and eventually with the reader, which produces narrative authority. The text in its performance seems to control the narratees, to provide them with what I earlier termed a map of the territory in the form of self-reflexive segments. However, the virtual reader's acceptance of this authority is not regarded as automatic. Also mapped into the text are the variables of reception which remain a matter for negotiation, since a hearer must accept the *point* of a story.

As the field of negotiation has changed, as literature has become a more and more private experience, relived as such by each individual reader, so performance has become less a matter of the pulpit, the minstrels' gallery, or the trestles and more a matter of the sitting-room or the bedroom. Chambers sees this situation mirrored, particularly in nineteenth-century literature, in narratives where the narrator must use his or her skill at story telling in such a way as to persuade the narratee of the interest and point of the story, thus regaining control of the narrative situation, which, at any rate in the case of listening for pleasure, normally belongs to the narratee.[13]

> This, in short, is a matter of recruiting the power of the narratee in such a way as to produce what is called 'authority' for the narrator; it is a seduction of the pre-existing desire for narration in favor of the desire to narrate. The power of the other is not challenged, but used; and the improvisational and adaptational character of what is, in essence, a feed-back situation, is most evident in the case of oral narrative.
>
> What written, and especially printed narrative, makes most evident, however, is a peculiarity of discursive 'authority' that I analysed in *Story and Situation, I* as a function of textual redundancy, which substitutes in this case for oral feed-back. This is a feature of authority whereby, once it is achieved – once the hearer's interest has been recruited, once a reader has 'gotten into' a book – retains a certain effectiveness beyond the storytelling moment, an effectiveness most clearly exemplified by the phenomenon of 'readability' (as the ongoing interpretability of a text).
>
> (Chambers, 1987b)

To put this in other terms, textual interplay is seen as being constantly open to negotiation, just as is erotic interplay. The relationships between narrator and narratees in the fictional world of the text and the more subtle dialogue between a speaking subject and a hypothetical listening subject, which constitutes the *énonciation*, must all constantly solicit the co-operation of the reader. The field of the textual *énonciation* is in constant but varying relationship with the desire of the reader, and on this complicated three-way exchange depends the phenomenon of interpretability. The field of the *énonciation* subsumes the various spaces and desires of the spoken subjects, actors or characters, but it is much more than they.

> *Enonciation* . . . recognises that language is an immense halo of implications, of effects, of resonance, of turns, returns, salients; . . . words are no longer illusorily considered as simple instruments, they are projected as missiles, explosions, vibrations, machineries, tastes: writing turns knowledge into a festival.
>
> (Barthes 1978b: 20)

It is this 'festival', this shifting performance, which is in its turn exposed to a readership that constantly changes and renews itself. Every new reader must be persuaded to new interpretation. Thus the narrative contract, like the sexual contract, is constantly open to re-negotiation.

THE ENERGETIC MODEL

The recent preoccupation of philosophers such as Gilles Deleuze and Michel Serres with the relationship between literature and science has yielded some new and exciting models of narrative performance. Deleuze and Guattari (1975, 1980) see the text in terms of the vital machine, or *agencement machinique*, an energetic model which enables an appreciation of narrative in terms of a dynamics of performance. The interplay of the text is comparable to that of a human body, an infinite interlocking of parts, each of which has its own vitality and its own energy. The running down of these energies, the forces of diffusion and stasis, is countered by the constant subversion of the pattern. The points of control and the points of escape are always shifting within the system.

Michel Serres, working rather with information theory, genetics, and physics, sees in literature a balance of entropy and negentropy similar to that in any system of communication. However, the entropic tendencies at work in such systems are countered by the negentropic effect of 'noise' or the parasite. Interference in an energetic field produces mutations in it, new measures to counter the resistance to the message. The very forces which resist and complicate the transfer of any text, from the text of a genetic pattern to that of a narrative, are those which prevent its eventual dissipation. These models will be further explored, particularly in Chapters 2 and 8.

LINGUISTIC MODELS

To the model of narrative suggested in terms of linguistic structures, and particularly of sentence structures (Todorov 1969; Fowler 1977), other more dynamic models have been added. The social and ideological forces inherent in language itself are now seen as contributing, not to a series of individual unified linguistic performances in the Chomskian sense, but to a linguistic dynamism, a dialogism such as that found by Mikhail Bakhtin in the multiple voices of the text. This theory of linguistic multiplicity is developed in Deleuze's epigrammatic proposition that all speech is indirect speech. In our story-telling, as in our daily language, we each speak not only in our own voice, but in that of those who preceded us. Textual performance, like any stage performance, bears the traces of previous performances, and continues, whether positively or negatively, in action or reaction, their tradition. The importance of this model will constantly emerge from the pages which follow.

However, the linguistic model which has made the largest contribution to the study of narrative is the development of speech-act theory which has been subsumed into pragmatics. Since this was originally based on the study of performatives in language it naturally forms an important part of this study of performance in narrative texts.

Performance and performatives

The most promising development in the study of verbal performance in general, not just of narrative performance, was made possible by the work of J. L. Austin, and particularly by his *How to Do Things with Words* (1975), one of those critical *tours de force* which mark whole generations of succeeding theory. The seductiveness, to use Shoshana Felman's term (1983), of Austin's theory lies not only in his own dazzling linguistic performance, but also in his recognition of the dynamism of language. His analysis of the performative not only showed language in action, but made it clear that this action was only possible because of an interaction between the sender and the receiver of verbal messages. Performatives are verbal forms which have not only meaning, but also effect. They are always context-dependent, since they rely on shared convention and shared obligation between the partners in the verbal act. It is no good warning people who are no longer prepared to consider your warning a valid performance, as the boy who cried wolf discovered.

The obvious affinities of this with performance theory are traced in

Shoshana Felman's *The Literary Speech Act* (1983), in which she not only shows performatives at work in drama, but also conducts an effective rescue operation, snatching Austin back from the clutches of both his disciples and his translators. The application of speech-act theory to drama and narrative had been regarded as questionable for years because of the rigid and unimaginative interpretation of Austin's 'felicity' conditions, the conditions under which illocution becomes effective. Austin was considering the very pretty problem of the relationship between performance and action, between saying and doing, and was therefore forced to exclude verbal representation, which produces no effect in actuality; the actor who says 'I thee wed' is not marrying anybody. However, the implications of the theory for enacted performatives as well as performative acts were too interesting to be wasted. Some way had to be found of taking the theory beyond the valid/non-valid impasse set up by positivist thinking, and to make it applicable to fictional and represented speech acts and hence to a very large proportion of human discourse. Susan Lanser (1981: 283–94) gives an excellent summary of the debate which attended this project.

The first important way in which we can develop and extend speech-act theory is the recognition that, instead of a single level of 'act' which is either valid or non-valid, we may be considering equally 'serious acts' which are merely valid in different contexts. The speech acts considered as 'serious' or 'valid' by Austin and, after him, by Searle (1969) were the performatives functioning in natural discourse, such as acts of promising, requesting, asserting, questioning, thanking, advising, warning, greeting, congratulating. These acts can only be performed in direct speech, and mostly only in the first person, since they involve doing with words. What is more, they are completely context-dependent. Involved in that context are not only the sincerity of the speaker and his or her sense of commitment to the hearer, but also the social and linguistic conventions to which both subscribe. It is true, as Thomas Pavel complains, that recent speech-act theorists have insufficiently considered the possible variations in these contextual conditions: 'By taking for granted the existence and stability of linguistic conventions, speech-act theory neglects the dynamism of their establishment and their inherent fluidity' (1986: 26).

However, I do not feel that this rigidity was a necessary result of the original Austinian speculations, which incorporated precisely the dynamism that both the logic of natural languages and their linguistics had lacked until then.

Since Mary Louise Pratt's initial attack on the absurd demarcations, imposed by logicians and literary critics alike, between natural language and literary language, it has been abundantly demonstrated that all performatives occur in both 'natural' direct discourse and in textual representations, and the latter cannot simply be dismissed as invalid and therefore of no account. Otherwise we would be in the logical but absurd position of the Roman lawmakers who refused Roman citizens the right to act on stage, because a Roman's speech acts had at all times to be valid. One solution that is both interesting and fashionable is to go to the opposite extreme and say that, since all discourse, by the very nature of language, is sign-based, symbolic, and therefore fabricated, the only way out of the impasse is to recognize that natural discourse, as a semiotic system, is in no way distinguishable from fictional discourse, and has equivalent reality claims. However, there remains a distinction which we all recognize, and which we learn to apply from an early age when we first ask 'Did that really happen or is it a story?'

THE TWO ORDERS OF SPEECH ACT

The solution to this impasse seems to be to posit two orders of speech act, both of which are language-dependent and hence can make reality claims only in relation to the context in which they operate. The first order would operate in natural discourse and in direct speech, and would correspond to the Austinian criteria for 'serious' performatives, the second would operate in fictional discourse and everyday narratives. This would acknowledge that narration changes the status of the speech act included in it.

A narration of any sort is inevitably a mediated experience. Even as we say 'I will tell you *the* story', we can promise no more than a mediation of reality. We enter into a narrative contract with our hearer when, for example, we undertake to give an objective account of the street accident which just took place outside our house. However, our account, our story, becomes just one of many virtual accounts, as any police officer can tell you. What is more, that account is governed by the forces of narrativity. William Labov (1972) has studied urban story-telling, the narratives of everyday lives, and shown how the arrangement of the story must follow its own rules, must be performed, if it is to maintain the interest of the audience.

Even when we promise a factual account, a reportage, which in theory should be 'representative illocution' (Pratt 1977: 80–1), the very fact that it is put in the shape of a narrative and is subject to the whims and selections of the teller means that the first-order illocution, the 'representation', is already a 'display text', that is, a text which foregrounds the manner as much as the matter, which is detached from its immediate circumstances, and which is capable of reduction or of elaboration as the need may be (Pratt 1977: 133–51). Any speech acts contained within a display text are already second-order speech acts, that is to say that they are valid only within the framework of the narrative. A telling is in the present, but any world it relates, even the seeming world of actuality, is really either a past world seen through the eyes of another or a future hypothetical world. Such worlds are already alternative worlds, as many stories of time travel bear witness.

THE NARRATIVE PERFORMATIVE

This is why I would go further than Susan Lanser (1981: 289–91) who rightly wishes to add the category of 'hypotheticals' (that is, fictional propositions) to John Searle's five categories of illocutionary activity, 'representatives', 'directives', 'commissives', 'expressives', and 'declaratives'. I believe that 'narratives' such as 'I will relate', 'I will tell', 'I will recount', are a special type of performative since, even when what is related is supposedly factual, the result is a display text rather than a mere assertion, the key factor being the creation of an *audience*. In fact, I share Mary Louise Pratt's view that everyday speech acts are not as materially distinct from literature as critics have claimed. The Russian studies of *skaz* referred to earlier (p.13) vindicate this view.

Indeed, it is in everyday vernacular narration that the effect of fiction, one of enhancement rather than radical change in the status of narration, may first be observed. We see the difference when we say not 'I will tell you *the* story', but cast off even the restrictions of the available choices from the referentiality of this world, and create another *possible* world. We allow ourselves the full freedom of the narrative contract when we say 'I will tell you *a* story'. This illocutionary act is, as I have said, a sort of performative, since it not only sets up a two-way contract between addresser and addressee, as all true speech acts do, but it also promises a performance and constitutes the hearers as audience. Implicit in every narrative performative is the double contract, '*Listen*, and I will tell you *a* story'. (See Figure 1.1.)

It seems to me that, although John Searle denies logical status to fictional discourse, he posits a performative when he speaks of 'a set of conventions which suspend the normal operation of rules relating illocutionary acts and the world' (1975: 326). The set of conventions is in effect the narrative performative which instructs one to differentiate between *énonciation* and *énoncé*, and more particularly between speaking and telling. For this differentiation to be made possible, what Erving

Goffman calls *keying*, the indication of a change in the status of discourse, is necessary. When this keying occurs in story-telling, both teller and hearer accept a new frame of reference, they accept the contract implied by the performative 'I will now narrate', and their situation is modified by the act of narration. Searle seems to admit this for the theatre while denying it to narrative performance:

> The playwright represents the actual and pretended actions and the speeches of the actors, but the playwright's performance in writing the text of the play is *rather like writing a recipe for pretense than engaging in a form of pretense itself.*
>
> (1975: 328; my emphasis)

What he is implying here by the expression 'recipe for pretense' is a form of illocutionary relationship between the author and the director, a relationship which will lead in its turn to the 'act' of performance, which is both 'acting on' the audience and 'enacting' the original script which is now displayed as a series of second-order illocutionary acts.

SPEECH ACTS AND FICTIONAL NARRATIVE

Narration is similarly paradoxical in the way in which the initial illocutionary relationship subsumes a further series of enactments. This is even more marked in the case of written fiction, which enacts not only the events but the *act of telling a story*, not only the *énoncé* but the *énonciation*. The fictional written text is in the first instance the representation of another narrative text, such as an oral story, letters, or diary. *David Copperfield*, as Barbara Herrnstein Smith points out, represents not a man's spoken reminiscences but his autobiography.

> *The Death of Ivan Ilyich* is not the biography of a fictional character, but rather a fictive biography. The fiction attaches no more to the narrated facts of Ilyitch's [sic] life than to the fact of someone's narrating them. Tolstoy is, if you like, pretending to be *writing* a biography while actually *fabricating* one.
>
> (Smith 1978: 30)

Thus the fictional text posits a double narrative contract, that between author and reader, and a second fictional contract between narrator and narratee. The relationship between author and reader usually takes the form of a first-order illocutionary act.

This illocutionary relationship of sender and receiver is shown by the fact that, in the theatre and in most published narratives, the performance is introduced by an authorial speech act or acts. The

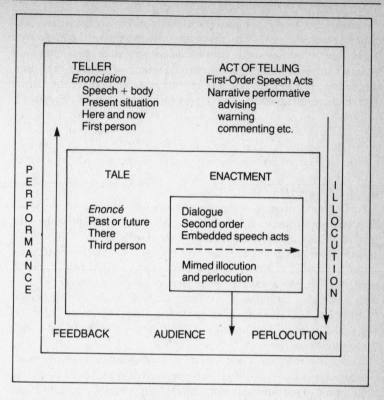

TELLER
Enonciation
  Speech + body
  Present situation
  Here and now
  First person

ACT OF TELLING
First-Order Speech Acts
Narrative performative
  advising
  warning
  commenting etc.

TALE

ENACTMENT

Enoncé
Past or future
There
Third person

Dialogue
Second order
Embedded speech acts

Mimed illocution
and perlocution

PERFORMANCE

ILLOCUTION

FEEDBACK   AUDIENCE   PERLOCUTION

Figure 1.1   Oral narrative: everyday narrative and folk-tales

audience's first introduction to the play is the billboard, a direct communication to them by the author – *Hamlet: a Tragedy*. In the same way, we are subject to the direct advertisement of *War and Peace: Book One*, or of course the ironical *Animal Farm: a Fairy Story*. It might be helpful to define what I mean by author. In spite of Barthes's much publicized essay (1977: 142–8) on the death of the author, the genus survives. It is just that we now realize that the author, like the reader, is a product of language, ideology, and context. The author's text, like all our texts, creates him or her, just as much as he or she creates it. *An* author, in fact, is a paradigm of virtual authors, from which *the* author of any given text is chosen.

The author of any given narrative text, one possible instance of the totality of the author, can opt for some forms of direct communication with the public as distinct from the narrator-mediated story itself. The most obvious example is if and when authors present themselves by name. The act of naming is a direct speech act, an act of ostentation, though what is named is again a virtual author, an instance of authorship. There is also of course a difference between naming the virtual author of an unknown text, who must be created from the beginning, and the naming of an author created by previous texts. This is in a way part of the general presentation of credentials which an audience demands from performers of any sort (Pratt 1977: 112), and the perlocutionary effect on the audience can be more easily calculated in relation to such illocutionary acts of ostentation as 'See the great Houdini' than to 'Joe Bloggs, Escapalogist'.

Apart from providing the name of the author, I consider the other direct authorial speech act, and the most important one, to be the title. It is the formalized rendition of the Labovian 'abstract' (1972: 104), and its relationship to the reader contains 'a zero grade of mediacy' (Stanzel 1984: 22). Along with the preface and certain public dedications,[14] it is in some ways the equivalent of the oral performer's 'come on', the fairground barker's 'You sir, you look strong/intelligent/discriminating. Will you fight a bout with the champion?/guess the secret of the hall of doom?/see one of the few stones ever brought back from the perihelion of Astyanax?'

This authorial speech act, which is paratextual in placing, must, though vital to any reading, be distinguished from the intratextual relationship of narrator and narratee. It is important to remember that, in the fictional written text, both the narrator and the narrative audience have become part of the fictional world (cf. Pavel 1986: 87–9). Thus the frequent narratorial performatives which advise, warn, or question the narrative audience, which Searle (1975: 331) wishes to attribute to the author and which Pratt (1977: 174) calls part of the authorial display text, are in fact second-order illocutionary acts belonging to the world of the text and produced by its narrator.[15]

THE THREE TYPES OF SPEECH ACT

In order to explain their effect on the reader, we must have recourse to the second major development of Austinian thought. Austin posited three types of speech act: the act of locution, of saying or producing a message; the act of illocution, in which the communication of the message is dependent on interaction between the speaker and the hearer and on their acceptance of the conditions of the verbal contract between them; and the act of perlocution whereby the message takes effect on the hearer. It may easily be seen that any verbal performance contains all three acts *in potentia*.

To take an example of Austin's (and to give some indication of the energy of his own performance):

> Suppose, for example, I see a vessel on the stocks, walk up and smash the bottle hung at the stern, proclaim 'I name this ship the *Mr. Stalin*' and for good measure kick away the chocks: but the trouble is, I was not the person chosen to name it (whether or not – an additional complication – *Mr. Stalin* was the destined name; perhaps in a way it is even more of a shame if it was). We can all agree
> 1) that the ship was not thereby named;
> 2) that it is an infernal shame.
>
> (1975: 23)

Here, an act of locution has taken place; whatever its purpose, however, the performative *I name* has not become a valid act of illocution because either: (a) there are no hearers, or (b) they do not accept the act, since the conditions are not right for it and the performer has not the requisite authority. In a proper naming ceremony the act of illocution would be followed by the act of perlocution. The hearers would accept the name as legitimate, and then it would be painted on the side of the ship, etc.

In these three divisions, I suggest that we can recognize the three major elements of performance: purpose, energy, and effect. I can shout 'Rape' with as much purpose as I like, but unless someone hears me it remains an act of locution. If someone hears me and accepts the message (energetic interaction), it becomes an act of illocution. The hearer may find the message irrelevant and so the act of perlocution will fail, or may experience belief, shock, fear, or outrage, in which case, from my point of view, the perlocutionary effect will be the correct one. If they shrug and say 'Oh God, not again!' there will still be an act of perlocution, an effect of sorts on the hearer.

It may be seen that the three elements are, in actual practice, as much indivisible parts of a whole as are, for example, signifier and signified which are the two sides of a single sheet, as Saussure put it. However, just as Barthes (1978a) was able to exploit the signifier/ signified distinction to show the existence of not one but multiple levels of signification, so a study of Austin's theoretical distinction allows an appreciation of double, even multiple, levels in speech acts. The breakthrough in exploiting the triple distinction between locution, illocution, and perlocution was made possible by the study of pragmatics in the theatre (Ubersfeld 1981). The relationship of actor to actor, and the way in which it combined with that of actor to audience, had always presented theoretical problems. The mimetic illocutionary acts in the theatre were originally considered by speech-act theorists not to permit perlocutions at all, since they were only representations of performatives. In that case, said the pragmatists in both senses of the word, what is happening to the audience? Enter the triple distinction. An act of locution may be seen in its original form in the script, where the words are written with purpose but still appear in the form of pure signifiers, a succession of marks in black and white which require reading to bring them to life. The performative locution, 'Give me the dagger' for instance, will be fully activated and energized only in performance and will then appear as a mimed illocutionary relationship between two stage characters, accompanied by mimed perlocutionary effects. It is these perlocutionary effects which are denied validity by the theorists, since Macbeth is an actor playing a part and only miming his reactions to his wife's commands. However, and this is where the distinction between the acts demonstrates its full value, the third factor, the audience, also hears the act of illocution, experiences it partly as though directed to themselves, and feels its perlocutionary effects. This is of course subject to the provision that the effects of perlocution, both in fiction and in actuality, are dependent on relevance. If the theatre bores me, or a dagger means nothing to me, I may be totally immune to the 'acts' on stage, although my negative reaction is in itself perlocutionary in nature. The effects of the triple distinction are equally operative in narrative speech acts, which are also mimetic in nature and which also have a double perlocutionary effect, fictive within the text, but genuinely experienced by the hearer or reader. Chapter 4 will explore the value of this distinction to narrative analysis.

It must be remembered, however, that performatives are not limited to directly mimetic *énoncés*, such as dialogue, but are also present in the narratorial relationship in which the narrator instructs, advises, warns, or persuades the narratee. Here again there is a double effect, within the text and beyond the text, but the narratee has been so frequently identified with the reader that narratorial performatives have been classed as 'valid' utterances. The narratorial speech acts mentioned earlier for instance, addressed within the text to a narrative audience, such as the opening remark of *Anna Karenina* about happy families which Searle classifies as a 'serious utterance' (1975: 331), or the opening remark of *Pride and Prejudice* about the need of single gentlemen for wives, are actually epigrammatic utterances directed by the

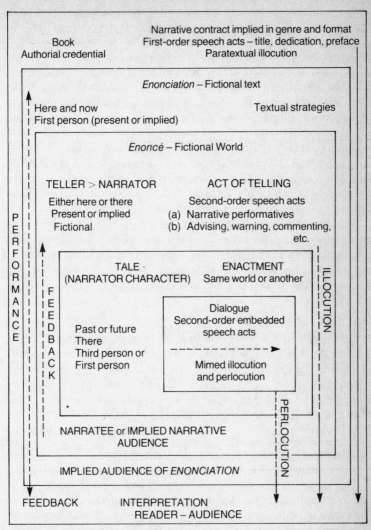

Narrative contract implied in genre and format
First-order speech acts – title, dedication, preface
Paratextual illocution

Book
Authorial credential

Enonciation – Fictional text

Here and now
First person (present or implied)

Textual strategies

Enoncé – Fictional World

TELLER > NARRATOR

Either here or there
Present or implied
Fictional

ACT OF TELLING

Second-order speech acts
(a) Narrative performatives
(b) Advising, warning, commenting,
etc.

TALE
(NARRATOR CHARACTER)

ENACTMENT
Same world or another

Dialogue
Second-order embedded
speech acts

Mimed illocution
and perlocution

Past or future
There
Third person or
First person

PERFORMANCE

FEEDBACK

ILLOCUTION

PERLOCUTION

NARRATEE or IMPLIED NARRATIVE
AUDIENCE

IMPLIED AUDIENCE OF *ENONCIATION*

FEEDBACK   INTERPRETATION
READER – AUDIENCE

* Further fictional worlds may be embedded within the world of the tale, thus
presumably creating further orders of speech act.

Figure 1.2   Fictional printed narrative

narrator to the narrative audience. The direct perlocutionary effect on the reader, which distinguishes these utterances and makes them seem first-order speech acts, is enhanced and facilitated, so that the reader can most easily identify with the narrative audience while at the same time remaining conscious that he or she is not a nineteenth-century Russian bourgeois or an inhabitant of Regency England.

Fictional illocutionary acts, whether those of the narrator or those of the characters in the story, are mimetic: they are produced by fabricated speakers, just as speech acts in drama are produced by its actors. The narratee of *Animal Farm*, being a purely textual construct, can only be presumed to experience disillusionment at the failure of the animal revolution; in the same way, the actor playing Oedipus is experiencing only hypothetical horror at the news of his parricide and incest. However, the audience can and does experience direct perlocutionary effects from the text presenting the speech acts of Napoleon or Squealer, Oedipus or Tiresias, effects controlled by the very nature of the presentation. *Oedipus Rex* provokes the pleasure and shock of catharsis, *Animal Farm* the 'What did I tell you?' of political wisdom after the event. Thus the audience may experience the double pleasure of *identification* (the direct perlocutionary effect) and *estrangement* (the appreciation of the performance or metatext as well as the effect of the mimed speech act):

> When we think of it in relation to social representations, we can say that mimesis is a particular case on its own, distinct from other modalities because it operates the *representation of representations*. In this formula we find again its paradoxical property. A representation of representations, mimesis presupposes between representations and its own scene a separation that makes it possible to appreciate, know and/or question representations.
>
> (Lima 1985: 461)

In other words, in the 'scene', on the stage of mimesis, the distancing from representation can be felt and interpreted as art.

The nature of the double relationship between narrative and its audience, that of identification and that of distance, is illuminated by the suggested developments to speech-act theory. The understanding of distance is enhanced by the postulate of two orders of speech act, the actual and the narrative, while the understanding of identification becomes clearer when we establish the split between sense, action, and effect. The narrative audience, like the dramatic audience, depends in part on the conventions of the speech act for both the pleasure obtained and the interpretation arrived at.

It is the audience's task to interpret the physical 'sayings' on stage as higher-order speech events in the dramatic world. In order to do so, it must project both a set of intentions on the part of the speaker and a semiotic competence (allowing 'uptake' to be secured) on the part of the listener. This is a major aspect of the spectator's role in 'constructing' the dramatic world.

(Elam 1980: 170)

This also helps define the reader's role. Great freedom of response (within the limits of congruity and competence) is permissible within the narrative situation, just as it is in the theatre. The reader/audience is as it were invisible, but at the same time both vulnerable and powerful: vulnerable to the strategies of performance, to the conditions of utterance, but powerful in the right to co-operate or not to co-operate. The teller/player on the other hand is eminently visible but protected by the 'framing', the contract, the conventions of unreality. A book or a play is not life; the publication, the footlights, create a barrier. The story-teller, whether identified as such or speaking through the narrative performers, has the pleasures and penalties of exhibitionism, but, except in the case of very naïve hearers, is not subject to an accounting in the real world.

The reader as spectator

One thing is clear, that the idea of the reader as a competent, serene, intelligent, and objective receiver of messages is just as much a myth as that of authorial 'intention' regarded as a single conscious act of sending a message. Both are myths of possession and control. When the notion of the author as proprietor of the truth of a text became no longer viable, another proprietorship was substituted, that of the ideal reader, the reader with the single perfect context, the privileged ideology, the repository of the truth of the text. The problem is that, while the text constructs narratees, it is readers who construct ideal readers. They can be viewed as yet another attempt by interpreters to limit the virtuality of the text.

Here again, the example of the theatre helps to clarify the situation, as does the spectator/stage relationship with its combination of inclusion/exclusion. The narratee/chorus on stage cannot and should not be confused with the audience which is both excluded from the stage and included in the dynamics of the auditorium, the sacred telling ground, or whatever the audience/hearer space may be. This is the case even in productions where the actors come and sit among the audience.

Always they create a performance space which is contiguous with and separate from audience space (Ubersfeld 1981). The reader too is one of a community of readers, separate from the text even as they help to shape it.

However, there are interesting examples of marginalization. Take that of the reader directly addressed by the first-person voice in written narrative, the one taken into the narrator's confidence in, for instance, *Tristram Shandy* or *Le Rouge et le noir*. While it is true, as Bal maintains, that in strict narrative taxonomy these are merely special examples of focalization, the fact remains that the reader is here placed in a particular and equivocal relationship. The reader directly addressed by the narratorial voice is rather in the situation of the Elizabethan nobleman who had a seat on the stage. He was simultaneously included in the performance space but excluded from the performance, excluded from the audience space but included in the audience. In the same way we, the 'gentle readers', are admitted to the intimacy of the narrator while at the same time distanced from the text by being refused facility of identification with the character there depicted.

The reader is thus made aware of the double nature of speculation, the double bind of spectatorship. He or she is tempted by the specularity, the mirroring, of identification but at the same time reminded that spectatorship, with the realization that one *is* a spectator, involves critical estrangement, and with it the penalties and pleasures of speculation.

However, the reader/spectator is also subject to another form of identification, the contagion of mass reaction. The all-pervasive effects of ideology, of fashion, of the prevailing horizon of expectation (Jauss 1982), are present in any audience, though experienced with more immediacy in the theatre. The mass response, the contagious reaction to a book or a play, will often precede the interaction provoked in a particular individual. Indeed, the expectations generated by the author's name, title, or publicity, and the ideological demands of a social group, may precede, generally do precede, the individual reaction to the actual text or performance. Audience response too is both immediate and deferred. Sometimes the deferred reaction of one audience is communicated to a second audience which then reads the text in a completely new way. A text like *Waiting for Godot* may be greeted with blank incomprehension by its original spectators, who then, by discussion and feedback, gradually reach a more informed appreciation. A later audience, aware of this, then approaches the text with different expectations.

This first aspect of spectatorship, the reaction of certain social groups to specified texts at specified periods in history, has been the one most explored by reception theory (Goldmann 1975; Jauss 1982). The interplay between the I and you of the speaking subject (*sujet de l'énonciation*) and the individual reader or spectator, has generally been put into the too-hard basket, although it has been attempted by such critics as Norman Holland.

THE READER AND DESIRE

A possible way to investigate this relationship is to remember with Virgil Tanase that: 'The stage is that privileged place where our ideology, our ideological condition, is in a spectacular manner checked by the force of desire' (cit. Pavis 1982: 86).

Just as the libidinal investment of the theatre spectator is enormous, so too is that of the individual reader. Indeed, according to Louis Marin (1978), one of the narrative traps consists in manipulating this investment, the desire of the reader, whether it be desire for power, for pleasure, for punishment, or for revenge.

Obviously there are many forms of desire. The libidinal investment of teller and of hearer and the relationship between them clearly allow for variations as infinite as those between the partners in that other contract, the sexual exchange. The narrative exchange too may be motivated by anything from curiosity to passion, may produce anything from revulsion to delight, may run the gamut of failure from fiasco to rape. Perhaps we need a Masters and Johnson, or even a Krafft-Ebing, of teller–hearer relationships.

Even before Marin, the critic who identified most clearly the forces of desire in narrative texts was René Girard in *Deceit, Desire and the Novel* (1965). It was he who pinpointed the triangular nature of desire in the nineteenth-century novel. He showed that the structure of desire in these texts is precisely that the hero or heroine most desires the object of another's desire, the archetypal schema of adultery, or, more subtly, expresses the desire for another by wooing the same object as he or she does, the archetypal schema of repressed homosexuality. Lacan expresses this idea in a more cryptic way when he says that our desire is always the desire of the other. Ross Chambers has extended this notion of the projection of desire and transferred it from the narrative subject to the reader's reaction to the seduction of text. One can either identify with the object of textual seduction and thus adopt the position of the narratee or, as with many first-person narratives, find one's satisfaction as reader in adopting the position of the narrator, thus in Chambers's terms identifying with the textual seducer. The most interesting reader reaction he postulates, however, is an identification of one's desire in the *process* of narrative, thus of course taking the position of estrangement which allows one to be alternately narrator and narratee, either the one who desires power over another or the object of that desire, or the textual utterance which subsumes them.

THE RETURN OF THE REPRESSED

Studies of spectator relationships in film and in the theatre (Mulvey 1975; Ubersfeld 1981) offer other possible models of the involvement of the reader by the manipulation of his or her own desire. Most spring from the Freudian notion of the return of the repressed, implying that spectators use performance to produce, as it were, a secondary revision of their own dreams and fantasies. To grasp this reader reaction we must appreciate

> the similarity and the difference between the dream discourse and any discourse based on the play principle: the former is directly related to the human primary process, whereas the latter, though also one modality of the discourse of the unconscious, differs from the dream modality by being a combination of both processes.
>
> (Lima 1985: 455)

The most common, or at least most discussed, manifestation of reader/spectator desire appears in the form of narcissism. Sometimes this narcissism takes the form of simple identification with the object or subject of desire in the narrative: we become the pirate or the pirate's bride, Anna Karenina or Heathcliff. It is the 'simple' pleasure of the mirror image, though, as we know, mirrors have many disconcerting characteristics, including those of perversion and inversion. A more subtle form of narcissism has been identified by Pierre Maranda, one in which readers see only themselves in the *text*:

> the text is the light on my face that enables me to see myself in the one-way mirror I hold in front of it; the text allows me, Narcissus, to marvel at my mind, to believe in myself and, consequently, to have the impression that I live more competently.
>
> (1980: 191)

While Laura Mulvey (1975) sees narcissism as most closely related to erotomania, she sees that other closely linked activity, voyeurism, as being related to scopophilia. Plays and books, narrative performances, allow us the pleasures of secret observation. We are the unseen, un-suspected, audience peeping through the lighted window at the private lives of others, peering through the keyhole at the doings in their bedrooms, having the vicarious pleasures of a thousand activities we either could not or would not dare indulge in. Of course, those who peer through keyholes and listen behind doors get some nasty shocks too. Peeping Tom should be coupled with Narcissus to become the two patron saints of spectators.

Another pair of commonly repressed desires which spectators can indulge to their heart's content are masochism and sadism. In catharsis we identify either with the punisher or the punished. Our repressed aggression can surface in sadistic delight in the casting out of the scapegoat (Girard 1977), or in permitted rejoicing at the misfortunes of others. It can enjoy transgression safely, revel in violence and violation. The spectator is not only the connoisseur of the scene, but also of the obscene, the nether side of the spectacle.[16] The spectator has another opportunity for sadism too: direct aggression towards the performance and the performers. Still safely anonymous, the audience can boo and jeer, or walk out ostentatiously. The reader can damn on hearsay, misrepresent, or attack with impunity. The text has no comeback.

In the long run, however, the masochistic tendencies of readers far outweigh the sadistic. One of the most common forms of repressed aggression is self-hatred. The enthusiasm of readers and spectators for self-punishment provokes the constant amazement and despair of the literally minded and didactic. 'What can you do', one hears them cry, 'with bourgeois who throng to a performance in which they are called idle grasping capitalists, with women who eagerly lap up the description of their sex as destructive sex objects, with adulterers who revel in the condign punishment or the abject humiliation of their like?' They forget the vital point that the force of desire, a force we do not even recognize, is far stronger than any overt political commitment.[17] And hatred is as strong a drive as love. Masochism goes so far with modern audiences that they have been known to co-operate enthusiastically with personal abuse and insult, although, even in the extreme case of cabaret, there is always the agreed formula of audience anonymity to match that of performance licence.

Perhaps the most conspicuous, and one of the most studied, instances of performance as the return of the repressed is that of the fairground or carnival (Bakhtin 1968; Kristeva 1982: 99–101). This is a return, a reversion as well, to the pre-Oedipal in Freudian terms. We are no longer, as in sadism and masochism, punisher and the punished. We have reverted to polymorphous perversion, to the longed-for reign of the chaotic and the imaginary (Jackson 1981), of disorder and the grotesque. One interesting feature of this reversion is that the distinction between performers and audience is lost. In the carnival we are at once actor and audience, male and female, master and slave. The reader of the carnivalesque text, of which the classic example studied by Bakhtin is the works of Rabelais, has the right to share the permission of licence in a realm where transgression is made the rule. The carnivalesque text, such as *Ulysses* or *Ubu Roi*, permits the ordering of disorder, the inclusion of the excluded, the eruption of the repressed.

THE EXCLUDED READER AND THE ENFORCED READER

A further aspect of the forbidden, imbued with the force of desire, is that of the excluded audience. By this I do not mean simply the reader excluded from the text or the audience excluded from the stage, the meaning given by Vincent Kaufman in his study 'Le tiers-lecteur' (1982). I mean the subjects of a much more specific prohibition, those highly ambiguous spectators who, either by reason of such authorial prohibition as 'This book, this performance is intended for men/women alone' or by reason of social convention or legislation, *should* not be present, or are discouraged from being present, at the performance, just as they may be discouraged from reading the text. What, for instance, are the reactions of women at a female strip show, or teenagers at a film clearly marked 'For adults only', or any of us devouring a book marked 'Banned by the censor'? What is the mixture of guilt and pleasure? Is the attraction/repulsion made stronger by interdiction and by disapproval? The presumption is that these spectator/readers interpret in function of their transgression. This can be a danger. We have all wondered if we have enjoyed a book because of censorship or in spite of it. On the other hand, as I hope to show, the excluded reader can play a very positive role by bringing a new and frequently ironic perspective to bear on performances designed for others. Yet another possibility is that the excluded reader has what one might call the 'taboo' reaction to the prohibited text, viewing it as either a 'sacred' object to be revered, or as a 'sacred' object to be vilified. So the response may be either that of the mind, irony, or that of the emotions, respect or transgression.

Equally interesting in its relation to transgression is that other audience which critics tend to forget, maybe because they have a vested interest in *not* thinking about it. This is the enforced audience: those who have to hear the performance of a narrative whether they like it or not. Part of the problem here is precisely that enforced readers are not allowed to interpret the text according to their own desires. The text is both performed and interpreted for them by a mediator, an enforcer, the interpreter of institutionalized literature or the voice of the prevailing ideology. One of the most interesting ways to study reader response would be to follow the reactions of those who, in congregations or classes, have had to follow the biblical narrative by command. What too are the varied reactions of those bus-loads of children taken to bad productions of Shakespeare, of the students who dutifully con the canonical texts?

The lucky few will feel the surprise of pleasure when least expected. In many readers, the least interesting, dutiful acceptance will mask boredom and forgetfulness. But what of those who feel and repress resentment and aggression? The imposition of an unwanted relationship can be felt as a form of violation. The more obvious forms of reader transgression which arise from enforced reading are the vast stores of parody which bear witness to the lasting effects of the imposition of this 'droit de seigneur'. I call parody *reader* transgression, because theories of intertextuality have thrown new light on the role of readership in the writing process (Riffaterre 1983b). Parody shows us this role in its most extreme form because the reading process is reproduced in the text itself, as the original syntagm is cast in new paradigmatic mould. Thus this 'authorized transgression', 'both textual doubling (which unifies and reconciles) and differentiation (which foregrounds irreconcilable opposition between texts and between text and "world")' (Hutcheon 1985: 101–2), sheds as much light on reading as on writing. Bakhtin (1981) suggests that parody represents a sort of Oedipal relationship, in which the child both rebels against the rule of the father and yet is forced to relive it in altered form. Enforced reading can produce an extreme version of this model.

Even more interesting are the cases where the return of the repressed in the enforced reader takes on new and explosive forms. Rimbaud's reading of the Bible emerges in the most violently transgressive yet creative transformations in *A Season in Hell*, and all of us can cite other examples from our private lives or from our reading. Some literature seems to feed on the flesh of dismembered texts. The force of this desire, to violate the very texts one once experienced as a violation, seems to me immensely important in the history not just of literature but of society. I do not feel Julia Kristeva has allowed for it sufficiently in her monumental study of transgression in literature, *Revolution in Poetic Language* (1984).

The recent emphasis on the *sujet de l'énonciation*, while beneficial in clearing away naïve pictures of the single omnipotent author and substituting a study of the workings of discourse, together with the to and fro of you and I *within* the discourse, still carries the danger of all *subject* orientation. We do not seem to have an equivalent term for the other active partner in the act of the creation or destruction of the text.

For instance, in the transgressive readings I have just been suggesting, it is quite clear that denunciation and renunciation complement the original enunciation. Of course, each contains within itself the original sign and thus a further discourse, a further performance.

The cases of the excluded reader and the enforced reader raise very central questions about reading as a whole. Reading has often been viewed in terms of satisfaction, of passive absorption, of submission to the authority of the text. Since the reader is an outsider to the consensus of the text, just as the audience is always an outsider to the consensus of the stage, we must ask if he or she is not always a transgressor, a breaker of boundaries and an intruder into the world of the other. Since the reader's desire is always the desire of the other, which wants what the other wants as much as it wants what the other is, and can never attain either, it must always involve the transgression implicit in the desire of the other. The extra exclusion of 'taboo' thus doubles and reinforces the barriers of the text, and stimulates reader desire confronted with a double lack. The betrayal by enforcement, on the other hand, which forcibly couples reader and text, stands to free reading as rape stands to love. Both can produce some quite sensational results.

A taxonomy of reader motivation and the force of reader desire, a study of the Eros and Thanatos of textual relationships, would be a vast undertaking.[18] A key to the directions it could take is Barthes's hypothetical typology of reading pleasure:

> We can imagine a typology of the pleasures of reading – or of the readers of pleasure; it would not be sociological, for pleasure is not an attribute of either product or production; it could only be psycho-analytic, linking the reading neurosis to the hallucinated form of the text. The fetishist would be matched with the divided-up text, the singling out of quotations, formulae, turns of phrase, with the pleasure of the word. The obsessive would experience the voluptuous release of the letter, of secondary, disconnected languages, of metalanguages (this class would include all the logophiles, linguists, semioticians, philologists: all those for whom language *returns*). A paranoiac would consume or produce compli-cated texts, stories developed like arguments, constructions posited like games, like secret constraints. As for the hysteric (so contrary to the obsessive), he would be the one who takes the text *for ready money*, who joins in the bottomless, truthless comedy of language, who is no longer the subject of any critical scrutiny and *throws himself* across the text (which is quite different from projecting himself into it).
>
> (1975b: 63)

I would propose that we will not understand the reader's part in the production of the text until we analyse the reader/spectator libidinal input as carefully as that of the author has been studied in countless works of psycho-criticism.

Coda: theory in performance

There is a more general meaning to performance: an implementation, and where possible a successful implementation, of a certain set of conditions of knowledge, skills, techniques, rules, or vocabulary. The classic distinction drawn by Chomsky is between the knowledge of vocabulary and of syntax, the paradigmatic and syntagmatic structures of a language, which is competence, and the use of those structures to produce a particular discourse, which is performance. As readers of narrative we are constantly acquiring more competence, competence which we put into performance in individual reading. Each reader, as we have seen, participates in an activity which gives the printed text an individual life, just as a director creates a performance text for an individual production. This may be seen in our reactions to illustration (unless the illustrations actually form part of the text as in children's books, Blake, Lear, or Lewis Carroll). We tend to reject illustration because we already have formed quite a clear picture in our minds.

We have just been looking at some of the elements which affect the transfer from competence to performance in various aspects of narration. Each reading puts the narrative into effect, fulfils the narrative contract, a contract of performance, which involves both the teller and the audience. However, this discussion has been largely theoretical, a demonstration rather of competence (or at least a display of competence) than of performance. Later chapters of this book will endeavour to show in precise concrete detail how the different elements of narrative theory, structural, pragmatic, hermeneutic, psychoanalytic, which have been sketched out here, can be applied to texts chosen for their relevance. Louis Marin, in his study of Poussin's *The Arcadian Shepherds* (in Suleiman and Crosman's edited collection of essays, *The Reader in the Text* (1980), which I regard as obligatory reading for *my* readers), has put the matter extremely well. I quote him in full, merely asking you to substitute narrative for painting as you read.

> It seems to me that all studies of pictorial and literary texts are exposed to such a tension between the pole of theoretical and methodological generalization and that of unique and individual

description, an opposition I might rephrase as that between *the structure of messages* in painting in general and *the system of a pictorial text* in particular. The concrete reading–viewing of a painting and the practical position of its reader–viewer thus have a twofold nature, a bidimensional constitution: on the one hand, *competence*, whose structure is constructed from the messages produced by codes and received by the viewer in the process of reading that particular painting as an example among many others or as a cluster of visual 'quotations' of several pictorial and extrapictorial codes; on the other hand, *performance*, whose system depends on that painting as a unique object of contemplation, which organizes it as an individual reading and is appropriate only for it in a unique situation of reception. The main problem such an approach encounters is the connection between these two dimensions, the determination of a level of analysis – and consequently a set of notions and relationships – intermediate between competence and performance, structure and system, messages and text, codes and individual reading–viewing. In a certain sense, the analyses that follow are attempts to construct such a level and to determine such relationships and notions.

(Marin 1980: 294)

Just as an actor participates in the making of a text by his performance, so we can participate in the making of that metatext which is critical theory by performing it. Each enactment, like each reading, is itself an interpretation of that theory. Our reader response, our enactment, our interpretation will modify the text and produce a new response among its readers in its turn. Performance, like revolution, is an act which must always be renewed.

2 · *The writer as performer*

Submitting narrative theory to the exposure of practice, one has the alternatives of examining structural and thematic devices from a wide range of texts, or of examining the process, the performance, of entire narratives in detail. I have chosen the latter path. I propose to examine a wide range of theoretical problems and narrative processes within a small corpus of closely related texts, each of which will be presented in full, so that my readers may conduct their own analysis and interpretation in parallel with mine.

The texts chosen are ideal for the purposes of demonstration as on the one hand they embody a distillation of a wide variety of narrative forms and structures and on the other they form together a liminal text, marking the threshold of modernism in literature. Over the period from 1855 to 1865 and particularly from 1861 to 1865, Charles Baudelaire, one of the greatest poets of France, experimented with a new form of literature which he called 'prose poems'. Most of these texts appeared in dribs and drabs in small journals and reviews[1] but several were not published until after Baudelaire's death in 1867.[2] The work, entitled either *Petits poèmes en prose* or *Le Spleen de Paris*, did not appear as a whole till the posthumous edition in 1869 where the order of printing of the texts was the arbitrary order of publication. This edition comprised only 50 of the 100 or more planned pieces. Frustratingly, we have only the titles and a few notes for the remainder.

THE TEXT AS KALEIDOSCOPE

Baudelaire's stated aim, and the aspect of the work which has been explored by most critics, was expressed in these lines of the dedication:

> Which of us has not, in his days of ambition, dreamt of the miracle of a poetic prose, musical without rhythm and without rhyme, supple and broken enough in cadence to adapt to the lyrical movements of the soul, to the undulations of day-dreams, to the convulsive starts of conscience?
>
> (*Oeuvres complètes*, I: 275)[3]

However, the really revolutionary aspect of the work, clearly expressed by the poet, has been accorded singularly little attention, perhaps because it was so foreign to the spirit of the time. This is how the dedication begins:

> My dear friend, I am sending you a little work of which one could not say, without injustice, that it has neither head nor tail, since, on the contrary, everything in it is both tail and head, alternatively and reciprocally. Consider, I beg you, what admirable advantages this combination offers all of us, you, me, and the reader. We can cut where we want, I my day-dream, you the manuscript, the reader his reading; for I do not make his restless will depend on the interminable thread of a superfluous plot. Remove a vertebra, and the two pieces of this tortuous fantasy will join together without difficulty. Hack it into numerous fragments, and you will see that each can exist separately.
>
> (I: 275)

In other words here we have a series of texts which have cohesion in that each text is a perfectly conceived and executed whole, but no syntagmatic closure in their arrangement, since any 'combination' of these 'fragments' is possible.[4] They can and should be read by changing the order and making different selections according to the choice of the individual reader. Thus the reader creates new possibilities of interpretation according to the order and number of the vertebrae joined together. In the rough notes to the dedication (I: 365) Baudelaire compares the work to a kaleidoscope. When I was a child I had a nineteenth-century kaleidoscope which differed from those seen today in that the viewer could place any selection of objects desired on the disc which rotated beneath the triangulated mirrors. One created ever-renewed pictures by the reflected combination of each choice of objects. In the same way each time one reads the prose poems in a different combination new and surprising elements emerge. This is why I have not hesitated to hack out and rejoin some of the pieces. As Patricia Waugh says in *Metafiction*:

> Writers employing such techniques, through a heightened sense of the randomness of the world, have come to see its configuration . . . as just as correspondent with reality as the paradigms of realism. . . . Combinative play in metafiction is concerned with the self-consciously performed reintroduction into the literary system of previously outworn modes and the exposure of present exhausted forms often unrecognised as such. Further, the element of chance in

combination may throw up a whole new possibility which rational exploration might not have discovered.

(1984: 43–4)

THE EXPERIMENT WITH NARRATIVE

It is precisely this recycling and recombination of 'outworn modes' which constitute the largely unrecognized originality of the 'prose poems'. The name 'poems' attached to them seems to have blinded critics to their most obvious feature, that they are in the first instance a dazzling display of many varieties of narrative. It is this that makes them so suitable for the testing of narrative theory. Only about nine of the texts would not qualify as stories in the generally accepted sense, as they deal rather with the description of emotions or places. (Any rigid categorization is useless: Greimas has shown us how fragile is the boundary between lyric and narrative.) The others comprise a compendium of traditional narrative forms, but in each case the quintessence of the form. Each genre is both refined and subverted, subject to ironic manipulation and recombination. The author of *Concerning the Essence of Laughter* . . . here examines the essence of narrative but does it in practice. The distillation of each narrative form and the incongruity of their juxtaposition are left to the reader to recognize. If this 'Hypocrite Reader, – my like, – my brother!', as he is called in the liminal poem of *Les Fleurs du mal* (1857, 1861), is equal to the task (see Brooke-Rose 1980), the new narrative possibilities will become apparent.

These texts include in perfect but minimal form the *Märchen* or wonder-tale, the *Sage* or anecdote,[5] the fable, the allegory, the cautionary tale, the tale-telling contest, the short story, the dialogue, the novella, the narrated dream. In the *Little Prose Poems* these narrative forms undergo what Gilles Deleuze and Félix Guattari have called *deterritorialization* (1975, 1980). A text which uses conventional forms in a conventional way is *territorialized*, it embodies the majority discourse and reflects the obtaining ideology of the society from which it springs. This is the case with most forms of popular narrative even though they may reflect that ideology from an oppositional standpoint.[6] However, just as popular thought may be revitalized by a new context or a new reading, suddenly revealing what Baudelaire called 'The immense depth of thought in vulgar sayings, holes dug by generations of ants' (*Oeuvres complètes*, I: 650), so too the accepted forms of narrative contain within themselves the mechanisms for possible *deterritorialization*. When one uses the traditional genres of narrative as a foreigner or a member of a minority uses language, then one changes the rules to one's own advantage and shakes the proprietorial bonds of discourse. The Baudelairean narrator is always defined as a stranger, a foreigner (see p. 52) and shakes the bonds of traditional narrative by turning its built-in structures to new uses.

> Proust used to say: 'masterpieces are written in a sort of foreign tongue'. It is the same thing as stuttering, but being a stutterer in language and not just in speech. To be a foreigner but in one's own tongue, and not simply as someone speaks another language than their own. . . . One only arrives at this result by sobriety, creative subtraction. Continuous variation has only ascetic lines, a little grass and pure water.
>
> (Deleuze and Guattari, 1980: 124–5)

Deterritorialization may thus be brought about by *recontextualization*, putting the traditional among the new or the products of one ideology alongside those of another; by *decontextualization*, as when a tale belonging to a cohesive corpus is isolated and judged purely on internal criteria; or most importantly by *self-contextualization* when unexpected paradigmatic structures work against the syntagmatic structure or vice versa.

Baudelaire for instance recontextualizes the traditional *Märchen* or wonder-tale by placing it amid other quite incongruous texts, and he self-contextualizes it by subtle paradigmatic shifts, as well as by an internal incongruity of discourse between the restricted code of the *Märchen* and the elaborated code of a nineteenth-century littérateur (see Fairlie 1976: 402–4). In 'The Gifts of the Fairies' (XX),[7] presented in a perfect pastiche of traditional oral performance and complete with asides to the audience, the motif of the supernatural gift-giving where one recipient arrives after all the gifts have gone is turned into irony at the expense of the small shopkeeper, the average Frenchman, who is incapable of understanding that his almost-forgotten son has finally been given the greatest gift of all, that of charm. In a cautionary tale, 'Loss of a Halo' (XLVI), a minute *Sage* in itself, the old motif of the angel who loses its halo is transformed in a few lines into that of the proper man of letters, who, having lost his halo in the mud of a Paris street, is found happily ensconced in a house of ill-fame, enjoying the vices of ordinary mortals and hoping that his joy will be made complete by the sight of an inferior poet in his discarded halo.

What is exploited in these texts is the immense variability which the very uniformity of traditional tale structure permits. The father of narratology, Vladimir Propp, repeatedly emphasized this multiformity, yet only his findings about the invariable sequence of functions (actions given meaning by their context) are usually remembered. He claimed that what gave the syntagmatic structure of the tale such power of transformation was that any function could be positive, negative, or contradictory (1968: 128–48). For instance, a contest could end in a victory (positive), a defeat (negative), or a victory which was really a defeat (contradictory). An action could be rewarded, punished, or given a reward which was really a punishment, and the same pattern applies to most of his thirty-one identified functions. Of course, in most *Märchen*, the structure is symmetrical; a story-line (or *move* as Propp called them) which has negative or contradictory features is usually followed by one with positive features. For instance, the heroine loses her husband in a battle of wits but regains him in the following contest. This traditional symmetry in no way prevents the modern tale-teller from making unexpected use of contradictory functions (such as the ones we have just seen, where the poet finds his descent to a den of vice not a punishment for his carelessness but a reward, and the shopkeeper views his gain as a loss). This device may be used to subvert and at the same time to highlight the conventionality of the basic structure.

> The parodist/metafictionist, using an established mode of fiction, lays bare the conventions that individual works of the mode share (which therefore define it) and fuses them with each other to extrapolate an 'essence'. This is then displaced through exaggeration and the substitution of a new content, so that the relationship of form to content . . . is itself laid bare.
>
> (Waugh 1984: 78)

This is so throughout the various genres and subgenres of narrative which Baudelaire employs, but particularly in the numerous stories in which he employs allegory. If we take allegory to be a narrative structure which suggests a coherent set or sets of paradigmatic variations which can be substituted within the same syntagmatic series, we see that in the traditional allegorical mode the alternatives are firmly guided by the text (see Fineman 1981). From Spenser's *The Faerie Queene* to Camus's *The Plague* with its epigraph from Defoe ('It is as reasonable to represent one type of imprisonment by another as to represent anything which really exists by something which does not exist') the allegorist usually draws the parallels clearly. Spenser's characters function as both moral and historical allegories, both abstract virtues and vices and real people of the Elizabethan world. Camus's are both the people of Oran, the people of any plague-stricken city, and the people of occupied France. Baudelaire's allegories are sometimes also clearly spelled out, as in 'Which is the True One?' (XXXVIII) where a laughing and vicious imp emerges from the sepulchre of the recently buried glorious beauty. When she mocks the poet's blindness, he stamps and his foot sinks – to be trapped for ever in the grave of the ideal. However, the more interesting and more modernist of Baudelaire's allegories are those in which the reader is left to supply a parallel story. Such 'open' allegories can be the subject of endless speculation, of endless mirroring between the text and the virtual texts it suggests. The patterning and constraints of the text work in constant interplay with the varied intertextualities – literary, historical, social – which inform the reading process. At the same time, the tropes of the text constantly turn the reader's mind back on itself, preventing any possibility of closure. 'Open' allegories have been examined with great subtlety by Paul de Man, and Chapter 8 will use aspects of his method to examine one Baudelairean allegory in detail.

THE ROLE OF THE READER

Baudelaire, as we have seen, was always acutely aware of the presence and power of both individual readers and his general reading audience. He realized the importance of establishing the initial narrative contract which provides the shared obligation and expectation between the text and its readers. In published work, that contract is confirmed by the title, a first-order illocutionary act, which is in itself a promise of performance and to which the reader responds by embarking on the text. An awareness of this bond is reflected in the particular importance of titles in the Baudelairean opus. The title is always highlighted by paradigmatic variations within the text, and usually contains great density of meaning. The statement in the notebooks 'I sought for titles' (*Oeuvres complètes*, I: 365) is borne out by the fact that sixty-three titles of further prose poems exist, with no more than a few rough notes extant as to their contents.

The prose poems reflect the many possible variants of the writer–reader relationship, ranging from full reader participation in the creation of the text at one extreme to almost total incomprehension or misdirection at the other. The multiplicity of possible readers ranges from the authorial audience (Rabinowitz 1977) of the full *alter ego* figure, such as the fraternal 'Hypocrite Reader' mentioned earlier, to the least desirable, the general public, 'which must never be presented with delicate perfumes which exasperate it, but with carefully chosen filth' ('The Dog and the Flask' (VIII)). The relationship between a writer figure and a reader figure is mirrored in the narrator–narratee relationships presented in many of the texts themselves. They experiment with a wide variety of narrative voices and focalization (Bal 1977), but the preferred voice is that of the first-person narrator who represents different recorder/observer figures, such as the *flâneur* or the poet.

This type of narrator figure suggests that the complementary figure of the narratee – and by narratee I mean a hearer or audience explicitly designated by the text (see Chapter 4 for a discussion of audiences) – would represent such different aspects of the reader as, for instance, the recipient of a letter, the browser, the self-improver, or the self-satisfied rationalist. The narratees are sometimes specified as female, such as the lady to whom the charmingly pretentious 'madrigal', 'The Clock' (XVI), is addressed, sometimes as male, such as the strolling gentleman who is advised to fill his pockets with penny toys for poor children in 'The Toy of the Poor' (XIX). More often the reader is left to deduce the implied narrative audience from the promptings of the text without a narratee being actually specified.

Often, however, two internal audiences are constructed by the text. The first we might call the audience of the *énoncé*, one we might regard as being constituted by the narrative world and as sharing its ideology, as well as knowledge of its interrelated happenings and characters. The other audience is one who is also aware of the textual strategies of the *sujet de l'énonciation*,[8] an audience to whom the text is not transparent communication, not a matter of course but a matter of discourse, to use Susan Stewart's formulation (1978: 19). The incomprehension of which Baudelaire complained, and the frequent attempts to censor his texts in whole or in part (several of the more scandalous texts, such as 'The Gallant Marksman' (XLIII), 'Mademoiselle Bistouri' (XLVII), and 'Let's Knock out the Poor!' (XLIX), were published posthumously for this reason), had made him acutely aware of the difference between the two audiences. He appreciated the gulf which divided the implied narrative audience, the average readers of his class and generation, from the ideal or potential reader who could grasp the *énoncé*, but, at the same time, be aware of the subtleties of the *énonciation*. As we shall see, he often exploited this by ostensibly addressing his texts to the average self-satisfied bourgeois, while at the same time using the intricacies of the *énonciation* to appeal to the 'happy few', to use Stendhal's term.

The power of the audience, who literally hold in their hands the life or death of the text, is most clearly portrayed in the novella 'A Heroic Death' (XXVII), which also demonstrates the difference between the audience of the *énoncé* and that of the *énonciation*. The jester hero of the tale, an incomparable actor, is tempted away from comedy by 'serious matters' and conspires against that budding Nero, the Prince, his friend and master. Arrested, he is commanded to give a last performance. Many of the court interpret this as potential clemency, but the narrator of the story, more 'clearsighted', sees it as an aesthetic and physiological experiment by the Prince. The actor, Fancioulle, gives the performance of a lifetime (quite literally) and shows himself 'a perfect idealization', the supreme embodiment of his role. The Prince, jealous of this power which exceeds his own, orders a page to interrupt the performance brutally with a piercing whistle (the ultimate sign of disapprobation of French audiences).

> Fancioulle, shaken, woken in his dream, at first closed his eyes, then reopened them almost immediately, unnaturally widened, then opened his mouth as though to take a convulsive breath, stumbled forward a little, back a little, and fell stone dead on the boards.
>
> (I: 322)[9]

Fancioulle, the actor, may be seen as the representative of the world of fiction, who has been tempted by the 'serious' world of actuality and is paying the penalty for transgression, for attempting to cross the barrier between the two worlds. The courtiers represent the audience of the *énoncé*, who judge the Prince's command for a final performance by the prevailing codes of the court, hence as a sign of approval and clemency. The narrator, on the other hand, represents the audience of the *énonciation*, the 'penetrating' witness who sees through the surface text to the possible multiple readings of the Prince's actions. When the performance takes place, Fancioulle is supreme 'on the boards', a perfect idealization in a fictional world, but the Prince, the reader/spectator excluded from the fictional world of the stage, still possesses the audience's ultimate power, which is to destroy the fictional world by denying it. The whistle represents the negative reading, which 'closes the show' and demonstrates the audience's command of the performance.

THE ARTIST AS OBSERVER

The particular role of the narrator in 'A Heroic Death', who qualifies as the teller of the story precisely because he is also the perfect audience, receptive both to the *énoncé* and to the *énonciation*, is characteristic of the figure of the artist/writer in *Little Prose Poems*. Jean Starobinski (1967) has presented the actor jester, who entertains and yet judges his master, the Prince, who appreciates and yet condemns him, and the writer/narrator, who tells their story, as all three doubles of the artist. The artist is both part of society and outside it. In the same way, the Prince, a spectator and dilettante, is excluded from the stage; the jester, an actor and artist, is excluded from reality which he aspires to by conspiracy; and the narrator, a witness in the wings, is excluded from the executioner–victim relationship which links the Prince and the jester in a bond of love and hate. This relationship of simultaneous exclusion and inclusion, of seeing and being seen, hearing and being heard (Chambers 1971b), is characteristic of performance. There is a shared bond between actors on stage from which the audience is excluded, yet there exists simultaneously a three-way bond between performer and performer and between performer and audience. The audience, excluded from the performance but included in the playing-space or auditorium, are doubly mirrored in 'A Heroic Death' by the Prince's (audience) relation to the actor and by the narrator-spectator's relation to the fatal drama enacted between them. Typical of the *Little Prose Poems* is this mode of the artist-narrator greedily observing the drama in which his other self, the artist-actor, is engaged. As Bergson remarked:

> Every moment of our life . . . offers these two aspects: it is actual and virtual, perception on the one hand and memory on the other. . . . He who becomes aware of the continual doubling of his present into perception and memory . . . will compare himself to the actor who automatically plays his role, listening to himself and watching himself act.
>
> (cit. Deleuze 1985: 106)

According to Bergson it is the visionary who is able to see the movement of time in terms of this constant doubling or division. Baudelaire had this visionary capacity, he was always 'the self insatiable for the non-self'. In his texts this doubled self becomes the narrator who is both actor and observer.

In his function of observer the Baudelairean narrator also frequently reflects the position of the reader *vis-à-vis* the written or printed text. In the performance of oral narrative, as we have seen, the audience was excluded from the performance space itself but included in the circle of the telling as one of a group of hearers. Like the audience at a theatre they were both set apart from and, at the same time, participated in a framed space which temporarily contrasted with the 'reality' outside the frame. However, the relationship of the reader to textual performance has changed with the switch from the oral to the written mode. This change may be gauged by the way in which ancient oral formulas and traditional narrative structures acquire new dimensions in some Baudelairean texts.

This is because these texts are intended for a changed audience. The audience for a written performance is differently placed. The shared experience of readership is *experienced* as a solitary pleasure. The reader no longer feels part of the combined audience but a 'voyeur' peering from the wings through a keyhole or a lighted window. *Little Prose Poems* is a crucial work for reader-orientated studies because many of the texts reflect the role of the reader, a reader alienated from life by immersion in the text, as 'The Stranger' (I) is alienated from family, friends, and country, and lost in the text of the clouds that pass. Such a reader too is passionately, but purely mentally, involved in the activities and emotions of others: 'What men call love is very small, very restricted and very weak, compared to this ineffable orgy, this holy prostitution of the Soul which gives itself entirely, poetry and charity, to the unforeseen spectacle, to the passing unknown' ('The Crowds' (XII)).[10] Could a better description of the 'pleasure of the text' be found?

The key to this relationship between narrator, 'voyeur', and reader is very clear in a short text which I quote in full, 'Windows' (XXXV).

> He who looks in from the outside through an open window never sees as many things as he who looks at a closed window. There is no object deeper, more mysterious, more fruitful, more shadowy, more dazzling, than a window lit by a candle. What one can see in the sunshine is always less interesting than what goes on behind a pane of glass. In this black or lighted hole life lives, life dreams, life suffers.
>
> Beyond waves of roofs, I perceive a mature woman, already wrinkled, poor, always bent over something, who never goes out. With her face, with her clothes, with her gestures, with almost nothing, I have rewritten the story of this woman, or perhaps her legend, and sometimes I tell it to myself with tears.
>
> If it had been a poor old man, I should have rewritten his story just as easily.
>
> And I go to bed, proud of having lived and suffered in others than myself.
>
> Perhaps you will say to me: 'Are you sure that this legend is the true one?' What does it matter what the reality which exists outside myself may be, if it has helped me to live, to feel that I am and what I am?[11]

The text starts distanced by a generalized third-person narration which informs and yet excludes the narratee. This necessary relationship of exclusion resembles that of the voyeur to the *closed* window, so preferable to the open. On this little lighted stage the passer-by can read the text of the life which yet remains cut off by the pane of glass. With the second part of the poem the voice moves to that of the first-person narrator now *including* the woman he watches in *his* fiction since he is excluded from her life. Just as he constructs his narrative metonymically, from a face, a dress, or a gesture, so readers construct their stories from the partial, metonymic, clues offered by the text.

Baudelaire is one of the writers who most skilfully evoke compassion. His texts can inspire tears or more frequently a 'throat choked by the terrible hand of hysteria' (*Oeuvres complètes*, I: 296). He is at the same time the writer who has analysed compassion with the most merciless clarity. Compassion is a simulacrum of passion, a feeling *with* another but also a vicarious feeling *of* the emotions of another. The emotion may be real but it is experienced at second-hand, it is essentially an observer's emotion, or, as in 'Windows', a telling to oneself of other people's stories. Compassion is a way of using life as a text to be read, just as the narrator here sardonically observes his pride in having 'lived and suffered in others than myself'. So the very experience which many readers find most fulfilling is shown as the most literary of experiences. It is, of course, none the worse for that, but the truth is an uncomfortable one.

The move into the last section of 'Windows' directly addresses and confronts the narratee, an implied bourgeois audience with the bourgeois preoccupation with veracity and reality. The final question-answer, which directly engages not only the implied audience but the actual reader, contains in itself a whole theory, not only of compassion but of text–reader relationships. The nineteenth-century (and after!) demand for textual realism is confronted by another 'truth', that of the text which helps one to know what one is and that one is, but at the same time renders the fixed reality of the subject as problematic as that of the text (see Johnson 1979: 68–9).

Just as one must be a spectator of the drama of others before one can feel compassion, in which one mentally re-enacts the performance of others, so too only a spectator can define obscenity. Obscene is a word one applies to the activities of others. In 'The Cake' (XV) the relationship of the two concepts is well expressed. The narrator has given a piece of white bread to a starving peasant child (who calls it cake). The child is attacked by his brother desperate to have the treat and a no-holds-barred fight breaks out, described in the most cruel and bloody terms. The narrator merely observes with clinical interest the gradual disappearance of the bread in the course of this battle, judging the fratricidal effects of starvation as an obscenity. The very com-

passion he feels for the poor is tempered by his self-centred reaction to
the story: 'This sight had clouded the landscape for me' (I: 299).

The wonderful story 'Mademoiselle Bistouri' (Miss Lancet)
(XLVII) is analysed in full in Chapter 7. We twentieth-century
readers see it as a compassionate and acute portrayal of sexual
fetishism, but it was seen as unpublishable by a nineteenth-century
editor, no doubt for its direct expression of 'perverted' sexual desire.
The judgement in each case, whether seeing it as psychological wisdom
or gratuitous pornography, is that of the reader, governed by his or her
own social and ideological context. The label of obscenity is a spec-
tator's view just as the 'feeling-with' of compassion is close to that
catharsis which results from the *spectacle* of pity and terror.

The discrepancy between spectator-judgement and actor-judge-
ment of the same event is one of the possible allegorical readings of 'The
Mirror' (XL). Here the minimal narrative (situation: the mirroring;
complication: the query about the reason; resolution: the answer that
one needs have no reason for a right) is present in the characteristic
form of the narrator observing an actor who is in turn observing
himself.

> An appalling man comes in and looks at himself in the glass.
>
> 'Why are you looking at yourself in the mirror, since you can only
> see yourself with displeasure?'
>
> The appalling man replies to me: 'Sir, according to the immortal
> principles of '89 all men are equal in rights; so I possess the right to
> gaze at my reflection; whether I do it with pleasure or displeasure is
> a matter for me and my conscience.'
>
> In the name of common sense, I was probably right; but, from the
> point of view of the law, he was not wrong.[12]

What is clear in any reading is that the word 'appalling' expresses the
view of the narrator; only to this spectator/reader is the 'appalling' text
an 'obscenity'. The man himself views his pleasure or displeasure in his
own reflection as a matter for his 'conscience', a typical play on words
as the French means either 'consciousness' or 'conscience', and leaves
open the matter of how aware the man is of his own appearance.

THE ARENAS OF PERFORMANCE: REALIST, SYMBOLIC, FANTASMIC

The *Little Prose Poems* were tentatively divided under three headings by
their author (though he added 'Other classes to be found' (I: 370)).
These three classes were *Choses parisiennes* ('Parisian Matters'), *Symboles
et moralités* ('Symbols and Moral Stories') and *Oneirocritie* ('Dream

Judgement'). The fifty poems we have divide more or less evenly between these classes though there are overlaps. Do we class 'Counterfeit Coinage' (XXVIII, see pp. 80–8) as a Parisian story or a moral story? 'Which is the true one?' (XXXVIII) as a dream or a symbol? In fact, as will become apparent, these classes are more an indication of possible alternative readings, since, as we have seen, any division of *Little Prose Poems* into generic types is subverted by the kaleidoscopic nature of the collection. Depending on reader, order of reading, and context, a Parisian story may be read *also* as a symbol or a dream, and vice versa. However, if we add the sixty-odd further titles which Baudelaire himself classed under these three heads, 'Parisian Matters' come out well ahead, with about fifty, compared with about thirty each in the other two groups. This agrees with the alternative title for the whole collection which is *The Spleen of Paris* and with the fact that its equivalent in verse poetry, which may also be roughly divided into 'Pictures of Paris', 'Dreams', and 'Symbols', is called *Tableaux parisiens* and forms one section of *Les Fleurs du mal*. Each of these three classes is developed in the text in close relation to actual performance, 'Parisian Matters' seen reflected in street drama and street theatre of various kinds, 'Symbols and Moral Stories' in relation to morality plays (*moralités* means 'morality play' as well as 'moral' in French) and allegories, and 'Dream Judgement' in relation to the concrete enactment of desire and lack which is portrayed in dreams and nightmares.

THE STORIES OF THE STREETS

'Parisian Matters' is the section which will concern us most. I have chosen to take all the examples for detailed study and demonstration from this section, partly because of the greater internal unity provided in this way to my own study, partly because the parallel between written performance and enacted performance is particularly clear and diverse in these poems. Baudelaire's role as a poet of the big city has been studied by many critics, following in the footsteps of Walter Benjamin in his *Charles Baudelaire: a Lyric Poet in the Era of High Capitalism* (1973), and I do not propose to try to cover the ground yet again. Rather, I will concentrate on two things: the particular role of the observer or 'voyeur' as reader of the drama of the streets and the use of the real theatre of the streets as parallel and self-reflexive play within the play of the text.

There are sixteen poems in prose which may be classified as 'Parisian Matters' and of these thirteen are set wholly or partly in the street. Some context must, I think, be given to the extraordinary emphasis on this particular setting to help in the reading of the poems. In the street the voyeur becomes a *flâneur* (see Nies 1976), a person who strolls the streets in search of entertainment. Baudelaire, like many other inhabitants of Paris, never had a private home and mostly lived in a succession of hotel rooms. People in these conditions spend many hours in the street in search of meals, of entertainment, of company and life, and, of course, of sex. The *flâneur* (defined in *Robert*, the French dictionary, as 'one who walks without haste, at random, abandoning himself to the impressions and the sights of the moment') will have hasty meetings with the busy bourgeois who cross his path and longer ones with all the other 'street walkers', the beggars, the prostitutes, the old men and women also living in one room on an almost non-existent income, the rubbish collectors and street-sweepers, the itinerant vendors and open-air stall keepers (particularly the sellers of prints and books along the Quais), and, last but not least, the buskers and *saltimbanques* (itinerant clowns, singers, acrobats, and mimes).

The *flâneur* then is constantly reading the text of the streets and, in the case of the Baudelairean narrator, constructing his own narrative from the signs he finds there. The narrative may grow metonymically, from a face, the lift of a skirt, a strange snatch of conversation, or it may grow metaphorically as some moment of the drama of the streets is seen to parallel and illustrate the telling of a tale. Walking then is a double activity: on the one hand it is conning the signs amidst which one moves, as the eye cons the signifiers of the text, caught in the patterns of the streets as in those of typography, pausing before a shop window as one pauses before a felicitous piece of rhetoric; on the other hand it is movement, rhythmic activity, the rise and fall of the breath, but punctuated by stops and starts, a parallel in fact to that rhythmic prose Baudelaire dreamt of: 'supple and broken enough in cadence to adapt to the lyrical movements of the soul, to the undulations of day-dreams, to the convulsive starts of conscience' (Dedication).[13] The *flâneur*-narrator then both absorbs and produces art as he moves through the streets.[14]

We have already noted how the *Little Prose Poems* are intended to be read in different selections and combinations according to each individual reader.[15] This possibility of permutation and juxtaposition gives an extraordinary quality of self-reflexivity to the texts. Individual texts have their own self-reflexive embedded segments or *mise-en-abyme* but whole texts also function as *mise-en-abyme* to other combinations of texts, casting light on the *énonciation*, the *énoncé* or both (Dällenbach 1977; see also Chapter 3).

'Crowds' (XII) acts in this way to cast light on both the telling and the tale of all the 'Parisian Matters'. It comments on the relationship of the *flâneur* and the poet:

> It is not given to just anyone to take a bath of multitude: experiencing the pleasure of the crowd is an art; and he alone can revel in vitality, at the expense of the human race, into whom in his cradle a fairy breathed the taste for fancy dress and masks, the hatred of home and the passion for travel.
>
> Multitude, solitude: equal terms convertible by the active and fruitful poet. He who does not know how to people his solitude, does not know either how to be alone in a busy crowd.
>
> The poet enjoys this incomparable privilege, that he can at will be himself and others. Like those wandering souls who seek a body, he enters, when he wishes, anyone's character.[16]

The poet then remains a *flâneur* so long as he is developing the text for himself and by himself. Let him publish, however, and thus put himself in the position of being read and of wishing to attract readers, and he becomes a performer. No longer an ambulating amateur, he becomes a strolling player. He is no longer merely involved in a desultory way in the everyday drama of the streets but becomes a professional, his work self-compared to the theatre of the streets (Mauron 1966), with its buskers, showmen, and acrobats. As a professional artist he is also a kind of prostitute, a street walker succumbing to the need to share himself with the reader, unable to remain one and alone (I: 650, 700).

But the teller of tales must first of all be an actor, a *saltimbanque* mouthing his words, showing his wares, turning handsprings for the entertainment of the public. The world of the fairground, the busker, the circus, becomes in Jean Starobinski's words 'a derisory epiphany of art and the artist' (1970). Only two of the prose poems, 'A Heroic Death' (XXVII) and 'Vocations' (XXXI), deal with court or bourgeois theatre and the traditional analogy between the actor and the artist; the others deal with popular entertainment. One, 'The Jester and the Venus' (VII), is an adaptation of a Deburau sketch from the *Théâtre des Funambules* (see Jones 1984), a working-class mime show 'discovered' by Baudelaire and his friends and seen by them as the apotheosis of popular art, but more especially as a kind of lost or 'innocent' model for all art. This was the period of the Romantic revival of folk art and a renewed interest in oral performance, clearly seen in the styles and genres chosen for *Little Prose Poems*. Most people have seen the film *Les Enfants du Paradis* which gives a vivid impression of this theatre of the people and its intimate relation with the life of the streets. Other poems invoke the fairground with its naïvety, its obscenity, its skills and its smells, its flares and its noise. In perhaps the most poignant of these, 'The Old Acrobat' (XIV), the analogy between the *saltimbanque* and the artist is clearly drawn.

> At the end, at the very end of the row of booths, as if, ashamed, he had exiled himself from all these splendours, I saw a poor acrobat, stooped, aged, decrepit, a ruin of a man, leaning against one of the posts of his shanty; a shanty more miserable than that of the most mindless savage, where two candle-ends, dripping and smoking, still cast too much light on the distress.
>
> Everywhere joy, profits, carousing; everywhere the certainty of bread for the days to come; everywhere the frenetic explosion of vitality. Here absolute destitution, destitution decked, to crown the horror, in comic rags, where necessity, rather than art, had introduced contrast. . . .
>
> And, going away, obsessed by this vision, I sought to analyse my sudden pain, and I said to myself: I have just seen the image of the old man of letters who has survived the generation he so brilliantly entertained; of the old poet without friends, without family, without children, degraded by poverty and by public ingratitude, whose booth forgetful society no longer wishes to enter![17]

Starobinski (1970) sees this new view of the artist as the tragic clown as being a self-depreciation characteristic of the shift towards modernism in the nineteenth century, a self-depreciation which culminated in such pictures of the artist as clown as those drawn by James Joyce and Henry Miller. Characteristic too of the modernist writer is the fragmentation of self whereby the poet becomes both the fairground *flâneur* and the poor clown he spies upon, both the I observing and the I observed.

THE MUTATIONS OF MORALITY

The arena of performance evoked in 'Parisian Matters' is linked with very public spaces and very public performances. The arena of performance of 'Symbols and Moral Stories' can be a similar public space or something more generalized and more abstract, as befits an allegory or a morality play. One example must suffice, which is also a Parisian story, since it is based on a true happening in the life of the painter Manet and dedicated to him. 'The Rope' (XXX) (*la corde* also means 'the hanging') ironically purports to illustrate mother love and moralizes on that theme. It is the tale of a child from a poor family who lives with an artist as helper and model. The artist threatens to send him home because of repeated petty thefts and the child hangs himself. The artist is stricken with guilt and remorse. However, the father says his son would have come to a bad end anyway, and the mother weeps and begs, not for the child's body but for the rope with which he hanged himself. The punch-line comes after repeated money offers from the neighbours to buy the rope, since the noose of a hanging is a well-known good-luck charm. Only then does the artist know with 'what trade she intended to console herself'.

The tale contains a classic *mise-en-abyme* which helps us to follow the symbolic similarity of the story to the greatest morality play of all, Christ's crucifixion. The artist narrator says:

> He posed more than once for me and I transformed him now into a little gypsy, now into an angel, now into a mythologic Cupid. I made him bear the fiddle of the vagabond, the Crown of Thorns and the Nails of the Passion, and the Torch of Eros.[18]

The child, spurned by his father, martyred by society, choosing death, is finally granted a sort of blasphemous *pietà* as his mother clasps to her bosom, not the body, but the rope whose fragments have acquired a miraculous value almost like those of the Cross.

It will be seen that Baudelaire's allegories and moralities are not just your conventional moral tale but rely on the mechanisms and formulas of convention to produce a new parodic variation on the genre. A self-reflexive juxtaposition of texts serves a similar function to the *mise-en-abyme* and generates further readings. Read together with the bitter misogyny of some prose poems, 'The Rope' may be seen as a vitriolic attack on the bad mother, contrasted with the ideal mother who appears in 'Widows' (XIII). On the other hand, if read in conjunction with 'The Cake' (XV), we see the moral as an attack on the dehumanizing effects of extreme poverty.

This new open-ended approach to that most closed of all genres, the moral tale, clearly illustrates the creative function which Michel Serres (1982) assigns to 'noise', or what he calls the 'parasite', the interruption in the channel of communication which necessitates a change or re-duplication of the message, the penicillin which produces new strains of bacteria thanks to its interference with the genetic code, the 'snow' in a visual signal which forces a redisplay of the picture. Baudelaire, as an enforced reader of the moral texts of his society, whether they took the form of sermons, of newspaper editorials, of court judgements,[19] or of fashions, was a producer of 'noise'. He set up reader resistance, he accepted the moral and ideological messages of the discourses of power only in a mutilated or a radically altered form. This 'noise', this 'parasite' attacking the messages of chauvinism, of patriarchy, of bourgeois morality, produced in its turn, as the reader became the writer, mutated messages which used the old channels in new ways (see pp. 166–8).

A symbol was after all originally a token, a substitute for a voice; in *Little Prose Poems* the tokens remain but they stand for new voices. The morals of stories like 'Loss of a Halo' (XLVI) or 'Counterfeit Coinage' (XXVIII) are mutant forms of bourgeois morality. As a reader or receiver of the bourgeois values of, for example, the press, the narrator may be presumed to have displayed resistance, or noise. This in turn has radically influenced the production of the text. The very notion of intertextuality implies that we must all read before we can write, and one activity cannot be divorced from the other. We are always using the discourse of others, but mercifully the parasite, 'noise', exists to ensure constant mutations in the reproduction of that discourse (see Chapter 8). Baudelaire's are considerably more radical than most. The minute morality plays enacted in these texts have all the shocking un-expectedness of Harold Pinter's *The Homecoming* or *The Birthday Party*, which similarly promise conventional forms only to present them monstrously mutated. These displacements at times resemble the work of dreams, and indeed dreams can always be read as symbols after the work of interpretation has taken place.

DREAM PLAY: VISUAL AND VERBAL

The third arena of performance, which is named in 'Dream Judgement' but extends throughout the texts, is the most private of all, the one we all share and yet in which we are always alone, the drama of desire, the drama of dreams. Indeed this was a primary focus of the whole collec-tion whose first title was 'Nocturnal Poems'. The dramatization of desire and lack is obvious in the poem 'The Double Bedroom' (V), a room double in both senses of the word as it is evenly divided in the text between the delicious eternity of dream and the nightmare of reality. This double scenario is the legacy of sleep where the soul 'takes a bath of laziness, made aromatic by regret and desire'. The concrete rep-resentation of power, the eternal moment, found in the dream when desire seems on the verge of fulfilment, is contrasted with the power-lessness of the narrator, enslaved to the past, to drugs, to depression, in his everyday nightmare. In the same way dreams of erotic and artistic plenitude such as 'The Invitation to the Voyage' (XVIII) contrast with such nightmares of powerlessness as the poem fragment 'Symptoms of Ruin':

A tower-labyrinth. I have never been able to get out. I dwell for ever in a building which is going to crumble, a building eroded by a secret sickness. I calculate, in my own mind, to amuse myself, if such a prodigious mass of stones, of marbles, of statues, of walls, which are going to crash into one another, will be very soiled by the multitude of brains, of human flesh, and crushed bones.

(I: 372)[20]

Even more striking than the mere evocation of dream states is the textual exploitation of the processes of 'dream work' later analysed by Freud: condensation, displacement, visual representation, and secondary revision (1982: 204–19). To give one example, not generally recognized as such: 'The Bad Glazier' (IX) contains a story of violent sadism against a poor glazier unable to supply 'pink glass (*verres roses*), red, blue, magic panes, panes of paradise . . . panes which make one see life as beautiful (*la vie en beau*)!' This is an obvious displacement and a visual representation of the cliché '*la vie en rose*' probably condensed with the English 'to see life through rose-coloured spectacles'.[21] The secondary revision, translating the visual signs into verbal signs, stresses the manifestation of lack. The narrator, who, by the doubling characteristic of dreams, may be presumed to be attacking a manifestation of self in the person of the glazier, resorts to aggression to obliterate the panes (*vitres*) which refuse to transform life:

> Knocked backwards by the shock, he finally broke under his back his poor walking wealth which produced the resounding noise of a crystal palace shattered by lightning.
>
> And, intoxicated by my madness, I shouted to him furiously: 'Life as beautiful! Life as beautiful!'[22]

The terms of my present enterprise do not permit a linguistic study of the processes of condensation and displacement in *Little Prose Poems*, since this would require close examination of the texts in their original language. The best study of these processes, though not expressed in the Freudian terms of dream work, is Barbara Johnson's brilliant deconstructive analysis of 'The Gallant Marksman' (XLIII) (1983: 85–96) where she shows conclusively how the growth of the poem arises from the displacement and condensation of two expressions, 'killing time' (*tuer le temps*) and 'you are my muse' (*tu es ma muse*) which is also (*tuer m'amuse*) 'killing amuses me'.

Baudelaire's own summary of this poem runs:

> A man goes to a pistol shooting gallery, accompanied by his wife. – He aims at a doll, and says to his wife: 'I'm imagining it's you.' He

closes his eyes and hits the doll. – Then he says, kissing his companion's hand: 'Dear angel, how I thank you for my skill!'

(I: 660)[23]

In this particular type of exploitation of the 'dream work' of textual creation, Baudelaire is the precursor of Kafka, the Kafka who transforms a cliché such as 'My home is my castle' into the dream convolution of 'The Burrow' or 'Your words are engraved on my heart' into the sadistic nightmare of 'In the Penal Settlement' (see also Mehlman 1974). The other main form of the narrative of desire, the analytic text, is discussed in detail in Chapter 7.

PERFORMANCE IN THE TEXT

As we have seen, in her study of the performative in *Don Juan* (1983: 29) Shoshana Felman points out that performance must be seen in literature under three connotative categories: erotic, theatrical, and linguistic. The Baudelairean text also displays a fourth: physical or energetic. Each of these categories is exploited in a very particular way in the prose poems, with the different forms of textual performance so precisely outlined that they can be seen as exemplary.

Physical performance: the moving body of the text

Baudelaire was very conscious of the functioning of texts not as static structures but as networks of moving parts. This involves a gauging of the movements and stresses, the structures and systems. There is a geometry of poetic art just as there is a geometry of the dance, a perfect combination of line and curve. The poetic performance involves the flawless interpenetration of the network of content and the network of expression. Such an interplay is what Deleuze and Guattari call an *agencement*, a network in which the physical and energetic actions of bodies and feelings are transformed into the combination of signs produced by *énonciation*, by the action of the speaking or writing subject. Just as Baudelaire foreshadows Kafka's use of the dream processes of displacement, so he also foreshadows the *agencement machinique* which Deleuze and Guattari see exemplified in Kafka's work:

> On the one hand the machine-boat, the machine-hotel, the machine-circus, the machine-castle, the machine-tribunal: each with its parts, its cogs and gears, its processes, its mixed, embedded, disjointed bodies. . . . On the other hand the system of signs or *énoncia-*

tion: each system with its incorporeal transformations, its acts, its death sentences and its verdicts, its trials, its 'law'.

(1980: 113)

It must be understood that Deleuze (1983) establishes a strong distinction between the *machinique* or energetic, and the *mécanique* or mechanical. The *machinique* involves an interplay of dynamism, rhythm, and process, whereas the *mécanique* is lifeless and artificial, not part of an organic whole.[24] The ship to Baudelaire is rather an *agencement géométrique*, an interplay of lines and curves with the logic of the work of art:

> I believe that the infinite and mysterious charm which lies in the contemplation of a ship, and especially of a ship in movement, belongs, in the first place, to the regularity and symmetry which are one of the primordial needs of the human mind, to the same degree as complication and harmony, – and, in the second place, to the successive multiplication and generation of all the imaginary curves and figures formed in space by the real elements of the object.
>
> The poetic idea which emerges from this operation of movement in the lines is the hypothesis of a vast, immense, complicated, but eurhythmic being, an animal full of genius, suffering and sighing all human sighs and ambitions.

(I: 663–4)[25]

Perhaps the most beautiful expression of this notion of the physical performance of the text is the tribute to the musical texts of Franz Liszt, 'The Thyrsus' (XXXII). The Thyrsus is the emblem of the text, a pole entwined with vines and flowers.[26]

> The pole is your will, upright, firm, and unshakeable; the flowers are the stroll of your fantasy around your will; the feminine element performing around the male its prestigious pirouettes. Straight line and arabesque line, intention and expression, stiffness of the will, sinuosity of the word, unity of the end, variety of the means, all-powerful and indivisible amalgam of genius, what analyst would have the detestable courage to divide and separate you?[27]

This notion of the text as a moving thing, an interplay of energy and action, carries with it a very modernist fusion of science and magic. The perfectly balanced text is like a prayer wheel, generating a mystical force of its own. One plan for a prose poem concerned a rosary with its combination of the mystical and the energetic, performance made text, text made performance. Baudelaire saw the manipulation of language with skill as 'practising a sort of sorcery by evocation' (II: 118), unleashing the power of the word as one unleashes the power of electricity by the correct balance of energies. Play in all meanings of the word is a key term for these works and the double meaning of play, both an activity of freedom and yet a strictly rule-governed progression – the play of the imagination and the play of the machine—is vital to both the writing and reading of these experimental narratives.

Sexual/textual relationships[28]

Sexual union is something both intensely physical and intensely abstract in the poetry of Baudelaire. Union with the beloved is a union with the forces of nature, with the infinite and the eternal, but above all fusion and identification with the other represent the apotheosis of self. The ideal woman reflects the desires of men who:

> love the sea, the immense, tumultuous, green sea, the shapeless and many-shaped water, the place where they are not, the woman they do not know, the sinister flowers which resemble the censers of an unknown religion, the scents which trouble the will, and the wild and voluptuous animals which are the emblems of their madness.
> 'The Benefactions of the Moon' (XXXVII)[29]

The love of a woman can be seen to be closely analogous to that 'sorcery by evocation', the creation of the poetic text, described as follows:

> It is then that colour speaks, like a deep vibrating voice; that monuments stand upright and are profiled against deep space; that animals and plants, representatives of ugliness and evil, display their unequivocal grimace; that scent provokes the corresponding memory and thought; that passion murmurs or roars its language, eternally the same.
>
> (II: 118)[30]

The poetic text, like the eyes of the beautiful woman, is the mirror in which the poet seeks his own perfect image, the mediating instance which permits a fusion with the infinite. However, it is borne in upon the disillusioned poet that the text, like the woman, remains irreducibly other. Like her, it must be shared with others, soiled by contact with other minds and other hands. The perfect self-image is only possible if unity is preserved; duality, the duality of text and reader, lover and lover, is prostitution.

> Invincible taste for prostitution in the heart of man, whence is born his horror of solitude. – He wants to be *two*. The man of genius wants to be *one*, so alone.

Glory is to stay *one* and to prostitute oneself in a particular manner.

It is this horror of solitude, the need to forget one's *self* in outside flesh, that man nobly calls the *need* for love.

(I: 700)[31]

Barbara Johnson has ably analysed the shift in focus in the view of the love-relationship apparent in this notebook entry, contemporaneous with *Little Prose Poems*, and has related it to the movement in Baudelaire's writing from poetry to prose. She shows how the move from metaphor to metonymy reduces the seduction of the metaphor and displays the artificiality of the poetic process. The subject seeking to construct his own identity by reflection in the mirror of otherness is instead trapped by the disparate play of metonymy. The reflection in the woman/mirror 'is neither himself nor an other, but what prevents the "I" from constituting itself other than *divided* – other than *fiction*' (1979: 50). The lack of true communication, of true unity, the invincible duality of man and woman even in the moment of orgasm, produces a constant admixture of pleasure and pain; indeed Baudelaire regards it as no accident that intercourse is accompanied by the noises of the torture chamber. The power that lovers have over one another is compared to the mutual bonds of torturer and victim. A similar reciprocal bond, the violence that it permits each to inflict on the other, is also the bond that links author and reader. 'What is Art?' asks Baudelaire, and answers 'Prostitution' (I: 649).

The theatricalization of self: enactment and concretization

A celebrated passage from *The Invitation to the Voyage* (XVIII), a *mise-en-abyme* which self-reflexively sheds light on many of the other texts, also provides a clue to the particular status of the first-person narrator in *Little Prose Poems*.

Dreams! Always dreams! and the more ambitious and sensitive the soul is, the more dreams distance it from the possible. Each man carries within himself his dose of natural opium, constantly secreted and renewed, and, from birth to death, how many hours can we count full of positive enjoyment, of successful and decided action? Will we ever dwell, will we ever pass into this picture my mind has painted, this picture which resembles you?[32]

Here we see the problem that action, for the dreamer, always becomes enactment. Putting a dream into action resolves itself into putting on an act, just as reaching the beautiful Utopia which reflects the beloved merely means passing into a picture, the concretization of the dream. What the narrator portrays may be a picture, an enactment, or a performance, but he himself always stands upon the stage of the text, framed by its confines. Where, however, the *mise-en-scène* of narrative differs from that of the theatre is that it permits a dramatization of self as both observer and observed, a mental multiplication which can be achieved on stage only by such devices as the interplay of voice and recorded voice in Beckett's *Rockaby* or *Krapp's Last Tape*.

The growing alienation of self produces the theatricalization of self in many Baudelairean texts. The vision of the self as other, as performer on a private stage, foreshadows the fragmentation of the unity of 'self' characteristic of modernism. The self splits into two or more virtual selves, each a mask, a fabrication, and performs a particularly neat disappearing-act behind the narrator in the first person. As John Fowles acutely remarked, 'the pronoun is one of the most terrifying masks man has invented' (cit. Stanzel 1984: 155), and the narrative *I* can produce the perfect illusion of presence, while actually foregrounding the self as other. One step further, and even the split *I* ceases to command the whole and disintegrates into a 'voice' among many others in those texts which consist completely of dialogue.

The display of a virtual self as a performer produces a sense of intimacy which is totally illusory, since the interposed person of the narrator actually maintains a greater distance between text and audience, and between author and reader. If the figure of the actor may be seen as a reflection of the figure of the narrator in *Little Prose Poems*, the choice, which we have already observed, of the condemned jester, Fancioulle, and the desolate figure of the old acrobat (*saltimbanque*) certainly argues an existential as well as a narrative alienation.[33]

However, I would be rather more positive than Barbara Johnson about the *mise-à-mort*, the reflection of the doomed performer in the doing to death of traditional poetic language. What she sees as the de-figuration, even the disfigurement, of poetic language I see as the 're-figuration' of narrative. Prose narrative is itself dependent on an elaborate system of tropes, but the emphasis changes from the metaphoric condensation of poetry to the more concrete processes of displacement and contiguity, the theatrical game of substituting the part for the whole and the attribute for the person. The crown stands for the emperor, the knife for the assassin, and three windows and a door for a house. Heavily theatricalized narratives, such as we find in *Little Prose Poems*, many of which are reminiscent of, and indeed modelled on, oral performance, are particularly dependent on metonymy. This may take the form not necessarily of a recognizable verbal trope, but of a particular significance given to concrete objects. It is not just that the irreality of the theatrical speech act is compensated by the extremely concrete reality of bodies and props, but rather that their iconic solidity in each case suggests a larger whole. In the same way, a highly condensed narrative text, like those of Baudelaire, may not need to use figurative language, because each concretization is in itself a figure. The shattered glass of 'The Bad Glazier' or the guttering candles of 'The Old Acrobat' are not so much metonymic of 'reality' as parts of a potential figurative whole which can take place only in the mind of the reader. Certainly the dazzling display of metaphor found in the verse poems has given way to a more sober form, the *essence* has given way to the *attributes* (Johnson 1979: 156). Yet these 'attributes', concrete in form and dramatic in function, have a particular role in the developing relationship between text and reader. The metonymic narrative involves an intellectual challenge which triggers in its turn a deeper response. The movement, as Prévost puts it (1953: 121), is 'from amusement to intelligence, then from the mind to the heart'. The interplay of actions and objects, condensed into a seemingly conventional narrative framework, can be seen to develop into an open-ended allegory which involves the full co-operation of the reader. Indeed, as Barbara Johnson's practice has demonstrated more than any other, the metonymic force of the narrative is such that each story provokes a range of intellectual and emotional responses which may properly be called metaphoric.[34] In these enactments 'everything . . . becomes allegory' (I: 86).

Competence and performance in language and in art

Performance in the linguistic sense of the word is opposed to competence, competence being the acquired vocabulary and grammar of a language, the capacity to form sentences and to participate in communication. Performance, on the other hand, is the actual putting into practice of the knowledge so acquired. This division does not just apply to language as a whole, to natural languages or mother tongues, but also to each specialized discourse which belongs either to a class, a period, or a profession. I may have considerable verbal competence and be extremely ignorant of the discourse of logic, motor mechanics, or cooking. The relationship between artistic competence and performance is very well displayed in the rough notes for a prose poem entitled 'Elegy of the Hats'. Here we see the meticulous acquisition of competence at work: shapes of hats, names of the parts of hats, types such as bonnets, pokes, caps, berets are enumerated. Every sort of trimming, ruching, pleating, biasing, puffs, feathers, and pompons is described in minute and picturesque detail. The appearance and furniture of the milliner's shop is summed up. Most of this vocabulary and information would not even have been used in the final text but it provides, as it were, a fluency in the language.

Only on the second page of the text are we given some idea of what would have been the aim of the actual performance:

> General aspect: freshness, light, whiteness, lively colours of a flower-bed.
> Ribbons, trimmings, tulle, gauzes, muslins, feathers, etc. . . .
> Hats make one think of heads, and look like a gallery of heads. For each hat, by its character, demands a head and makes it visible to the eyes of the mind. Severed heads.
> What sadness in solitary frivolity! Heart-rending feeling of sprightly ruin. A monument of gaiety in the desert. Frivolity in abandonment.
>
> (I: 373)[35]

Then of course the meaning of the carefully chosen title 'Elegy of the Hats' begins to emerge.

This pursuit of competence is also the pursuit of excellence, rather like the immense amount of 'language', that of the body, the context, the space, as well as the text, that an actor has to acquire to play a part really well. Brecht has admirably described this acquisition of competence in his picture of the long deliberations of a young actor tortured over the choice of a hat from a theatre wardrobe for his four-minute appearance as a beggar:

> There were shades of dilapidation invisible to the careless eye; the one hat had perhaps once been expensive when new but was now in even worse condition than the other. Had Filch's hat once been expensive, or at least more expensive than this other? How dilapidated might it have been? Had Filch looked after it when his fortunes declined, was he in a position to look after it? Or could it have been a hat which he had not worn at all in his good times? And how long ago were those good times? How long did a hat last? The collar was gone, that was decided during a sleepless night, dirty collars are worse than none at all (God in Heaven, is that really so?) anyway it was decided, what then might the hat look like?
>
> (1967: 1001–3; trans. H. Maclean)

So runs the painful acquisition of competence for the artist determined 'to find the *only* way of presenting his character'. Brecht concludes: 'This, I thought blissfully, is an actor of the scientific age'. What one must bear in mind is that the Baudelairean narrator who is taking shape in 'Elegy of the Hats' is like the Brechtian actor, acquiring competence not for performance in the Chomskian sense, but for *a* performance. His performance will involve a specialized vocabulary but also a specialized knowledge of the syntax of narrative, the grammar of stories. The unused expertise, the discarded paradigms will remain essentially part of that performance, which will consist as much of the choices made as of the final combination.

THE PART OF THE READER IN THE PLAY OF PARTS

The Baudelairean narratives may be assessed as performance in any one or several of these connotative frameworks, the physical, the erotic, the theatrical, the linguistic. Our choice of a reading strategy may work with or against the strategies of the text. The strategies of the text are variable, however, and depend on the juxtaposition of texts, what whole we make from the sum of what parts, and of course what parts we exclude from that whole. Our reading depends on the extent of our knowledge of the language of literature as well as of our knowledge of the language of our society: 'The infinity of texts, of languages, of systems: a difference of which each text is the return' (Barthes 1974: 3). The network of quotation or of 'indirect discourse' (Deleuze and Guattari 1980: 95–109), which underlies not only literary discourse but all discourse, varies from text to text and from reader to reader (see also Riffaterre 1983a: 117–32).

Censorship and self-censorship, the negative functions of ideology, are important in the choice of texts we read, but also in the way we read, what we highlight, and what we conveniently ignore. One example of the function of ideology in reading and text selection can be clearly seen in the history of three prose poems: 'Beautiful Dorothy' (XXV), 'Portraits of Mistresses' (XLII), and 'Mademoiselle Bistouri' ('Miss Lancet') (XLVII). They seem at first quite different in intention and construction: a portrait of a mulatto prostitute written in the third person by an impartial aesthete (XXV), a worldly misogynist's account of a bragging-contest between four men (XLII), and a first-person reminiscence of a female fetishist by a compassionate *flâneur* (XLVII). Yet they were subjected to a similar judgement by nineteenth-century ideology, and censored by nineteenth-century editorial readers. They were all sent to the *Revue nationale et étrangère* which published XXV with cuts which provoked a furious letter from the author (dated 20 June 1863). XLII was kept in a drawer for two years and published only after Baudelaire's death, and XLVII was considered unpublishable by the *Revue nationale* and did not appear until the complete edition in 1869 (Kopp 1969: 420–2).

Why were these texts singled out (and thus united) by the editor of a journal whose circulation depended on the acceptance of contemporary readers? The answer is their outspoken, but differing, treatment of female sexuality. It is precisely the new-found interest in theories of desire and sexuality, and their links with a present-day ideological commitment which is just as deeply felt, that will make a twentieth-century reader, and particularly a feminist reader, once again single out these texts for special attention.[36] This is but one of many examples of how the kaleidoscope of the text may be constantly readjusted by the vagaries, the commitments, the censorship, and the fashions of its readers.

Little Prose Poems provokes such wildly disparate readings, as do the individual texts, that one can only feel that its stated aim of allowing the will of the reader free play has been successful. It is like a modern sculpture incorporating beautiful precision-tooled parts which nevertheless are linked only by an electrical field, a field energized by the spectator to produce random and yet harmonious conjunctions. Each different reading, each different interpretation of the whole, is but one possible performance compared to the infinitely varied play of the parts.

3 · *True coin and false coin: narrative acts and narrative contracts*

All performance implies shared conventions, implies a contractual relationship between the performer, who undertakes to meet certain expectations, and the recipients, whether participating or passive, judge or audience. These receivers in the transaction are active as decoders rather than encoders in the case of a verbal or visual performance. Such a contractual relationship is also a necessary prerequisite to the functioning of performatives and speech acts in general.[1]

However, as Jacques Derrida has suggested (1977a, 1977b), all performatives are in their turn dependent on shared linguistic conventions and on an acceptance of the transactional and contractual forces of language itself. It is the arbitrary nature of the symbolic order which permits and encourages the arbitrary convention-governed behaviour characterizing all human systems, including literature. Since we are dependent on the contractual nature of language itself for our ability to 'do things with words', it is probably more true, as recent theorists have observed, to regard words as doing things with us (see Johnson 1980: 52–6). Thus narrative may be seen to have arisen as one result of the evolutionary potential of language, which made it capable of such linguistic splitting as that between the first and second persons on the one hand and the third person, the abstract 'non' person, on the other (Benveniste 1971: 217–22), or the splitting which permits the differentiation between *oratio recta* and *oratio obliqua*. The conventions governing such types of linguistic doubling enabled the doubling which characterizes representation. The possibility of performing 'acts' of language exists only because humans are divided *from* language by the gap between the arbitrary and the natural. Indeed, this gap itself is produced linguistically, as the 'natural' is a cultural category. Thus we can narrate only because language permits the conventions of narrating which are shared by members of our culture.

NARRATIVE TRANSACTION

When we relate, when we say 'I will tell you . . .', we are using a performative and initiating a contract which must itself be seen in the perspective of the transactional and hence shifting nature of language and the realm of the symbolic. The acceptance of a conventional relationship belongs to the very nature of contract, but an arbitrary relationship, unlike a natural one, can be changed, a contract can be renegotiated. The narrative contract differs from other linguistic contracts in that it initiates a transaction which is both an 'act' and an enactment, both a doing and the representation of a doing. Narration, whether it be the re-enactment of reality or the enactment of virtuality, is always a representation. Telling a story involves the relay effect of setting up a 'display text' (Pratt 1977: 136–45), and the distinction between reportage and fiction is less important than the fact that both are subject to the selective whim of the teller, the structuring effect of point of view, and the necessities of narrative cohesion. The performative 'I will relate' guarantees nothing but a verbal representation by the teller even when he or she purports to be conveying a factual experience.

> The shapes taken by stories and the reasons for their telling suggest the need to explore more fully the narrative situation – narrative *in situation* between teller and listener – and the kinds of reaction and understanding that narratives appear to want to elicit. All story-telling, Roland Barthes maintains, is contractual: it asks for something in return for what it supplies. . . . In fact, we shall see that 'contract' is too simple a term, and too static; something more active, dynamic, shifting, and transformatory is involved in the exchange.
>
> (Brooks 1984: 216)

The audience to a narrative experience an obligation to respond and feel cheated if they cannot do so. The response may be positive or negative, it may confirm or contest the expectations of the teller. Audience anticipation and reaction arise precisely because of the transactional nature of narration. The audience, whether willing or unwilling, feel that they have entered into, or sometimes that they have been forced into, a contractual relationship. The narrative act sets up a frame in which, whether the story informs, entertains, teaches, challenges, or asserts, certain minimal contractual obligations must be observed. These obligations are what distinguish narrative from reported speech.

It is expected that a story should obey the basic conditions, the 'logic', of narrative (Brémond 1973; Prince 1973a). These conditions in natural narrative are perhaps best summed up by Labov: 'A complete narrative begins with an orientation, proceeds to the complicating action, is suspended at the focus of evaluation before the resolution, and returns the listener to the present time with the coda' (1972: 369).

As the term 'focus of evaluation' indicates, a story should have *point*, as Labov puts it, if the audience are to feel the transaction has been a successful one. The point of a story is not necessarily that anticipated by either teller or hearers, since, like other discourse, narrative is subject to transactional shifts and stresses:

> For discourse is not the transmission of information between two minds located at opposite ends of a channel but, rather, a series of complex transactions between two persons who are located in a rich world of objects, events, experiences, and motives, including *reasons* for speaking and listening to each other.
>
> It is important that we recognize not only that discourse is a transaction, but also that it is an *economic* transaction, and one in which the functions or value of an utterance differ significantly for the speaker and the listener. It is especially important for literary theory, because the dynamics of that transaction, and the value of an utterance for both 'speaker' and 'listener' can, under certain conditions, change radically; and we can begin to identify the characteristic functions of language in poetry or literature only when the nature of those conditions and the consequences of those changes are appreciated.
>
> (Smith 1978: 83)

However, in spite of the shifting and transformatory nature of the narrative exchange, one contractual feature remains invariable. This is the status of the speech acts contained *within* and defined *by* the narrative frame. As we have seen, a feature of narrative is that it enacts and it represents. Hence any speech acts within the story itself are relayed as second-order speech acts with a different status from those of everyday transactions. For instance, any direct speech incorporated in narrative is a form of mime, a ploy of the narrator, an overlap of fiction and non-fiction (Pratt 1977: 142). The words, 'Then he said, "Let's get married"', and I believed him', in a woman's story to her friends contain a second-order performative which is emphatically not the same thing as a valid proposal. It may even be fictional. We have only the woman's guarantee of her story. For the teller–audience contract to function, the audience must be capable of distinguishing between first-order and second-order speech acts. The convention of the represented speech act paves the way for the convention of the fictional speech act since both belong to the second order.

> the assumptions of natural discourse may . . . be deliberately sus-
> pended or replaced by other conventions operating for both
> 'speaker' and 'listener'. In such circumstances, 'counterfeit' – that
> is, fictive – utterances will, like stage money, have a positive value,
> as will also the listener's *not* crediting the speaker's words or *not*
> taking what he 'says' as meaning what made him 'say' it.
>
> (Pratt 1977: 101)

This ability to recognize the markers which distinguish the two orders of speech acts in narrative and to appreciate that individual per-formatives are valid only within their own level is a basic skill which users of language acquire at a very early age. Between the levels a deliberate engendering of confusion is possible, as for example when a television 'judge' is asked to give advice on the merits of real courses of action. This may be seen as the deliberate substitution of non-valid for valid currency, of stage money for the coin of the realm. The use of this analogy is one way in which this chapter will explore the narrative 'act'.

FICTION AND THE VIRTUAL WORLD

In the case of written fictional texts the contract is further complicated by the fact that they are a representation of a representation. The narrator, from being a teller, an active performer, becomes an encoded entity or merely the narrating function of the text. The written fictive story is founded on a situational presupposition, the acceptance of a linguistic structure as the enactment of an enactment, a representation of the performance of story-telling (Smith 1978: 29–30; Warning 1979: 328–9). Appreciation of the functioning of this structure, in which the narrator, a convenient fiction, is used to present a virtual world, makes it easier to understand the second-order, relayed status of the illo-cutionary acts within it (cf. Hamburger 1973: 176).

Ever since Austin pointed out that 'Go, and catch a falling star' has absolutely no status as a command (1975: 104), there has been a tendency among speech-act theoreticians to deny logical status to fictional and theatrical texts (Searle 1975).[2] That there is a *difference* in status is quite clear in the theatre, where it is obvious that the actor who says 'I thee wed' is not performing an action but acting a performance: 'A performative utterance will, for example, be in a *peculiar way*, hollow or void if said by an actor on the stage, or if introduced in a poem, or spoken in soliloquy' (Austin 1975: 9).

On the other hand communication does occur: not just the feigned, illocutionary/perlocutionary transaction on stage but a transaction between actors and audience who are subject to the perlocutionary effect of the staged speech act. In fact, as Barbara Johnson points out, the Austinian distinction between valid and non-valid 'acts' of speech, the serious and the non-serious, is undermined by the very language he uses:

> That the logic of language renders some kind of discontinuity between speaker and speech absolutely inescapable is in fact demonstrated precisely by Austin's attempt to eliminate it. For the very word he uses to name 'mere doing', the very name he gives to that from which he excludes theatricality, is none other than the word that most commonly *names* theatricality: the word *perform*. As if this were not ironic enough, exactly the same split can be found in Austin's other favorite word: *act.* How is it that a word that expresses most simply the mere doing of an act necessarily leads us to the question of – acting? How is it possible to discuss the question of authenticity when that question already subverts the very terms we use to discuss it? Is it inevitable that the same split that divides the referent from itself the moment language comes near it should divide language from itself in the very same way? And can language actually refer to anything other than that very split? If Austin's unstated question was, What are we really *doing* when we speak? it becomes clear that, whatever else we may be doing, we are at any rate being 'done in' by our own words. And it is precisely the unknowable extent to which our statement differs from itself that performs *us*. Decidedly, 'leaving the initiative to words' is not as simple as it sounds. Left to their own initiative, the very words with which Austin excludes jokes, theater, and poetry from his field of vision inevitably take their revenge. But if, in the final analysis, the joke ends up being on Austin, it is, after all, only Poetic justice.
>
> (1980: 65–6)

According to Johnson, all performatives in fact fictionalize their utterers by making them the mouthpiece of a conventionalized authority. Our speech 'acts' derive their validity only from a long history of accepting the convention of speech acts (1980: 60). Thus, rather than making a distinction between the natural and the unnatural, the valid and the invalid, we should be seeing each as 'serious' within its appropriate context; we should rather refer to parallel linguistic transactions, some actual, some virtual.

SELF-REFLEXIVITY AND THE FICTIONAL

By virtue of the narrative contract, valid in the real world because of the precedent of narrative convention, fictional speech acts are on the one hand perceived to be illusory, but on the other seen to be valid within their own virtual world.

Another aspect of the narrative performance examined in this chapter is one particular role of self-reflexivity in fictional narratives. This role is to foreground the arbitrary nature of the fictional world and its transactions and, by the very fact of highlighting the status of the second-order speech act, to make us aware of the truth of the virtual world as opposed to its reality. Anne Ubersfeld proposes that the theatrical speech act be marked with a minus or negative sign (1977: 261),[3] precisely because a situation of self-reflexivity, such as a play within a play, will juxtapose two negatives and thereby reveal a positive, the truth of the fiction.

The opposite of the self-reflexive endeavour, and the perversion of the contract, is the one which attempts to persuade us that the fictitious is real. This is where textual fabrication merges into the domain of forgery. To deny the existence of the fictional level is, as Mary Louise Pratt points out (1977: 174), to deprive oneself of the major benefit provided by fiction, which is the doubling of experience. When we recognize the double nature of the experience and knowingly use the verbal currency of the alternative world, we are in the realm of the true, but any attempt to confuse this with natural discourse will produce a debasement of the currency at both levels.

NARRATIVE AS LEGAL TENDER

The contractual aspect of narrative has been made easier to grasp, as Barthes has pointed out, by the fact that fiction itself is traditionally a commodity. 'Meaning', says Barthes, 'is golden' and narratives are 'legal tender, subject to contract, economic stakes, in short, *merchandise*' (1974: 89). We may pay the producer of fiction with money, with goods, with praise, with love, or with understanding, but, at whatever remove, the receiver of fictional narratives is involved in a transaction with the producer. A written narrative is both 'product and production, merchandise and commerce, a stake and the bearer of that stake' (Barthes 1974: 89).

However, what is not made clear in *S/Z* is that the economy of narrative is rather that of the gift than of the commodity. Narrative is indeed subject to contract and a basis of exchange, but its worth stands in no fixed relationship to what we pay for it. Only in the case of such fictional merchandise as Mills and Boon stories or those of the Harlequin press do we get a narrative package exactly calculated as what we pay for. Literature, both oral and written, partakes of the nature of the gift, as Lewis Hyde (1983) has pointed out. The gift economy is more flexible than that of merchandise: you can choose not to enter into it, you may even choose not to reciprocate, as the lady in 'Sarrasine' chooses not to reciprocate by giving her person in return for the gift of the story. The worth of a narrative, like the worth of a gift, has nothing to do with its value, as the later Barthes of *The Pleasure of the Text* would be the first to admit. In pointing out that a commodity has value but a gift has worth, Hyde quotes the distinction observed by Marx:

> In the seventeenth century many English authors continued to write 'worth' for 'use-value' and 'value' for 'exchange-value', this being accordant with the genius of a language which prefers an Anglo-Saxon word for an actual thing and a Romance word for its reflection.
>
> (Hyde 1983: 60)

A gift is of course also a transaction, but one different in nature from a transaction in commodities and, as we will see, subject to different laws. The traditional nature of narrative is seen by Barthes as self-reflexively mirrored in the structure of many stories which use transactions thematically, since a contract of exchange featured within a story is a *mise-en-abyme* of the condition of production of literature itself. From this springs his perception of the framing promise in 'Sarrasine', 'a night of love for a lovely story', as a *mise-en-abyme* of the fictional contract as a whole.

The stability of meaning, like the stability of performatives, is seen by Barthes as an equivalent of economic stability, both being dependent, as we have remarked, on contractual and conventional relationships in the arbitrary world of signs. If meaning is golden, then, to continue the analogy, one basic question, in the world of literature as in the world of commerce, is 'who controls the gold standard?' Or even 'is the gold standard completely unnecessary?' One function of literature is to highlight the distinction between the true, which belongs to the world of signs and only functions within the realm of discursive propositions, and the real, which has reference in the natural world (cf. Prendergast 1986: 90–110). The true – and of course its obverse, the false – functions within a closed system, a fabricated system *parallel* to that of the real, and the signs of literature must not be confused with natural discourse, in which the convention is that the referent *does* have reality.

> [fictional] discourse has no responsibility vis-à-vis the real: in the most realistic novel, the referent has no 'reality': suffice it to imagine the disorder the most orderly narrative would create were its descriptions taken at face value, converted into operative programs and simply *executed*. In short . . . what we call 'real' (in the theory of the realistic text) is never more than a code of representation (of signification): it is never a code of execution: *the novelistic real is not operable*.
>
> (Barthes 1974: 80)

The naturalization of the sign led to an illusion of reference when mimesis, rescued from the actors and vagabonds, became part of cultural orthodoxy. The resultant confusion about the nature and purpose of 'realism' has led to the widespread modern preoccupation with the 'gold standard' of literature. Writers strive through various self-reflexive devices to obviate the confusion between the fictional and the natural which threatens to debase the currency.

MONEY AND LANGUAGE

In order to obtain the maximum relevance to the functioning of language within the narrative contract, I have chosen to examine a text whose theme is money, both counterfeit and real. My reason for the choice must already be apparent: it lies in the almost perfect homology which exists between those two symbolic forms of communication, that through money and that through words. To see this, we have only to superimpose one on the other as in the Jakobson model, admitting of course the over-simplification of that model and its insufficiency in terms of the functioning of discourse (see Figure 3.1).

Mary Douglas discusses an equally valid homology between money and ritual. I propose to use her statement for my own purposes, substituting each time the word 'language' for her 'ritual:

> The metaphor of money admirably sums up what we want to assert of [language]. Money provides a fixed, external, recognizable sign for what would be confused, contradictable operations; [language] makes audible external signs of internal states. Money mediates transactions; [language] mediates experience, including social experience. Money provides a standard for measuring worth;

[language] standardises situations and so helps evaluate them. Money makes a link between the present and the future, so does [language]. The more we reflect on the richness of the metaphor, the more it becomes clear that this is no metaphor. Money is only an extreme and specialised form of [language].

(1966: 69)

Like language (to put it in Baudelaire's words), money is 'what obtains everything, what gives the worth of everything, what replaces everything' ('The Temptations' (XXI)).

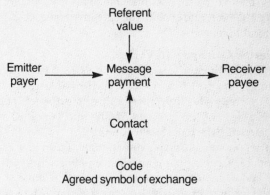

Figure 3.1 Symbolic communication (simplified model)

However, to return to our schema, it is clear that money and language function only within an agreed code. When we change the context we change the currency, thereby invalidating our initial means of exchange. This truth about signs and about narrative is spelled out in concrete form in folk-tales. Marcel Mauss refers to the 'false coin' of magic (cit. Douglas 1966). We might well use a similar analogy of literature. When we enter the world of narration we enter the other, negative, mirror world. In this parallel world words and coins are always *fairy gold*.[4] The means of exchange and communication *seem* to exist, the coins of the unreal world function, yet as soon as the rules of belief are broken, the coins are revealed as simulacra: fairy gold becomes dead leaves, stones, charcoal, shavings. In Bulgakov's *The Master and Margarita* the fairy gold, roubles (produced by black magic in a Moscow theatre), becomes in the real world old bottle labels *and* American dollars, causing equal consternation in both cases.[5]

A title, as we have seen (p. 28), is the most important instance of a paratextual first-order speech act which indicates a performative relationship between virtual author and virtual audience and so announces the narrative contract. Thus titles such as 'Counterfeit Coinage' or *The Counterfeiters*,[6] with their reference to forging, acknowledge at the first level of illocution, the narrative contract, what is always true of the second level of illocution. What happens when we, the readers, as well as the actors in the narrative, consciously make use of false coin? I intend to read Baudelaire's text exploiting to the full the homology[7] I have just outlined. It should be made clear that this is a perverse reading, in the Freudian sense of the term; indeed it may be that no other readings are possible. I believe, with Baudelaire, that we as readers should draw all possible deductions from all possible hypotheses. My intention is to explore the narrative contract, using the text as exchangeable coinage.

Counterfeit Coinage (XXVIII)[8]

As we were leaving the tobacconist's, my friend carefully sorted out his change; into the left pocket of his waistcoat he slipped little gold coins; into the right, little silver coins; into the left pocket of his trousers a heap of coppers, and finally, into the right, a two-franc silver coin which he had closely examined.

'A strange and painstaking distribution!' I said to myself.

We met up with a poor man who tremblingly held out his cap to us. – I know nothing more disturbing than the mute eloquence of those imploring eyes, in which a sensitive man, who knows how to read them, can find at once so much humility, so much reproach. One finds something approaching this depth of complicated feeling in the tearful eyes of dogs that one whips.

My friend's gift was much greater than mine, and I said to him: 'You are right; after the pleasure of being astonished, there is none greater than that of giving a surprise.' 'It was the counterfeit coin,' he replied calmly, as if to justify his prodigality.

But into my miserable brain, always complicating the issue (with what a tiring faculty nature has endowed me!) there suddenly entered the idea that such behaviour, coming from my friend, was only excusable by the desire to create an event in the life of this poor devil, perhaps even to know the various consequences, disastrous or not, which can be engendered by a counterfeit coin in the hand of a beggar. Could it not multiply into true coins? Could it not also lead him to prison? A tavern keeper, a baker, for example, would perhaps have him arrested as a counterfeiter or as a passer of counterfeit coinage. Just as possibly the counterfeit coin would perhaps represent, for a poor little speculator, the source of a few days' wealth.

And thus my whimsy took flight, lending wings to my friend's mind and drawing all possible deductions from all possible hypotheses.

But he abruptly broke into my day-dream by repeating my own words: 'Yes, you are right: there is no sweeter pleasure than to surprise a man by giving him more than he expects.'

I looked him right in the eyes, and I was appalled to see his eyes shining with undeniable candour. Then I saw clearly that he had wanted at one and the same time to dispense charity and do a good deal; to win forty sous and the heart of God; to enter paradise at cut rates; finally to earn for nothing the reputation of a charitable man. I should almost have pardoned him the desire for the criminal satisfaction of which I had recently supposed him capable; I should have found it strange and odd that he should amuse himself by compromising the poor; but I shall never forgive him the ineptitude of his calculation. There is no excuse for being nasty, but there is some merit in knowing it; and the most irreparable of vices is to do evil through stupidity.

THE CONTRACTUAL ROLE OF THE TITLE

Of particular interest in the functioning of narratives is the role of the title, the first-order illocutionary act. Here I wish to explore the functioning of a title in which the sign or signs are *themselves* negated; in other words a direct speech act which contains *two* contractual features, a promise of narration and a warning. The title 'Counterfeit Coinage' (*La fausse monnaie*) presents the reader with a double contract, since it promises both a story *and* a universal truth about 'coinage'. It also contains a double warning: once in clear, in the word 'counterfeit', and once in code, since *la monnaie* (in French both the mint and its product) was originally the temple of Juno Moneta, the goddess of warning.

THE TRIPLE NARRATIVE STRUCTURE

A first-person narrator presents the second level of illocution, the tale itself, and his speech acts belong to that level. The narrator is himself a fabrication, the textual facsimile of a living teller; he can either form part of the world he narrates, as here, or introduce yet another world at a third textual level. As Peter Rabinowitz remarks: 'all fictional narrators are false in that they are imitations; but some are imitations of people who tell the truth, some of people who lie' (1977: 134).

The narrative takes the form of a triple series of sortings out, gradings, pickings through, whose aim is to distinguish truth from falsehood. These siftings also form a structural triptych. First comes the incident of the false coin, then the two sides, head and tail as it were, of that incident. Thus *triage*, or sifting, and *triade*, or triple structure, are interdependent in this narrative. Each of the three panels consists of a different form of sifting, which yields a varying number of categories depending on the criteria applied (see Figure 3.2).

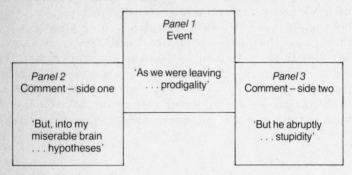

Figure 3.2   The triptych* of 'Counterfeit Coinage'

*This is a recurrent situation in *Little Prose Poems*. See Johnson (1979: passim) and Mauron (1966: passim).

The first panel shows the triple sorting of the genuine money into gold, silver, and copper, and the recognition/exclusion of the forged. This is followed by the triple narrative kernel, the meeting with the beggar, his declaration of lack, the gift, which also shows us:

donor $\longrightarrow$ payment $\longrightarrow$ recipient

sender $\longrightarrow$ message $\longrightarrow$ receiver

But of course the liquidation of the beggar's lack is *negative*: 'It was the counterfeit coin.' As I remarked earlier, narratologists have never paid enough attention to Propp's provision for negative and contradictory functions.[9] This is a clear example of their possibilities, reinforcing at the level of the *énoncé* the negation present throughout.

MISE-EN-ABYME AND THE FICTIVE

Self-reflexivity, while not necessarily an inherent characteristic of the fictive, has become a salient feature of such narrative experiments as those we are examining. It is said to provoke reader participation in the construction of the text and to highlight the hermeneutics of the performance. It is also a way of reminding us of the true nature of the currency we are using in the fictional transaction.

Lucien Dällenbach (1977) has produced the clearest definition of the different forms of *mise-en-abyme*, that internal mirroring which is the most obvious self-reflexive device. He finds three sorts of *mise-en-abyme*. The first reflects the *code* which narrator and audience must share, since, unless we are using a shared code, we have no entry into the text. The second reflects the *énonciation*, the textual strategies of the speaking and organizing subject. The third reflects the *énoncé*, all or part of the spoken message of the text. We have clear examples of all three here and can judge their part in co-opting the audience in the true reading of fiction.

The introduction of the 'counterfeit coin' in the story is a *mise-en-abyme du code.* It reminds us of the promise of the title. The importance of our understanding of the symbolic code of money and its relationship to the equally symbolic code of language is enhanced by the paradigmatic clustering, since no less than fifty-four words in the short text belong to the semantic set of *payment/currency*.

An important feature of the first narrative panel is the parenthesis in the present tense from 'I know nothing' to 'that one whips'. We have here a *mise-en-abyme de l'énonciation* in which the narrator is shown to lay claim not just to the power of understanding, but to that of *reading*. He is the sensitive man who can read the message, 'the mute eloquence of those imploring eyes'. (At least fifteen words in the text belong to the semantic set of *interpretation*.) This 'faculty' with which the narrator is endowed will be used in the narrative in various ways. For instance, he will, at a later stage, again read a message in eyes, this time those of the donor, the actantial subject of the first and last section. This reflects the implied relation between the text and its readers.

One example of the *mise-en-abyme de l'énoncé* is the parenthesis – 'with what a tiring faculty nature has endowed me!' – since it repeats in ironic form the central function of the gift; for both gifts, that of nature and that of the friend, are two-edged. It may also be remarked that the first section ends appropriately with the word 'prodigality'.

THE TRANSACTIONAL IMPLICATIONS

The second panel, the left-hand one of the triptych, can also be seen as the first side of the forged coin. It shows the second *triage* of the text. This is the sorting out of possible meanings of the transaction by the narrator, who has already claimed status as a skilful reader, even if, like all of us skilful readers, he complicates the issue (the French idiom here is *chercher midi à quatorze heures*). So he interprets what he thinks is his friend's act by asking himself what sort of a contract is implied by an honest offer of counterfeit coin. What are the possibilities for the receiver, particularly if he in turn passes on the coin/message? Here, with the mathematical precision of *la conscience dans le mal* (*Oeuvres complètes*, I: 80), the narrator explores the combinations:

a) the forged accepted as genuine, passed on as true, undetected: the naïve *and* lucky receiver;
b) the forged accepted as forged, passed on as forged at a profit: the manipulator, the cynic;
c) the forged accepted as genuine, passed on as genuine, detected: this leads to tragedy, but perhaps to wisdom;
d) the forged accepted as forged, passed on as genuine, undetected: a few days' riches for the poor little speculator.

This breakdown anticipates in its effect Greimas's basic tool of semantic analysis, the semiotic square (1983: 222–56). If we apply the 'possible hypotheses' to the more general question of the fictional we get the semiotic square shown in Figure 3.3. Thus the notion of the forged or fabricated and the genuine or legitimate presents the vital critical questions of the status and effects of: a) fiction given as reality; b) fiction given as non-reality; c) reality given as fiction; d) reality given as non-fiction.

Figure 3.3 Semiotic square of fiction

The importance of the figure of the forger in twentieth-century narratives, such as *The Confidence Man* (the film) or *Felix Krull*, is seen by Deleuze to reflect the breakdown in implied notions of 'truth' and 'reality' which opens the way to an 'irreducible multiplicity'.

The power of forgery only exists in the form of a series of powers, which always refer back from one to the other and pass from one into the other. To such an extent that investigators, witnesses, innocent or guilty heroes, will participate in the same power of forgery whose levels they will incarnate at each stage of the narration. Even 'the truthful man ends up understanding that he has never ceased lying', said Nietzsche. So the forger will be inseparable from a chain of forgers into whom he metamorphoses. There is no single forger, and if the forger reveals something, it is the existence behind him of another forger, who may even be the State . . . . The truthful man will form part of the chain, at one end, as will the artist, power of forgery to the nth degree, at the other. And narration will have no other content than the display of these forgers, their shifting from one to the other, their metamorphoses one into the other.

(Deleuze 1985: 175)

Forgery is here seen as the Baudelairean narrator sees it, as part of a transformational chain with multiple future possibilities. As such it is easily assimilated to art. The gift of a forgery, its exchange value, and its implications for the receiver are analogous to the 'gift' of fiction, its value, and its implications for the reader.

THE ACCEPTANCE OF THE NARRATIVE CONTRACT

Two assumptions are made about narration and especially about the narration of fiction: that the teller is expected to ensure that his or her tale is 'worth' the audience's attention, and that the hearers or readers expect the tale to be 'worth'-while (Pratt 1977: 106, 148). In the *Little Prose Poems* the beggar is frequently chosen as a receiver of polyvalent gifts/messages, particularly in the paradoxical 'Let's Knock out the Poor!' (see Chapter 8). The beggar is literally the person who 'asks for it' and, since he has asked for it, has no right of refusal. Begging, in other words, involves accepting whatever is given, with all its implications. In 'Let's Knock out the Poor!', for instance, it turns out to be a good hiding as well as half the narrator's ready cash. Here, the end result of the gift is left open.

The beggar is like the *potential* reader/hearer who demands a story (without specification) or who accepts the offer of a narrative (*any* narrative). This relationship of the potential receiver to the sender is the same as in that illocutionary contract we all know from the playground: 'Open your mouth and shut your eyes / And Johnny will give you a big surprise.' Sometimes we got a sweet and sometimes we got a sheep dropping, thus learning in one swift lesson about contractual ambiguities. Baudelaire would say, and shows it amply in the prose poems which play obsessively with the notion of *contract*, that either result is a valid experience.[10] In the same way, when we accept the narrative contract, which is a contract of gift rather than a contract of sale, we may get the sweet (like the mellifluous certainties of Tolkien's *Lord of the Rings*) or the shit (like the scatological uncertainties of Pynchon's *Gravity's Rainbow*) *but* we get what we bargained for as partners in the illocutionary act of narration. Unless we opt out of the contract (we have what Baudelaire termed 'the right to go away') we may undergo *either* what Ross Chambers (1984) calls 'the seduction of the reader' *or* what Anne Ubersfeld (1981) calls 'the rape of the spectator'. The motto appears to be not only *Caveat emptor* but *Caveat lector*. Of course *Caveat auctor* also applies, since, when the multiple possibilities of the currency and the message allow for multiple reading, they may also involve the rape of the writer. The power relationship may always be reversed in the constant dynamism of textual relationships. Panel two of our narrative thus rightly ends with the stress on polyvalence, and its last words are 'drawing all possible deductions from all possible hypotheses', which shows the narrator as speculator, the traditional role of the critic when dealing in literary currency.

DEVALORIZATION AND NARRATIVE REVERSAL

The third panel, the right-hand one of the triptych, is also the second side of the false coin. It is the sorting out of the motivations or intentions of the actantial subject of this section, as the expert reader gets the message from his friend's words and more especially from his eyes: the message of stupidity, of the fact that the *false coin was given falsely*. This *triage* applies specifically to the sender/donor and hence reminds us of the varying roles of that rather forgotten partner in the narrative act, the author.[11] Here we have, in the bargain at cut rates, the attempt to 'win forty sous and the heart of God', a set of possible interpretative variations, not so much of the textual counterfeiter (*le faussaire littéraire*) as of the literary fake. For forty sous, try reading a million dollars, and for paradise, the Nobel Prize. This is also the main thrust of Gide's analogy, that of the devalorization of literature, of bad money driving out 'good', as *homo faber* turns into *homo fabricator*. The words 'I shall never forgive him the ineptitude of his calculation' neatly unite the semes of finance and of interpretation as they lead into the moral about doing 'evil through stupidity'. With this moral, and the text's return to the present tense and the universal, we can see the full action of the *mise-en-abyme du code*. We realize the story is not just about making and passing false coinage (double implications of *monnaie*), but more specifically about *devalorization*. The subject has the intention of increasing his *own* value: a charitable reputation *and* a good deal are what he seeks to acquire. In fact, of course, he decreases his value, and this devalorization constitutes the narrative reversal. The question raised in this whole discussion of exchange, exchange of money, exchange of value, exchange of words, exchange of pleasure, is whether the *énonciation* has achieved yet another reversal in the perlocutionary effect on the reader. The narrator has been forced to speculate on the use and misuse of the counterfeit: he assumes a certain perlocutionary effect of his story on his narrative audience, an effect dependent on shared conventions which are not those of the stupid. Is the reader, sharing the conventions of the fictional narrative, now similarly forced into full awareness of the special nature of fictional speech acts? This awareness is ensured not only by the direct warning about the counterfeit but also by the *mises-en-abyme* which stress the interpretation of the message.

THE TRUE AND THE REAL

The fictional text functions similarly to the poetic text in its 'valid non-validity', 'work of image on image, of the construction of an image which is the image of an image, image to the second degree' (Ubersfeld 1981: 68). As both Johnson and Ubersfeld remark, when we acknowledge the fictiveness of the poetic functions we at the same time enable ourselves to acknowledge their truth in the world of literature. This is what makes us, as spectators and receivers, ready to accept counterfeit coin as legal tender.

> We know since Freud that when we dream we dream, the dream within the dream tells the truth. Through double negation, the dream of a dream is what is true. In the same way the 'play within the play' speaks not the real, but the *true*, changing the sign of illusion and denouncing both the illusion and the stage context which surrounds it.
>
> (Ubersfeld 1977: 52)[12]

Note the words, 'not the real, but the *true*'. She is claiming that the self-reflection of the two fictive acts, the two negatives in her terminology, produce a recognition of illusion, of fiction, and hence a positive perlocutionary effect on the spectator. Self-reflexivity, by foregrounding the special status of the narrative 'act', is one device which maintains the 'gold standard' of literature.

The text of 'Counterfeit Coinage' can thus be used to explore the nature and value of the contractual relationship as a whole. This is always dependent on convention and relies, like any arbitrary relationship, on an understanding of and obedience to the rules. Even the gift relationship, fluid and variable as it is because of its basis in worth (not value), is subject to strict conventions which we disobey at our peril. The parallels between the arbitrary systems of money and of language allow one to observe both the possibilities and the dangers of substituting the conventional for the real. As Umberto Eco points out:

> A sign is . . . something . . . which stands in place of something which is absent, which could not even exist, or at least not be present anywhere at the time at which I use the sign. This means that the fundamental characteristic of the sign is that I can use it to lie. So that everything is a sign that can be used to *LIE* (since everything that serves to tell a lie can also be used, in the right circumstances, to tell the truth).

(1975: 12)

Thus natural discourse, like currency, is in itself a fabrication, only 'true' if we agree on its use.

Fictive discourse is also a fabrication but of a different sort, a simulacrum of the natural, produced by the conventions of audience creation which allow us to accept and interpret the represented sign so long as it remains within the performance framework. It is distinguished from natural discourse by socially acceptable criteria of validity, just as the distinction between forged money and genuine money is made by the ruling social institutions. Thus forged money, like fictive discourse, can become a powerful means of testing those conventions and establishing their limits, since, unlike fairy gold, it does not disappear when used within the framework of the genuine but assumes new possibilities.

Baudelaire's text originally valorizes but then devalorizes the function of the forged or fictional. The narrator first reads his friend's gift of the counterfeit coin with positive perversity. Used in any one of the four hypothetical ways suggested in panel two of the triptych, the forgery will 'create an event' and 'engender consequences'. The enlargement of experience, whether happy or unhappy, is a goal positively to be desired. The valorization, however, is short-lived. It becomes all too clear that the counterfeit is merely being used as if it were genuine, thus allying evil to stupidity and effectively devalorizing the function of the gift. In the same way, an attempt to pass off the fictional world as the natural world must be either naïve or deceptive, constituting a betrayal of trust and a devalorization of the true worth of the fictional narrative.[13]

4 · Scene and obscene: the constitution of narrative audiences and gendered reading

Narrative always implies mediation, dramatization, and speculation. Since it presents the listener with a second-hand, a mediated, experience it involves an exploitation of the triadic nature of the speech act, which is always split between locution, the message itself or the sense, illocution, the force of message transfer between interlocutors, and perlocution, the effects of the message. The recognition of this distinction between illocution and perlocution has given us new precision in coping with the definition of audiences and their relation to addresser–addressee interaction, both internal and external to the text.

The notion of perlocution is particularly important to the narrative speech act, in which, as we have seen, the direct performative is the act of narration itself. It is a performative which can also subsume other performatives and contain within itself second-order reported illocution. The special characteristic of such illocution is that it can produce, as well as any reported perlocution, real first-order perlocutionary effects on the hearer or reader. It is precisely this relay effect of what Mary Louise Pratt calls display texts, which include all narrative, whether non-fictional or fictional, that permits the vicarious experience which constitutes the audience mode of perception.[1]

The aim of this chapter is to examine the different orders of speech act and the different types of audience contained within narrative and constructed by that narrative. It will examine also the relationship of those audiences to different types of reading audiences with their varying interpretations of the text.

The question of the receiving partner in narrative acts has provoked a great deal of attention, particularly since Gerald Prince's study of the narratee (1973b) and Wolfgang Iser's *The Implied Reader* (1974). Unfortunately the resultant terminology varies according to its user, and the categories overlap. I will indicate the categories I find most useful and endeavour to show how these relate to the better-known classifications. Within the text, we may distinguish:

1) The interlocutory audience, the characterized hearer or hearers within the text who are the receivers of embedded narration in dialogic form. These may participate in the tale not only as active receivers but may also take part as narrators in their turn. This phenomenon will be studied in Chapter 5 together with the question of power relations in narrative. Roland Barthes has examined the active role of the interlocutory audience closely in *S/Z* (1974). However, the interlocutory audience may also be presented as purely passive, indeed as non-speaking receiver, as is the case in the text used for demonstration purposes in this chapter (cf. Rousset 1982).

2) The narratee (Prince's term) constructed by the text but to whom the *tale* is *explicitly* addressed. This may take the form of a named individual: for example Walton's tale in *Frankenstein* is addressed to his sister Margaret, who is pure narratee, while Walton is himself both a narrator and also an interlocutory audience to Frankenstein's tale. The narratee may be indicated by an honorific, Sir or Madam, or by some other form of address such as Gentle Reader or Idle Reader. Alternatively these narratees may only be addressed by the narrator in the second person as 'you' or admitted to complicity with the use of the first person plural 'we'. (See Piwowarczyk 1976: 176 for a full diagram of narratee indicators.)

3) The implied narrative audience as constructed by both the *énoncé* and the *intertext of the énoncé* to whom the *tale* is *implicitly* addressed. Prince does not make this distinction, allowing only the narratee constructed by the internal evidence and logic of the text. However, I agree with Rabinowitz (1977) that we must grant what he calls the narrative audience (which he limits to the audience of the *énoncé*) an ideological, literary, and historical context while at the same time seeing them as confined to and by the world of the tale: 'Anton Lavrentevich, the narrator of the *Possessed*, is an imitation historian. As such, he writes for an audience which not only knows . . . that the serfs were freed in 1861, but which also believes that Stavrogin and Kirilov "really" existed' (Rabinowitz 1980: 244).

I should prefer to call this implied audience that of the *énoncé*, but am prepared to use Rabinowitz's term, narrative audience.

On these three audience levels the illocution is a second-order speech act. Perlocution within the text is merely a reported phenomenon, and the represented speech acts themselves are only exchanges of signs. Any perlocutionary effect on the reader is relayed through the various audiences internal to the *énoncé*. However, there is a more interesting interaction which takes place at the level of the *énonciation*.

4) Here we must account for the audience described by Iser (1974) and Chatman (1978) as the *implied reader* (although Iser's implied reader also contains elements of 2) and 3)), and by Rabinowitz (1977) as the authorial audience. It is the audience constituted by the *énonciation* and the intertext of the *énonciation*.

> The relationship . . . is established on internal grounds, that is, it is defined with respect to the particular [text], making neither concessions to nor acknowledgements of whatever external relation the poet may have to the reader. (This reader or audience, of course, is to be distinguished from whatever listener – mistress or nightingale – may be 'addressed' in the fictive utterance itself and also from any audience addressed by the poem offered as a *natural* utterance.)
>
> (Smith 1978: 115)

This 'reader', whom I shall call the audience of the *énonciation*, is the respondent to the processes of narrative and the focus of its textual strategies. This is the audience of the narrative performance itself, of the *telling* rather than the *tale*. Iser's seminal work shows how this audience is implicitly addressed not only by such formal features as style and rhetoric but also by the gaps or 'indeterminacies' of the text which challenge audience participation.

5) The actual reader in his or her context, who may have features of 3) or 4) or neither. An actual reader totally aware of narrative strategies, of context and intertext, would be that mythical figure, the ideal reader, who is usually evoked by critical wish-fulfilment. Actual readers must be defined according to their social, historical, and ideological status, and therefore belong to many different categories with sharply differing approaches to the reader's construction of the text (Ruthrof 1981).[2]

The actual reader's construction of the text may involve both complicity and contestation. This will be partly governed by the tactics of audience inclusion or exclusion employed by narrator or author, tactics which we are about to examine in detail. One may study, as I do here, women's actual reading of a text for which the implied audience is masculine, or men's actual reading of a text reserved by implication for a female audience. Such readings will be vastly more productive if the readers are aware that:

> among the cultural constructs which writer and readers traditionally bring to their interaction with discourse, are a strongly polarised sex-role system and a set of stereotypes about women and men. In fashioning a theory of point of view, social realities like gender, and their impact on the writing and reading of texts, cannot be overlooked.
>
> (Lanser 1981: 61)

It is at the final stage of the audience construction of the text that the concept of gendered reading becomes important. Actual readers aware, before approaching a text, that they themselves have been constructed *as* text, conscious of their own determination by the ideological, linguistic, and social forces of upbringing and context, will throw quite a different light on reading (see Culler 1982: 58). They will be aware that one can read either with the grain of the text or against the grain and, indeed, that 'conflict between reader and author/text can expose the underlying premises of a work' (Moi 1985: 24). Gendered reading can bring variations and subtleties to the process of interpretation, thereby both constructing and contesting the text simultaneously. This chapter involves a deliberate attempt to demonstrate gendered reading.

THE STATUS OF THE SPEECH ACT IN NARRATIVE AND DRAMATIC TEXTS

In order to demonstrate the relationship between speech-act theory and the constitution of audiences I have chosen to use a text in dramatic form to highlight the fact that in fiction, as on the stage, the change in the status of the speech act is produced by the presence of an audience, which adds a third factor in addition to the I–you, addresser–addressee relationship of valid speech acts, and creates a spectacle. Even in the conventions of everyday discourse, the presence of an audience is necessary to produce what Pratt calls a 'display text'. The audience helps create the necessary 'frame' (see p. 26) within which only second-order speech acts are possible.

In its simplest form the dramatic performance, like the fictional narrative, involves a filtering, a relay effect within the text. The locution is double, the original sender/author speaking through the actor who delivers the lines. Illocutionary acts are performed at one remove: when actor speaks to actor the words have only a mimed validity and in no way modify the real situation of the actors. Most interesting of all is the true perlocutionary effect which concerns not the interlocutor but the audience. This model presents an interesting analogy to the channelling of the author/reader relationship through that of the narrator/narratee. Here author communicates with reader through the relayed effect of the fictional narrative, although obviously he or she has more control over his or her protagonists than the dramatist over actors. Naturally the simple analogy must be further modified to allow for self-reflexivity, for *mise-en-abyme*, for overt presentation, in other words for those features of the *énonciation* which involve the audience directly.

We will get a little closer to the model of many of the *Little Prose Poems*, for example, if we look at the speech acts in Greek tragedy which is itself loosely related to oral narrative. (See Figure 4.1.)

Not only are the protagonists in this dramatic/narrative situation obviously not performing an act but rather acting a performance (Agave, the actress, in the *Bacchae* is in most cases not experiencing horror any more than she is carrying Pentheus' real head; the *audience*

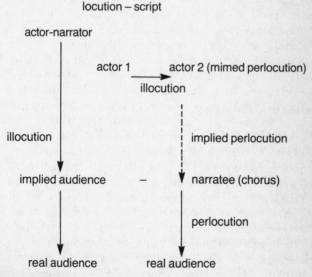

Figure 4.1 Speech acts in Greek tragedy

is); but also the seemingly valid illocutionary act where the leader of the chorus tells the audience something like 'Take warning, good citizens of Thebes' was, even in classical times, *not* addressed to Thebans but to a rather mixed bag of citizens of Athens. In other words the perlocution itself was mediated. There was an implied audience to whom the whole drama was directed and through whom it was relayed to the real audience.[3]

THE EXCLUDED AUDIENCE

To the implied audience I have added another equally important concept, that of the *excluded* audience (see p. 38). For example, nowadays the real audience for the *Bacchae* may consist completely of those specifically excluded from the original classical spectators, foreigners and women. They obviously read the performance differently. What would have been the reaction of the women of Athens to the *Bacchae*? This presents a whole new range of possibilities, one that modern authors have not been slow to exploit.

To take an example, how do I, part of the excluded audience, react when I read these lines from the poem 'Deirdre'? 'Do not let any woman read this verse!/ It is for men, and after them their sons,/ And their sons' sons!'

This is a textual strategy. When James Stephens, in the twentieth century, uses the formula of the oral tradition, he is not expecting it to be obeyed or even to function as an illocutionary act. The conditions, as Austin says, are not felicitous. Stephens uses it as a ploy to increase the perlocutionary effect on the readers, whether male or female, of the poem which follows, and in fact to attract female readership. In the same way, in a projected preface to the second edition of *Les Fleurs du mal* Baudelaire declares: 'It is not for my wives, my daughters or my sisters that this book has been written; and not for the wives, daughters or sisters of my neighbour either' (*Oeuvres complètes*, I: 181).

This was obviously an important note since it appears four times in various forms,[4] and of course it does not mean that Baudelaire expected only men to read his work. The tactic of the excluded audience works in many ways, filtering, distancing, justifying, tantalizing. I could write here 'Please do not read further if you object to the use of verbal crudity.' You would read on but would be aware of the ploy involved.

In this discussion of audiences, I want to look particularly at the interrelationships of the implied audience, the excluded audience, and the reader who may be one, the other, or neither. In order to see how these textual and contextual factors could be exploited, I chose as model one of the very small number of texts in *Little Prose Poems* where Baudelaire limits himself to purely dramatic utterance.

The Wild Woman and the 'Petite-maîtresse' (XI)[5]

'Truly, my dear, you exhaust me without moderation and without pity; one would say, hearing you sigh, that you are suffering more than sixty-year-old gleaners and old beggar-women who pick up crusts of bread at the door of taverns.

'If at least your sighs expressed remorse, they would do you some credit; but they only convey the satiety of well-being and the exhaustion of repose. And then, you constantly spread yourself in useless words: "Be loving to me! I need it so much! Console me here, caress me there!" Look, I want to try and cure you; perhaps we will find a way to do it, for two pence, in the middle of a fair, and without going very far.

'Let's take a good look, I beg you, at this solid iron cage behind which moves, howling like one of the damned, shaking the bars like an orang-utan driven wild by exile, imitating, in perfection, now the circular leaps of the tiger, now the stupid swaying of the polar bear, this hairy monster whose shape is a vague approximation of yours.

'This monster is one of the animals generally called "my angel!", that is to say a woman. The other monster, the one yelling at the top of his voice, a stick in his hand, is a husband. He has chained up his lawful wife like an animal, and he shows her in the suburbs, on fair-days, with the magistrates' permission, as goes without saying.

'Watch very carefully! See with what voracity (perhaps not pretended!) she tears up the living rabbits and the squawking hens which her keeper throws her. "Come now," he says, "one mustn't eat all one's goods in one day", and with these wise words, he cruelly tears her prey away from her, and its torn-out guts stay for a moment hanging from the teeth of the fierce animal, of the woman, I mean.

'Come now! a good whack with a stick to quiet her down! For she darts glances made terrible by greed at the food taken away from her. Dear God! the stick is not a theatrical prop, did you hear the flesh ring, in spite of the fake fur? And so her eyes are now starting from her head, she howls *more naturally*. In her rage, she sparks all over, like iron being beaten.

'Such are the conjugal customs of these two descendants of Eve and of Adam, these works of your hands, oh my God! This woman is incontrovertibly unhappy, although after all, perhaps, the titillating pleasures of glory are not unknown to her. There are forms of unhappiness more irremediable, and without compensation. But in the world where she has been thrown, she has never been able to believe that woman deserved another fate.

'Now, let's have it out, my dear *précieuse*! When I see the hells with which this world is crowded, what do you expect me to think of your pretty hell, you who only rest on materials as soft as your skin, who only eat cooked meat, and for whom a skilled servant carefully carves the portions?

'And what can all these little sighs which swell your scented breast mean to me, you sturdy coquette? And all these affectations learnt in books, and this tireless melancholy, calculated to inspire in the beholder any other sentiment than pity? Truly, I sometimes long to teach you what true unhappiness is.

'Seeing you thus, my delicate beauty, with your feet in the mud and your eyes turned hazily towards heaven, as though to ask for a king, you may fairly be compared to a young frog invoking the ideal. If you disdain the log (which I am now, as you are well aware), beware of the crane *who will snap you up, gobble you up, and kill you when he feels like it*!

'Though I may be a poet I am not such a fool as you would like to think, and if you tire me often enough with your *précieuse* whining I will treat you as a *wild woman*, or I will throw you out of the window, like an empty bottle.'

THE TITLE AND THE AUDIENCE OF THE *ENONCIATION*

In this text the narrator is completely eclipsed, and the *sujet d'énonciation* is present only in the title and tone of the piece. As we have seen, valid illocutionary acts of particular importance in the theatre and in narrative occur at moments when the actual audience and that of the *énonciation* are directly addressed. Of these acts the title is the most important because it establishes the contract and ensures that the audience/readers accept the implications of the performance which follows. The theatrical experience begins with the billboard, the textual with the typographical impact of the heading.

The title 'The Wild Woman and the *Petite-maîtresse*' gives a contract of performance and specifically of theatrical performance, particularly to the audience of the *énonciation*. This is done by coded signs: partly by the fairground connotations of 'wild woman' but also by the extremely limited use of the expression *petite-maîtresse* (Deloffre 1955: 16–17). The audience seeks a point of reference and will probably find it in Marivaux's comedy of cured affectation, *Le Petit-maître corrigé*. Thus economically the title suggests a spectacle, a lesson, and most importantly a certain tone, which recurs in the *énonciation* as a whole. It was their tone above all, their linguistic affectations, which characterized the *petit-maîtres*. Their tone is claimed to be at the root of present-day society talk, the French equivalent of the English 'Darling, how divine to see you'[6] (Deloffre 1955: 107). In fact it is the tone indicated which will be important in the text itself ('Truly, my dear', etc., etc.) helping to construct both the implied narrator and the narrative audience. Baudelaire notes in his *Journaux intimes* at this time: 'The tone of the kept mistress (My loveliest! The coy sex!)' (*Oeuvres complètes*, I: 662).

Thus the text exploits a tone or code which helps define the context of both the implied narrator and the actual speaker, the *entreteneur*.[7] The narrator is one who knows the parallel, artificial world of purchased sexual relationships, the world of the nineteenth-century rich where keeping a mistress was a codified procedure, as was the expected behaviour of such women. This world preoccupied Baudelaire, as is shown by another note: 'The delights of the *entreteneur* belong at once to those of the angel and the landlord. Charity and ferocity. They are even independent of sex, beauty and animal species' (I: 650).[8]

Tone and subject matter will also help to define the narrative audience. Women were implicitly excluded from hearing the narration of this sort of discourse just as the note (p. 94) professed explicitly to exclude them from the intended readership of *Les Fleurs du mal*. The implied narrative audience here is the same as in 'Portraits of Mistresses' (see Chapter 6): experienced men of the world in the comfortable after-dinner intimacy of the male club. However, this text is unlike 'Portraits of Mistresses' since the whole of the narrative framework is here implied, and what Horst Ruthrof (1981: Chapters 2 and 8) calls the presentational process is left to the audience of the *énonciation* to deduce.

THEATRICALIZATION AND THE SECOND-ORDER SPEECH ACT

The theatricalization of the text is accomplished with the greatest economy by the insertion of quotation marks which stress the direct address from the first person–*entreteneur* to the second person–*entretenue* (the kept female). These quotation marks are a late reinforcement of the dramatic form. They were not used in the original publication in *La Presse*. So textually we move immediately to that second level of illocution where the split between act and effect takes place. But the perlocutionary effect is mediated by the narrative audience. We, the readers, are left to supply the presentational process, to imagine the knowing laughter from the stalls at the admonition of the *entreteneur* to the *entretenue*.

We can at this point construct a narrative/performance model for the first stage of 'The Wild Woman and the *Petite-maître*' (remembering that this is only the first level of the textual performance, the one which provides narrative unity and continuity, and in which the second level is embedded).

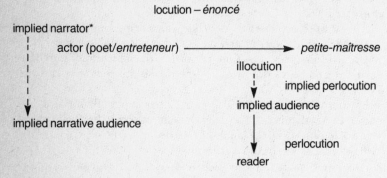

Figure 4.2   Stage one – schema of *La Petite maîtresse*

*It has been questioned (Genette 1983) whether the term implied narrator, or indeed implied author, is really necessary. We could see this as rather a case of an implied director or *mise-en-scène*.

THE INTERLOCUTORY AUDIENCE

Note that the *petite-maître* herself, the interlocutory audience of the *énoncé*, is never represented as speaking. The tone of the single actor, the *sujet de l'énoncé*, is all-important as it tells us not only about the speaker himself but about a partner who is only present dialogically, constructed only by *his* speech. This applies to her so-called utterances which are carefully marked as satirical deconstruction, *not* as exact quotation.

When a proprietor states that he should be exempt from having his belongings make demands on him, it tells you a lot about the owner as well as about the owned. The ambiguity of the word 'sighs' (used in a specifically sexual sense in many other Baudelairean texts) is the beginning of a series of underlying suggestions. The remarkable contrast between the 'satiety of well-being' which the kept woman is supposed to enjoy and the bitter quotation/distortion of her words: 'Be loving to me! I need it so much! Console me here, caress me there!' raises, as it is meant to, a number of questions about the relationship.

QUOTATION AND THE IMPLIED AUDIENCE

The use of quotation is never innocent in a text and is closely involved with the constitution of two implied audiences, those of the *énoncé* and those of the *énonciation*. That is why I stress that the intertext of both must always be considered.

> All verbal play as the representation of an utterance is bound up in the possibility of quotation – a repetition of discourse, a detachment of discourse from its context of origin. Quotation is a method of making texts, a way to give integrity to discourse and to focus interpretive procedures within a set of parameters defined by what is internal to the quotation 'marks'. Quotation involves an infinite regress and an infinite resource.
>
> (Stewart 1978: 122)

Three sorts of quotation are used here. Firstly, the *entreteneur*'s quotation of his mistress's words is not only meant to evoke a smothered guffaw. It also gives the statement ambiguity, making it both more authentic and more open to question.

> Quotation marks are marks of convention, marks of interpretation. Like any convention, they can work in either of two directions – they can mark the discourse as more real than real, . . . or they can mark the discourse as 'merely conventional', as a fiction among fictions.
>
> (Stewart 1978: 123)

Secondly, deliberate use is made of the intertext of the *Little Prose Poems* themselves, references to beggars at the doors of taverns or visits to fairgrounds suggesting narrator-narratees in common for a semantically related network of narratives (cf. Prince 1980b). Again this procedure involves considerable ambiguity.

The third stage in the hierarchy of quotation calls on a wider intertextuality and involves the quotation of other authors. 'Quotation from domains beyond the experience of the participants, beyond immediate context, has the force of an extended spatial and temporal boundary' (Stewart 1978: 122). Not only this, but such quotation may be used to make an ironic point about the *énoncé* itself, it may work against the apparent intent of the text. We may note for instance that in the Marivaux play it was the *man* who learnt his lesson (*Le Petit-maître corrigé*) and we will see that the quotations from La Fontaine are similarly loaded.

THE EMBEDDED PERFORMANCE AND THE COERCED AUDIENCE

The relation of man to woman, of the keeper to the kept, is shown as one of admonition and correction ('I want to try and cure you'). The method of correction involves subjection to a spectacle, a scene of obscenity. It is worth noting that the discourse addressed to *la petite-maîtresse* not only frames this obscene scenario but is itself of the same nature. The obscene is only so because it implies watchers. It is an act at second-hand. Like narrative, obscenity demands an audience. The act itself may be cruel, bestial, lustful, but it may only be obscene to those who view the performance. So the relationship of the poet and his mistress is already obscene with the narrative audience as its voyeurs. What follows, as we move from private to public, from house to street, and as the original pair of actors become themselves part of an audience, is an extension of the obscenity, but also a comment upon it.

So we move to the next stage, the second spectacle, and we may construct the schema of 'the wild woman' (see Figure 4.3).

It will be seen from this schema that the second framed spectacle

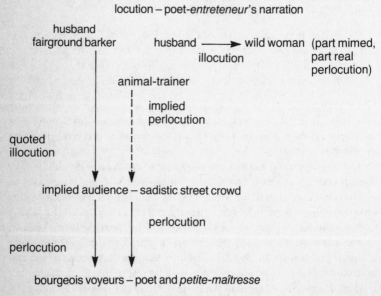

Figure 4.3   Stage two – schema of 'The Wild Woman'

presents the same relationships as the first, while at the same time presenting a tableau scene within a dialogue, thus framing one form of theatricalization within another. The implied audience is again basically one of voyeurs. However, there is a significant addition to this audience: the *précieuse*, who would normally be part of the excluded audience, is forced to become a spectator. The reactions of the 'delicate beauty' are left to us to imagine; she is merely present as watcher. This use of the excluded audience as coerced voyeur or *voyeuse* is typical of de Sade, and insufficiently remarked in studies of sado-masochism in Baudelaire (see Blin 1948; Mehlman 1974; Bersani 1977).

So we have in part a coerced audience watching a coerced performance (marked by the wild woman's 'natural' shrieks). The situation of the observer and the observed is gradually developed in sophistication in Baudelairean texts. The so-called intellectualism characteristic of his later work is in fact a theatricalization, a concretization of mediated experience. This redoubling may be personal, a situation in which the self splits to become both spectator and performer,[9] or observed in others. For example, a subject noted in his rough notes is: 'The drunk spying on and studying the drunk' (*Oeuvres complètes* I: 592).

THE FEMALE AND THE FEMININE: PARALLEL MIRRORING

So here woman is forced to study woman. The actress with her 'sighs' and 'useless words' is forced to study another actress with her 'howls', 'circular leaps', and 'stupid swaying'. Both women deform the natural by their very performance. Both play the part of animals: one that of the wild beast, the other that of the lap-dog (or rather bitch). One tears apart with her teeth the living animals thrown to her, the other picks delicately at the food cut up for her. One is imprisoned in a 'solid iron cage', the other in a 'pretty hell'. One is costumed in 'fake fur', the other in 'materials as soft as your skin'.

The 'monster' is a show, a demonstration of the doubleness of woman, woman who must always be an actress, doubling as and viewed as either 'angel' or beast. The effect of the wild woman's act is greatly enhanced by being framed in the degrading domestication of the kept woman. It is worth considering at this point whether the views of Anne Ubersfeld on the play within the play are applicable here. As we saw in Chapter 3, she sees such redoubled theatre as a form of double negation, which speaks not the *real* but the *true*.

If this is put in narrative terms, it means that a redoubling of the narrator–narratee relationship as well as that of the second-level illocutionary acts, as in the case of embedded narration, should produce a parallel mirroring and hence intensification of the perlocutionary effect.[10] The present example is particularly clear because both the original utterance and the framed event are specifically theatrical. The notion of the use of a representation, the embedded performance, to comment on the narrative performance itself, and hence to speak the truth about it, seems valuable. It is a way of driving home the impact and the implications of the rigorous parallels imposed between the two textual situations, the framing story and the framed story. These parallels are part of the *énonciation* and demand a special audience, alive to the strategies of the text.

THE *ÉNONCIATION*: COUPLING AS A TEXTUAL DYNAMIC

Before readers fall too easily into postures of outrage, reprobation, or satisfaction at the parallel established between the two women, they need fully to explore this Baudelairean minefield. A study of the *énonciation* reveals that, central to the parallel dualism, is a statement of complementary monstrosity: '*This monster* is one of the animals generally called "my angel!", that is to say a woman. *The other monster*, the one yelling at the top of his voice, a stick in his hand, is a husband' (my emphasis). The pairs then work in parallel. Just as the *entretenue* requires an *entreteneur*, the 'wild woman' requires a 'husband': the kept require keepers. Part of the strategy consists in the fact that in the actual text it is the poet-*entreteneur* who is playing the role and speaking the lines of the fairground barker: 'Let's take a good look, I beg you . . .' 'Watch very carefully! . . .' 'See with what voracity. . .' 'Come now! A good whack with a stick.' This in spite of the fact that it is the husband (significantly enough this is the only time the word 'husband' is used in *Little Prose Poems*) who is *said* to be shouting his lungs out. The legitimate proprietor, whose chaining of his wife is sanctioned by the magistrates, is textually linked with that other proprietor, the man who mounts a mistress, a procedure sanctioned by financial and social custom.

It is impossible to give a full account of the analysis by Samuel Levin (1959), Jean-Claude Coquet (1973), and their followers of coupling effects at the syntactic, prosodic, and phonetic levels but we can look at one example, the coupling of the two pieces of quoted direct speech: the 'useless words' of Scene One, 'Be loving to me! I need it so much! Console me here, caress me there!' and the 'wise words' of Scene Two, '"Come now," he says, "one mustn't eat all one's goods in one day".'

Both these exclamations seem to define the kept while by implication defining the keeper. By this link between the inner and the outer spectacle the text shows the relationship of woman to woman and man to man. In the husband's use of the cliché, 'one mustn't eat all one's goods in one day' one finds an unexpected depth of signification (see I: 650).

Let us examine this sentence in the light of the whole utterance. First comes the stamp of the proprietor, the illocutionary act of command, reinforced by the concrete act of snatching away the prey. 'Eat' stands for the whole seme of consumption, of digesting, absorbing, wasting, exhausting, the complementary opposition of *voracity and satiety*, and encompasses all of these in this sentence just as it does in the narrative as a whole. Mankind is carnivorous. Man consumes woman just as woman consumes man. Is 'all one's goods' merely her prey, that stock of shrieking rabbits and squawking hens? Or should the reader apply the husband's maxim to the man himself? Try and cash in on your property too quickly and it will cease to be economically viable. What are the implications of 'in one day'? Legitimate ownership requires continuity as does putting on a performance. A 'husband' does not indulge in a one-night stand, and this one puts on the show regularly 'in the suburbs, on fair-days'. A performance involves deferment, the expenditure of energy but the husbanding of resources. This '*différance*' (difference, deferment) suggested by folk wisdom may be seen as a counter not only to the appetite of 'the wild woman' but to that of universal woman: *quaerens quem devorat* was the motto Baudelaire inscribed under his drawing of *his* woman.

The multiplicity and insatiability of woman's appetite, so obscenely represented in this performance, is as 'natural' as are the screams of pain. In the diaries we find about woman:

> She is hungry and she wants to eat. Thirsty and she wants to drink.
> She's in rut and she wants to be fucked.
> What a claim to fame!
> Woman is *natural*, that's to say abominable.
>
> (I: 677)[11]

The pronoun 'she' (*elle*) is stressed in the same way in this text, and recurs in a most revealing phonetic coupling in the original French. The phoneme *elle* reappears in the adverbs *cruellement* and *naturellement*. She (woman) is an amalgam of the savagery of nature (*cru nature*), and the falsity she needs to survive (*ment*) – the raw and the cooked, you might say. It would obviously be *extremely* unwise to permit either the 'wild woman' *or* the *petite-maîtresse* to devour all her goods in one day.

The chains which bind the one are necessary for the other, the master and would-be master are coupled in syntactic wish-fulfilment.

'"Come now," he says, "one mustn't eat . . . "': this is the husband speaking. 'Come now! a good whack with a stick . . . ': this is the poet-*entreteneur* speaking, appreciating the *naturalness* and the barbarity of this living Punch and Judy show.

In the seventh paragraph, starting 'Such are the conjugal customs', the interlocutory audience changes. (The second-person pronoun stood until this point for the *petite-maîtresse*, now it stands for God, in 'works of your hands, oh my God!') The aside stresses the ultimate sanctioning of these marital customs. The church blessed the wedding, the magistrates licensed the show, and this couple are the descendants of Adam and Eve, who were personally created by the Almighty. Even if this God were to feel compassion, as, for a moment, does the poet, we must remember that this very Baudelairean emotion is also one experienced at second-hand. It is the replaying, the interiorization of the passion of others. It is essentially a theatrical experience – *true* rather than *real*, to use Anne Ubersfeld's terms. Thus the impact of the illocutionary invocation is emphasized by the all-pervasive dramatization, and *yet* this only enhances the strong perlocutionary effect, the emotional truth of the woman's suffering and of her inescapable destiny.

With the return to the frame narrative and the close of the tableau scene marked by the two shifters 'Now, let's have it out', the address to the *petite-maîtresse* takes the form of a declaration of war, and the effects of the coupling in parallel continue. There are two possible replies to the question 'what do you expect me to think of your pretty hell . . . ?' The reply of a surface reading is: You are lucky, as a woman you are *naturally* property, therefore make the most of being pampered and living in ease. However, the second reply, that of the syntactic and semantic coupling, is different: you too are an animal in a cage, but whereas she is wild and the *capital* of her keeper, you are tame and the *luxury* of your keeper. Barbara Johnson assesses what follows in terms of the non-coincidence of artificial signifier with real signified, as the poet reproaches his mistress for the belief that she can indulge in a game of signifiers, of empty simulation without any risk of real involvement (1979: 74). I agree with this reading but continue to describe the same phenomenon in terms of performance. The performance, 'affectations learnt in books' and '*précieuse* whining', of the mistress is assessed as unconvincing. Perhaps, as well as being forced into the role of audience-*voyeuse*, she can also be forced to act better, to sigh more naturally, to evoke real pity.

THE DOUBLE-EDGED WEAPON OF QUOTATION

The quotation from the La Fontaine fable, 'The Frogs who Asked for a King', is even more interesting in its intertextuality than the hint of Marivaux. I regard La Fontaine as being one of the main models of the textual strategies which Baudelaire adopts in his poems in prose, especially in the 'Symbols and Moral Stories'. The fable, by its very nature, remains close to the oral tradition where we see the still-active relationship of narrative and performance. This in its turn demands or implies a participating audience. La Fontaine spends longer than most poets in defining and involving his, and does so with an ironic consciousness equal to Baudelaire's own. The snares into which La Fontaine leads *his* implied reader have been examined by Louis Marin in his aptly titled *Le Récit est un piège* ('Narrative is a trap'). Here is part of the text of the fable:

> The frog nation, becoming bored
> With democracy, raised such a fractious cry
> That Jupiter appointed them an overlord.
> The king who came down was far from being harsh;
> Yet he made such a noise when he fell from the sky
> > That the people of the marsh
> > Rushed to hide . . .
> > > . . . In fact it was a log
> That had made the awesome splash . . .
> > . . . Before long the frogs were clamouring:
> > 'We want an active King!'
> By now nearly out of his mind
> With annoyance, Jupiter sent them a crane,
> Who breakfasted and lunched and dined
> On frogs whenever he felt inclined.
> And still the frogs continued to complain.
> This time Jupiter told them flat:
> 'Don't be silly. Do you think that my decrees
> Can be repealed just as frogs please?
> To start with, you should have kept
> Your own government.'
> > > (trans. Michie 1981: 37–8)

One notes with amusement that the frogs in this very fable had in fact enjoyed 'democracy' before being stupid enough to ask for a king, and wonders how La Fontaine's first readers reacted in the seventeenth century, the century of the Sun King, Louis XIV. Semantic coupling establishes a relationship between the 'log', which was the first king given to the frogs, and the rod used to beat the 'wild woman', the passive 'log' and the active 'stick'. Potency here is clearly equated with waving the big stick, or devouring the devourer. The lady's despised means of support may be galvanized into sudden activity. The ending, 'I will treat you like a *wild woman*, or I will throw you out of the window, like an empty bottle', echoes all too clearly 'But in the world where she has been thrown, she has never been able to believe that woman deserved another fate.'

The snag of course is that if the poet becomes aware 'of the necessity of beating women' (I: 701) and takes a stick to his pampered pet with her '*précieuse* whining', if the 'log' takes on the role of the 'stick', this can only be done at a price: the poet must equate himself with the *husband-keeper*. We do have Baudelaire's own word for it that 'Only brutes regularly get it up' (I: 702), but the price does seem rather a high one.

IRONY AND NARRATIVE REVERSAL

Here the audience of the *énonciation* can perceive the typically ironic use of the process of narrative reversal. Even if the poet-*entreteneur*, the actantial subject, achieves his object, the correction of the *petite-maîtresse*, he will reach his goal only at an even greater cost to his self-esteem. This reversal merely accentuates the fact that love, in the words of Baudelaire, is a crime for which an accomplice is indispensable (I: 689). In physical love there is always a victim and a torturer:

> Even if the two lovers should be greatly attracted and very full of reciprocal desires, one of the two will always be calmer or less possessed than the other. He or she is the operator, or the torturer; the other is the subject, the victim.
>
> (I: 651)[12]

Again we find the principle of rigorous complementarity. In fact, our poet, having set up a series of irresistible parallels, now presents a complete homology to 'the other monster'. The only result of the completion of the narrative reversal is that instead of being the victim he is now the torturer. 'What a claim to fame!'

THE FATE OF THE NARRATIVE AUDIENCE

We can now see that the coupling between the inner theatre and the outer theatre, between the fairground actors and the boudoir actors, is the way the textual strategy of the *énonciation* works, the way in which the trap is laid for the narrative audience of the *énoncé*.

The implied audience, the men of the world who recognize the 'tone of the kept mistress', who swap notes on unbearable mistresses and believe in asserting their rights, are neatly sucked in. They are presumably nodding agreement to the proposal that the man who mounts a mistress has a right to beat his property, his domestic pet. Spoilt, vain, affected, lazy, and selfish, why not treat her as a bitch like any other? The narrative audience, peering through the keyhole at the little drama, recognize their own desires. They see their own image in the *entreteneur* who asserts the power to administer correction to the nagging coquette. After all it is his right, the right of the 'log', the man who pays the bills. It is a known fact that 'A woman, a dog and a walnut tree, The more you beat them, the better they be.'

However, they are caught in the machinery of the play within the play, which forces the voyeur-spectator to identify himself with that other voyeur, the poet. The poet-*entreteneur* inflicts on the *petite-maîtresse* the spectacle of the fairground obscenity, so that she may recognize both her own animality and her own importance in 'the wild woman'. But by his very act of coercion, by the parallel he himself establishes, the poet is forced at the same time to recognize *himself* in the husband who chains his wife, clothes her in fake pelt, and treats her like an animal. Because of this fact, we finally see the narrative audience caught by means of the very prejudices sanctioned by their own society. The ideology of the society, the mechanism of power implicit in the textual structure, is an essential part of the textual trap, which is in a way a *miroir à alouettes*, a trap composed of mirrors.

In this trap each audience is reflected in another audience, just as each relationship of desire or power is mirrored in another. We find a similar situation in *A Midsummer Night's Dream* or in Peter Weiss's *Marat-Sade*. The series of audience levels in Figure 4.4, which views the text in performance terms, also corresponds to the series of levels in the narrative hierarchy postulated by Lanser (1981: 144).

THE ACTUAL READER AND THE EXCLUDED READER

At the final level, that of reception, each actual reader will appreciate differently the ultimate effect of this play of mirrors, one where the implied spectator, the 'veteran of joy' as he is called in 'Portraits of Mistresses', is drawn into complicity with the main actor. 'The spectator, lulled into a false security by the apparent legality of his surrogate, sees through his look, and finds himself exposed as com-

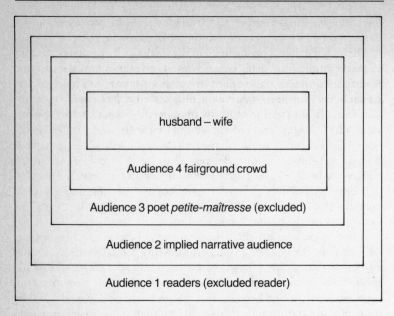

Figure 4.4   Audience embedding in 'The Wild Woman and the *Petite-maîtresse*'

plicit, caught in the moral ambiguity of looking', is how Laura Mulvey describes an analogous situation (1975).

By using a specifically theatrical form of narration, the text makes us acutely aware of the missing audience, forces us to speculate upon its nature. By redoubling the theatre, by constructing a play within a play, the text also redoubles this effect. The readers are forced to fill the slot, are themselves trapped into playing the role of audience. This demand that we recognize our role takes away our reader's anonymity. Such techniques 'destroy the satisfaction, pleasure and privilege of the invisible guest and highlight how film has depended on voyeurist active passive mechanisms' (Mulvey 1975: 16).

To return to my beginning, and of course to the last level of the game, there is a special fascination in being the *excluded* audience – a fascination the female critic knows only too well.[13] As we have seen, Baudelaire, in much of his work, plays an elaborate game of explicitly ('This book is not made for my wives, my daughters or my sisters' (I: 182)) or implicitly (by tone or choice of subject) excluding a female audience. If we peer through this particular keyhole we have only ourselves to blame, and, as intended, the temptation is almost irresistible. The very fact that the interlocutory audience of the text is a woman, as is the performer in the play within the play, sets up yet another trap, one of gender this time: the lure of being a woman watching a man watching women. However, we will fare no better than the male audience; the seduction of voyeurism will bring about our downfall. Righteously indignant at the social mores depicted, at the deformation of women by their 'inescapable destiny', we are gently reminded of those frogs, who, tiring of responsibility, demanded a king, and who, of course, deserved everything they got.

5 · *In the eyes of the other: the creation of narrative space*

In this chapter, I want to examine the question of spatialization. This has been foregrounded as an issue in literary criticism in America by the work inspired by the seminal essay of Joseph Frank, 'Spatial form in modern literature' (1945), and in France by that of Gérard Genette, 'La littérature et l'espace' (1969). However, the research in this area can be usefully supplemented and expanded by the work of Anne Ubersfeld in performance studies (1974, 1977, 1981) and that of Emile Benveniste on the relation of *énonciation* and spatialization (1971, 1974).

Narrative may be said to create an arena of performance, similar to an acting-space:

> A space not indefinite but marked by its limits. The stage is here and not there. A space which is defined by its relationship of exclusion with what is not itself. Even if naturally fluid, the limits of the space are virtually cut off as though by a razor.
>
> (Ubersfeld 1981: 51)

And yet written narrative, by the fixed nature of its signifiers and its pure textuality, is both more limited spatially than theatrical space and yet capable of architectures not available to the stage. The written text has a life as object, a synchronicity of its constituent parts, which resists a purely temporal unfolding and allows for the spatial interpretation of both signifiers and signifieds.

SPATIAL RELATIONSHIPS

There are five main types of spatial relationships operative in written narrative texts.

1) The spatial relationships constituted in the text by *deixis*. Deictics, or shifters as defined by Jakobson (*Essays in General Linguistics*, Chapter IX), are a class of words whose meaning varies with their situation, and which can never be defined except in relation to the message which contains them. The principal deictic relationship is

the I–you, speaker–hearer, relationship of both *énonciation* and *énoncé*. Any message must have a subject/sender and a subject/receiver even if these are obscured by the seeming impersonality of the voice used. Linked with this I–you and defined only by context are the relationships of here and now, past and present, the spatio-temporal framework contemporary with the instance of discourse. According to Benveniste (1974: 262) deictics 'organise temporal and spatial relations around the "subject" taken as a point of reference', and thus the illusion of life, of time, of space, flows in the first place from the text itself and not from anything exterior to it. The speaking instance of the text takes on substance, 'flesh and blood', in spite of its lack of any existence outside the boundaries of the text: 'This corporeal presence [of the first-person narrator] so emphatically determines the spatio-temporal orientation that an independent, autonomous system of orientation is established around this embodied "I"' (Stanzel 1984: 92).

The space so created can perhaps best be described by imagining an actor on an empty stage, or, better still, a voice on an empty stage. An *I* such as is presented in Beckett's *Not I* is almost purely deictic. The *I*, merely by being a presence, here and now, creates around itself a sense of space defined in relationship with that of the audience. This space may be modified and sharply delimited by the presence of a second actor or actors to whom the first relates (intimacy, hostility, indifference, etc.). Such a relationship has a past and a present even if only in terms of stage time, and it will eventually be modified by other spatial relationships such as those with objects or décor, or by textually defined relationships with imaginary or contextual spaces. However, it is the pure proxemic relation between actor and actor, and actor and audience, which is the physical equivalent of the space set up by the shifters in the text, a space both immediate and intratextual in nature.

2) The spatial relationships iconically specified in the text. These are the only ones normally considered in discussions of narrative space and include what is known as scene or setting:

> In the theory of the novel, scene may be defined in two ways; first, as setting or place; second, as a moment dramatized in a specific time/place location. Dialogue, which is temporal, therefore is relevant only 'in location' – for example, Isabel Archer at the staircase or Natasha Rostov at the ball or Andrey Bolkonsky at the window.
>
> (Kestner 1981: 107)

The extension here of scene from setting to dialogue in location still allows only for space as iconically defined. It is a purely mimetic definition of scene, and does not differentiate between mimetic space and deictic space. This is characteristic of much writing on narrative. It should be added that space is constituted by *all* the descriptive elements in a text, bodily characteristics as well as 'setting', and, to be fair, Kestner does deal with this in his discussion of 'volume' (1985: 115–20).

3) The relationships suggested to contextual space, the equivalent of the spaces 'off' in theatre. Historical and geographical allusions may add a whole extra dimension to a text, but so may references to fictional and mythological spaces. Each of these spaces constitutes what Bakhtin calls a *chronotope*, a semiotic space-time entity which interrelates with other such entities, both intra- and intertextual (1981: 84–258). In this way there exists an 'interspatiality' as a concomitant of intertextuality (Ubersfeld 1981: 69–77).

4) The spatial relationships suggested by the figures of the text. The word 'figure' is somewhat misleading here as spatially a distinction must be made between space *iconically* suggested by such figures as metaphor, simile, and metonymy and that other space which one might call the *architecture of rhetoric*. The first is a function of the signifieds of the text and particularly of that second level of signification, the connotative, where the signifieds become signifiers in their turn (Barthes 1978a: 89–94).[1] The second is a function of the primary signifiers in the text and the networks they constitute. Hence:

5) The spatial relationship of the textual signifiers to one another, syntactic, rhetorical, or typographic. The ordering of a sentence or longer text division, whether hypotactic or paratactic (Rabkin 1981: 79–99), embedded or sequential, is in itself a spatial device which may be related to any of the others I have mentioned. In the same way such rhetorical figures as antithesis, parallelism, ellipsis, and chiasmus are in themselves spatial arrangements which serve the architectural aims of rhythm, scale, sequence, and proportion (Kestner 1981: 123).

The typographic features of the text, the use of gaps, paragraphing, and layout, are also vital components of the spatial dimension of written narrative.

All these *signifier* relationships work hand in hand with the earlier network of *signified* relationships, since, when the *énoncé* takes on the physical semblance of text, the distribution of signs which bear witness to this production have in themselves an iconic value (Delas and Filliolet 1973: 88). Lastly, the title is a vital spatial element in any text. It is marked off, capitalized, at once part of the text and exterior to it. It is a boundary marker, a sign of territory and at the same time a liminal experience. The title exemplifies that relationship between the spatial and the visual which is seen in narrative in so many ways.

The text I have chosen to demonstrate the interplay of the different spaces of narrative performance is one where the visual has primacy and which is appropriately entitled.

The Eyes of the Poor (XXVI)[2]

Ah! you want to know why I hate you today. It will probably be less easy for you to understand than for me to explain to you; for you are, I believe, the finest example of feminine imperviousness which may be found.

We had passed a long day together which had seemed short to me. We had sworn to one another that all our thoughts would be shared between us, and that our two souls henceforward would make only one; – a dream which is not particularly original, after all, except for the fact that, dreamt by all men, it has been realized by none.

In the evening, rather tired, you wanted to sit in front of a new café which occupied the corner block of a new boulevard, still littered with rubble and already showing off the glory of its unfinished splendours. The café was brilliant. Even the gaslight displayed all the ardour of an opening, and lit enthusiastically the blinding white walls, the dazzling expanses of the mirrors, the gold of the beadings and cornices, the pages with plump cheeks dragged along by leashed dogs, the ladies laughing at the falcon perched on their fist, the nymphs and goddesses carrying on their heads fruits, pâtés and game, the Hebes and the Ganymedes presenting with outstretched arms the little amphora of mousse or the parti-coloured obelisk of Neapolitan ices; the whole of history and the whole of mythology in the service of gluttony.

Right in front of us, on the road, was standing a decent man about forty years old, with a tired face, a greying beard, holding by the hand a little boy and carrying on the other arm a baby too weak to walk. He was acting as nursemaid and taking the children out in the evening air. All in rags. These three faces were extraordinarily intent, and these six eyes were staring fixedly at the new café with an equal admiration, but with varying touches according to age.

The eyes of the father said: 'How beautiful it is! how beautiful it is! one would say that all the gold of the poor world has ended up on these walls.' – The eyes of the little boy: 'How beautiful it is! how beautiful it is! but it's a house where only people who are not like us can go in.' – As for the eyes of the littlest one, they were too fascinated to express anything but a stupid deep joy.

Popular singers say that pleasure makes the soul good and softens the heart. Song was right that evening, as far as I was concerned. Not only was I softened by this family of eyes, but I felt rather ashamed of our glasses and our carafes, bigger than our thirst. I turned my gaze to yours, dear love, to read *my* thought there; I was sinking into your eyes, so beautiful and so strangely sweet, into your green eyes inhabited by Whim and inspired by the Moon, when you said to me: 'I find those people unbearable with their eyes wide open like gateways! Couldn't you ask the head waiter to move them on from here?'

So difficult is it to understand one another, dear angel, and so incommunicable is thought, even between people who love one another!

DEICTIC SPACE

The opening paragraph is a stunning example of pure deixis, the first of my five types of spatial delineation. The relation of *I* and *you* in their present time *today* exists at first only as a field of emotion, of intimacy. I and you are two actors on a blank stage defined only by consciousness and by their closeness to or distance from one another. In terms of *énonciation* we have here a putative identity of speaking subject and spoken subject both situated in the *énoncé* of the *I* of the text. The *I* and the *you* are also put in a paradoxical position by the particular use of literary deixis. The dialogic form of the opening sentence seems to limit the *you* of the *énonciation* to the interlocutor or interlocutors and exclude the readers. But in spite of its form this dialogue is *not* on stage where the audience is clearly distanced from the performers, but a printed text. For a brief but important moment until the interlocutor is identified, the reader or readers tend to be assimilated by the deictic *you* and to read the message ambiguously.[3] The receiver is felt *both* to be the unknown *you and* the readers themselves who partially experience 'It will probably be less easy for you to understand than for me to explain to you' as a message to them. Thus the reader is momentarily involved, and, when deictically excluded from the text by the partial definition of *you* in the words 'example of feminine imperviousness', feels forced back into an exterior space gazing at the intimate interior situation of non-understanding. By the end of the first paragraph what we are left with is two presences, of whom all we know is that one is female, in what is already a highly energized space. They are bound by the intimacy of hatred, but divided by the woman's imperviousness, the 'road barred' sign of frustrated communication.

This deictic space embeds the rest of the text, as it is re-formed in the last sentence/paragraph. When it reoccurs to close the text it is re-defined by tense and anaphoric reference. The intimacy of the emotional field suggested in the first place by hatred is finally re-asserted by its complementary opposite, the ironically used 'love' which is the *last* word in the original French text.

THE HYPOTHETICAL SPACE

The change in the second paragraph, in tense from present to past perfect and in voice from the subject/object *I/you* pair to the shifter *we*, defines an anterior space, one governed by the apparent communication inherent in the use of the first person plural.[4] This space is still one of pure personal interaction which contains in its turn a *hypothetical* construct, a realm in which all thoughts would be shared and two worlds would be one. This construct has in common with the dream its spatialization of desire, where the double space of *I* and 'other', characteristic of consciousness, will contract to the single space of unity, characteristic of the oneiric (cf. Wright 1984: 108).

THE CONCRETE SPACE

In the third paragraph, another shifter, 'in the evening', heralds a new space, as does the change to the aorist as opposed to the past perfect. An unexpected use of tense (the formal past historic *vous voulûtes*, not the expected conversational *vous avez voulu*) marks the present narrative distance between the interlocutors, as does the use of *vous* rather than the more intimate *tu*. 'In front of a new café' marks the move from the deictic definition of space to the iconically marked scene or setting.

To understand the spatial divisions of this narrative it is particularly important to grasp that the man and woman are sitting not *in* the café but *in front* of it, that is to say at one of the tables set out on the pavement. They are in a relationship of contiguity to the café, but it acts as a backdrop to them, not a stage. The *terrasse* or pavement space thus represents a kind of hybrid space, both belonging to the café and not belonging to it, as an apron both belongs to the main stage and is set apart from it.

INTERSPATIALIZATION

Before looking at the iconic localization in the signs of the text, it is worth considering here my third category of space, contextual space or interspatialization. The mention of a 'new café' at the corner of a 'new boulevard' produces an off-stage space, the Paris of Napoleon III and Baron Haussmann, a Paris which was being ruthlessly remodelled, and where the new wide boulevards with their elegant buildings were achieved by the dispossession of the poor. The 'rubble' which still litters the scene is a historically potent signifier in Brechtian terms.[5] It is metonymic of the shattered homes of the poor, driven to the outer suburbs by the rising bourgeoisie, and the darkness of these remains contrasts with the exhibited brightness of the new café. In the same way, the pavement, theoretically the property of all, is dispossessed in favour of those who can afford to pay for their seats and their refreshments. Interspatiality, like intertextuality, is the category most subject to reader variation in the final construction of the text. It contributes to our need to distinguish between the reception of the implied narrative audience, the Parisian of the 1860s, and that of the actual reader in a totally different context.

ICON AND SETTING

The concrete setting of the café is described in terms of the utmost theatricality, in lighting, decoration, painting, hangings, statuary. Even the food is described as a representation, a *prop* rather than a comestible. The very brilliance of the gas lighting seems to permit penetration, to shed light into every corner. But this is a mere illusion. Just as a stage set permits only visual penetration by the audience and otherwise sets up an impervious barrier, so the café here is seen through glass, from the outside. It is a feast for the eyes, offering itself to the spectator as a stage set offers itself to the audience. It is from this narratorial perspective that the whole picture of the café is drawn. This is a tableau of consumption, a purely pictorial world where the gold, the gluttony, and the laughter have all been transferred to the walls in a series of figural and mythological representations. The stasis of this tableau scene (see p. 12) stands in sharp contrast to the anticipated narrative momentum.

There is nothing human, nothing moving. The depicted women and boys, the Hebes and the Ganymedes, are themselves objects of consumption to the eyes, frozen as they endlessly proffer their wares. They are the equivalent of the fruit, the pâtés and game, the mousse and the ices. This *setting* of fictional profusion, the second form of narrative space, is iconically coupled with the fifth form of space, the proliferation of the textual signifiers. The single long sentence from 'Even the gaslight' to 'gluttony' is a syntactic and rhetorical *tour de force*, where the cumulative effect of the elaborated binary and ternary patterns, an architecture of primary signifiers, parallels the semantic content. Both signifiers and signifieds accumulate in a build-up to the devastating final sign, 'gluttony', which sums up the whole space.

THE SPACE OF THE SPECTATOR

. At this stage, in the fourth paragraph, there is completed the construction of a triple material space. The first part consists of the café (or backdrop), the second of the pavement (or stage), reintroduced by the shifter 'in front of us', and the third of the road (or audience space) where stand the spectators, the poor. The narrator and his companion sit in the intermediate space between the backdrop and the spectators, between the light and the dark, the illusion of wealth and the reality of rags, the mythological carriers of food and the living carrier of the hungry.[6] The poor family's all-important function as audience is stressed by metonymy: they are mainly *faces*, 'three faces' and 'six eyes' looking in at the new café from which they are excluded, into which only their eyes can penetrate.

These eyes are the dynamic focus of the text, its source of energy, and they actuate a remarkable spatial reversal, which is the turning-point of the text. Attention is still centred on the poor family, but in the fifth paragraph the narrator reverses the roles of the spectacle and the spectator, the seen and the seer. This is the advantage of the drama of the streets, or the drama of narrative. Like the carnival it permits reversals between actor and spectator and between narrator and narratee, which are seldom possible in the one-way traffic of the theatre, and particularly of the bourgeois theatre with its Italian stage and segregated auditorium (Ubersfeld 1981: 54).

Prompted by that compassion, that fellow-feeling, which as we have seen (p. 53) is a form of self-projection, a way of extending one's own life by experiencing vicariously the emotions of others, the narrator turns the poor family from audience to actors, performers in a story which he has 'rewritten' just as he rewrote the life of the woman he glimpsed in 'Windows'. In his narrative the poor are made to express the fictional emotions he imagines for them, while he represents himself as audience to lines of which he is also the scriptwriter. The direct speech here helps to produce this imaginary space, localized by a series of deictics ('How beautiful *it* is', '*these* walls', '*it's* a house', 'like *us*'). These deictics have, however, as subject reference not the real poor, but the narrator's own ego projections.

IMAGINARY SPACE

The *eyes* of the poor, the putative speakers, produce different versions of the imaginary space. The father's eyes produce a figural space ('one would say that all the gold of the poor world has ended up on these walls') which is an expression of *condensation*.[7] The gluttony of consumption has sucked in all the gold of the poor world (and by extension all the money of the poor) to concentrate it in this one dazzling display. The attributed figure ('one would say') provides one more spatial dimension to the text, one that belongs to the fourth category of space. Next, the child's eyes produce a reinforcement of the theme of imperviousness ('it's a house where only people who are not like us can go in'). This emphasizes the sense of spatial hierarchy stressed throughout the text (cf. Ubersfeld 1981: 93). Lastly the baby's eyes enhance by contrast the frustration of desire common to all the other actors, since they express the satisfaction of desire, a 'stupid deep joy'.

In the sixth paragraph the focus then turns to the intermediate space, the pavement in front of the café, which should also be the space of mediation between the rich and the poor. Here the narrator's attention switches from his imaginary reconstruction of the feelings of the poor to an analysis of his own emotions *vis-à-vis* 'this family of eyes'. He frankly admits these emotions to be sentimental and egoistic in nature by his self-deprecating reference to popular song. Just as the pavement itself is spatially related to the café by contiguity ('in front of a new *café*') and to the narrator and his companion deictically ('in front of *us*, on the road'), so 'our glasses and our carafes, bigger than our thirst' stand metonymically and iconically for the café and its display of consumption, while the shifter *our* refers to the deictically defined interpersonal space of the man and the woman. Ironically, this is the only use of the second person plural in this part of the text. The dreamed-of communion of minds which was characterized by *we* is already known by the narrator not to exist. What he is telling is the past story of his disillusionment.

The next space explored is another purely imaginary one: 'I turned my gaze to yours, dear love, to read *my* thought there'. The Baudelairean narrator is obsessed with the mirror image, constantly seeking confirmation of self in the search for identity, in a sort of all-pervasive narcissism. As Lacan puts it:

When, in love, I solicit a look, what is profoundly unsatisfying and always missing is that — *You never look at me from the place from which I see you . . . what I look at is never what I wish to see.*

(cit. Wright 1984: 117)

In these texts the relationship with woman frequently displays what Umberto Eco (1984: 212) calls 'catoptric nostalgia', the longing for the mirror image. Woman, as 'other', is seen as the possible provider not only of the confirmation of identity, but of the *reflection* of identity. This search for the ultimate self-reflexive space is, of course, doomed to failure; woman remains irremediably other.

FIGURAL SPACE AND ITS REVERSAL

The figural space of the woman's 'green eyes', into which the narrator hopes to sink, far from providing the haven of identification, of shared thought, is immediately distanced. It is linked by the keyword 'beautiful' to the café, that frozen, dehumanized, glassed-off space. She is objectified too by her mythologization, bright, distant, and cold like the 'Moon'. Woman, like the 'ladies', 'nymphs', and 'goddesses' of the café, is in this context the ultimate object of consumption, staged and isolated, visible and inaccessible at the same time, doing everything to exhibit herself and yet claiming the right to refuse the gaze of the unauthorized. The narrator's 'angel', a true representative of this sexual reification, refuses to play the roles assigned to her by the 'gaze' of her companion and the 'eyes of the poor'. She is neither able to be the mirror to her companion's thoughts, nor willing to be an object of consumption to those who have not paid for the privilege.

The assertion of her identity in direct speech, where she is at once the speaking subject and a spoken subject contained in the *énoncé* of the narrator, comes as a considerable shock after the solipsistic nature of the direct speech attributed to the eyes of the poor. Far from the shared signs of compassion where the narrator spoke for the poor in the first person, she rejects the 'family of eyes' and reduces them to the 'non-person' (Benveniste 1971: 228–30) of the third person ('their eyes', 'them').

She also reverses the figural space. In place of the condensation of the figure attributed by the narrator to the eyes of the father ('All the gold of the poor world . . . on these walls'), *she* sees in the eyes of the poor the ultimate figuration of lack. The eyes, 'wide open like gateways', are waiting to swallow up those unwary enough to look into them. Far from expressing condensation, they express that other Baudelairean ex-

treme, *vaporisation (Oeuvres complètes*, I: 676), the dilution and absorption
of self into the 'other'. Her refusal of compassion is a more realistic
assessment of the meaning of those open eyes. They represent the space
of the excluded, always waiting to swallow up the little hermetic
enclosure of the privileged if once the barriers are lowered. The
distancing she demands between the field of the interlocutors, the
deictic *here*, and the *there* associated with the third person, is the only
solution to this figural attraction, this power of absorption, posited by
the manifestation of lack.

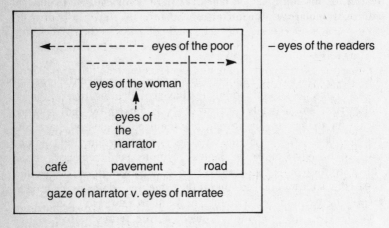

Figure 5.1 Relationships of gaze in 'The Eyes of the Poor'

Thus the final array of space in the sixth paragraph is one of the most
profound non-communication imaginable. The eyes of each par-
ticipant in this visual and narrative exchange are focused on a *different*
space from that of the others. The eyes of the poor are fastened on the
iconic space of the *café*, the eyes of the woman on the figural space of the
eyes 'wide open like gateways', and the eyes of the narrator on the
non-reflexive deictic space of 'Your eyes . . . beautiful . . . sweet'. As
well there is a total non-coincidence between the understanding of the *I*
and the *you* of the frame *énoncé*, the speaker and his 'dear angel'. His eyes
and hers perceive totally different aspects of the 'reality' they share,
and rather than being self-reflexive they are mutually repulsive.

As for the eyes of the readers, we have already seen the initial
ambiguity about the *I* and the *you* of the *énonciation*, and how the reader
is then deictically excluded from the text, and forced into an exterior
space spying on an interior situation of failed understanding. It will be

noted, however, that the reader, as *tiers exclu*, the excluded third party (cf. Kaufman 1982), is put in the same relation to the text as the poor are to the deictic space of the narrator and his companion. This leads to further interesting questions about the dynamics of exclusion and the role of the reader.

THE ARCHITECTURE OF RHETORIC

We will now return to the fifth aspect of space and the architecture of rhetoric. The figure most characteristic of the Baudelairean poetics of space is the chiasmus, the mirroring structure, the universally present *ab:ba* characteristic at once of such small polarities as the rhymes of a quatrain or of such major ones as the structure of the human brain.

> Chiasmus . . . can only come into being as the result of a void, of a lack that allows for the rotating motion of the polarities. As long as it is confined to objects, this structural necessity may seem harmless enough: the declining motion of a fountain or a ball, the reflection of a mirror or the opening of a window casement have, in themselves, nothing of pathos about them. But [this] figuration must also involve subject/object polarities, precisely because it has to put into question the irrevocability of this particularly compelling polarity. This implies the necessity of choosing as figures not only things but personal or subjective experiences as well, with the avowed purpose of converting them into impersonal over-things, but without being able (or wanting) to prevent that the subjective moment first function on the level of meaning. However, these experiences, like the figural objects, must contain a void or a lack if they are to be converted into figures.
>
> (de Man 1979: 49–50)

This particular figure represents a structural obsession recognized in *Little Prose Poems* by Mauron. He sees the characteristic form of the prose poems as two opposing spaces (he calls them *plages*), one bright, lit, happy, and one dark, unlit, unhappy, linked both by their mirroring in the two halves of the text and by the mediating function of the poet-narrator.

This is what he recognizes in 'The Eyes of the Poor' (1966: 56), and at first sight it would indeed seem to be the basic structure: dark/light, rich/poor, seen/seers, inside/outside. This is how I first read the text, but a nagging sense of dis-location made me realize I was not making allowance for the differences between the mirror and the eye. As Sartre remarked in a celebrated scene of *Huis-Clos* (*In Camera*), eyes *cannot* be domesticated to serve the function of mirrors. One's image, rather than being faithfully reflected, may be diminished, distorted, or lost in the eyes of another. It is this distorted chiasmus, with all its implications, that is found both in the signifiers and in the signified of 'The Eyes of the Poor'.

In order to realize the full implications of visual space in the text under consideration, we will compare it with part of another prose poem which presents an almost perfect mirror image on the dark/light pattern identified by Mauron. This is the ending of 'The Toy of the Poor' (XIX).[8]

> On a road, behind the railings of a vast garden, at the end of which appeared the whiteness of a charming manor bathed in sunshine, was standing a handsome well-kept child, dressed in those ever so smart country clothes.
>
> Luxury, heedlessness, and the constant spectacle of wealth make those children so attractive that one could believe them made from another clay than the children of mediocrity or poverty.
>
> Beside him, there lay on the grass a splendid toy, as well-kept as its owner, varnished, gilded, dressed in a purple gown, and covered in plumes and glass beads. But the child was taking no notice of his favourite toy, and this is what he was looking at:
>
> On the other side of the railings, on the road, between the thistles and the nettles, there was another child, dirty, puny, grubby, one of those stray brats whose beauty could be discovered by an impartial eye, if, as the eye of the connoisseur divines an ideal painting under a thick daub of varnish, he cleaned it of the repulsive patina of destitution.
>
> Through those symbolic bars separating two worlds, the open road and the manor, the poor child was showing the rich child his own toy, which the other was examining avidly as a rare, unknown object. Now, this toy, which the little ragamuffin was teasing, tilting and shaking in a barred box, was a living rat! The parents, probably to save money, had drawn the toy from life itself.
>
> And the two children laughed at one another fraternally, their teeth *equally* white.

THE POSITIVE CHIASMUS AND ITS SUBVERSION

Here one finds the establishment of two truly paraxial spaces, two mirror halves characterized by the balance, the *equality* (the emphasis is Baudelaire's, not mine) between the spaces and their components. The railing stands as the necessary denominator of lack in this chiasmic structure, and through this barrier the two children interact, each at once the seer and the seen, at once actor and spectator, at once subject and object.

The differences between light and dark, rich and poor, merely emphasize their similarities and their fraternity: 'just as reflective totalization must include both sides of the mirror, so the totalization of subjective experience must lead to a positive assertion that only chiasmus can reveal. The reversal of a negativity into a promise . . .' (de Man 1979: 50).

This reversal, which de Man finds characteristic of the work of Rilke, is clearly visible in 'The Toy of the Poor', an early work where the rhetoric is still Utopian and optimistically transgressive of the established order.

In 'The Eyes of the Poor', on the other hand, we are dealing with a subverted chiasmus, a failed reflection, due to the treachery of the human eye which refuses to return the desired image. At first sight the textual organization of space seems almost as perfect as the mini-chiasmus which stresses the keyword: 'this family of eyes', 'your eyes so beautiful', 'your green eyes', 'their open eyes'.

However, an examination of the spaces according to their division into paragraphs reveals a flaw in the patterning of the basic rhetorical trope (see Figure 5.2). This may be more clearly seen at the purely typographic level of lines and spaces between paragraphs (see Figure 5.3).

In this highly organized text, where all the paragraphs are repeated in reverse order but in slightly diminished form, an exemplum of de Man's paradigmatic bouncing ball, there is one omission. The mirror

I/you	We	Rich	Poor		Poor	Rich	I/you
						we	
now	together	pavement				separate	now
here	then	café	road		road	pavement	here
deictic space	iconic space				iconic space		deictic space

reversal
point

Figure 5.2 Space–paragraph relationships in 'The Eyes of the Poor'

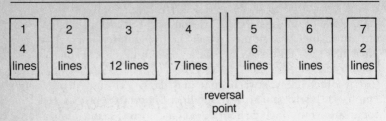

Figure 5.3 Typographical distribution

image of paragraph 2, the one which offered the dream of communion, is missing, or is only present as a momentary illusion in paragraph 6, which thus telescopes elements of paragraphs 2 and 3.

So the spatial disposition of the text, even at the concrete typographical level as an organization of signifiers, is a transposition of the problem of communication itself. The flawed chiasmus of the text represents the flawed relationship between self and other made apparent by the intrusion of lack, the energetic input of the excluded third. The purely narcissistic reflection desired by the narrator is shown to be a rhetorical dream not realizable in any relation between self and other, least of all that between man and woman or woman and man.

6 · *For men's ears only: narrative power play and the sexual/textual nexus*

Narrative space can become an arena, and performance can become a contest. Narrative contests involve not only tellings, but rivalry and even aggression. They display, in the clearest possible form, the basic problems of power relationships in the telling itself, because they offer an exceptionally complicated model of narrator–narratee interaction. Rather than a single or even a multiple sender–receiver story model, there is a permutation and alternation of roles between tellers and listeners. In this way the dynamics of narrative become closer to those of conversation, in so far as conversation implies a switching of roles, a constant turn-taking involving interplay with other speakers. Each contribution to a conversation necessarily modifies that of the other or others. Listeners must give power over themselves to a speaker, because they in turn want to claim power *as* speakers over others (Pratt 1977: 105–7). In any form of communication, modifications are imposed by a context which implies an interchange, and *a fortiori* by one which implies a competition.

The status of narrative is changed if a *mobile* relationship between narrators and narratees, in which there is turn-taking and switching of roles, is substituted for the *stable* relationship between a narrator and his or her audience (Rousset 1982: 32). It is the difference between such basic models as *The Decameron* on the one hand and *The Thousand and One Nights* on the other. The succeeding narrators in narrative contests address multiple narratees, many of whom will become narrators in their turn. One of the oldest and most compelling narrative forms, such a contest demands that each succeeding narrative must endeavour to outdo the one before, by capping, by undercutting, by inverting the story which precedes it. The narrative contest takes many forms. It may be a competition in ingenuity of insult, or in the degree of fear inspired; a derogation of another race or another gender; a competition in ingenuity of sexual fantasy or in exaggeration. It is interesting to us because it displays the basic problem of narrative which is one of control, and one of control by signs. As we have seen, any narrator enters into a contract, undertakes an obligation to the audience, even if it is only that of killing time. At the same time, the teller is given power by the listener or reader, the power to entertain, to shock, to offend, even to outrage. However, the contract is always reciprocal, because he or she also yields the power of judgement, of acceptance or rejection. In the normal narration, while there is always a narrator, we are frequently left to deduce the possible reactions of the narratee from the strategies of the text. In the narrative contest, however, the double nature of the narrative contract is actualized because each performer is seen in a double role. Apart from explicitly judgemental statements, each competitor also gives an implicit opinion of the previous narration by the tale he or she chooses to tell and the manner of telling it. So each is not only actor but audience, and simultaneously both counsel and judge.

THE TRADITION OF RHETORICAL AGGRESSION

This narrative form belongs to a tradition which Walter Ong, in *Fighting for Life* (1981), identifies with the channelling of aggression into accepted cultural forms. He sees this as mainly applying to masculine aggression, for the simple reason that men controlled literacy and culture. Thus the whole development of rhetoric and of the rhetorical tradition in both academic and popular forms followed a competitive and agonistic path. He points out that *ludus*, the Latin word both for game and for school, originally meant a preparation for war. The narrative contest is a highly developed cultural game, but a game which involves, in the same way as an academic debate, a symbolic execution, a verbal *mise-à-mort*.

In his discussion of games theory, Roger Caillois (1962)[1] distinguishes four different types of game: *alea* or risk-taking; *ilinx* or vertigo; *mimicry* or play-acting; and *agon* or competition. He sees *mimicry* as closest to interaction and *agon* as closest to warfare. The particularity of the narrative contest is that it takes story-telling, which is basically a form of *mimicry*, and converts it into a competition, thus giving it the characteristics of *agon*. It becomes a competition of performances. The ludic, in its original sense, and the agonistic are both basically concerned with maintaining control, dominating the opponents, and sweeping them from the field or the board.

Another feature of a story-telling struggle is that it takes on very different forms according to the sex of the participants. We will be looking at one example of an all-male contest, possibly the most common kind in everyday life. Then there is the contest in which both sexes participate, which can acquire strong overtones of either seduction or humiliation, as Freud suggests when discussing the use of the joke as a sexual weapon (Freud [1905] 1960: 97–102). The most notable example of the use of the war of words to express the war of the sexes is, of course, in Boccaccio. There are few artistic expressions of all-female story sessions which also have a strongly competitive element, although they have always existed, but in a marginalized rather than a literary form (Maclean 1987). A further question then arises. If story-telling is used so extensively as a form of competition, and even as a form of 'death-dealing', between tellers, as each story 'wipes out' its predecessors, how far can this be seen as characteristic of the narrative genre as a whole? Success may be seen as a matter of succession, and succession may cover the time-span of a convivial evening, or that of several generations of tellers. The fear of the generations as they confront each other is expressed as much by the anxiety of being superseded found in the story-telling contest as by the 'anxiety of influence' (see Wright 1984: 150–6). When Bakhtin talks about the Oedipal element in genre development, in which each generation of writers ceremonially 'murder their fathers', he too is seeing the text wielded as a literary surrogate for the *mise-à-mort*. In narrative, as in rhetoric or philosophy, texts are the weapons in the 'fight for life'.

BRAGGING: FICTION VERSUS ACTION

The bragging contest, of which we are examining an ambiguous example, is a world-wide phenomenon. The space of such contests is often clearly marked as masculine territory, and such classic signs as drinking and smoking unite the included participants and proclaim a state of licence. The rituals of licence indicate that the contest is one of empty signs. Any speech act in a bragging contest is known to be contained and neutralized by the framework of the performance. Narratives swapped, after drink has been taken, exclude reality; the drink and the stories merely 'kill time'. In such speech acts signs display their basically arbitrary nature, since it is unimportant whether they are used to lie or to tell the truth (see p. 88).

Indeed, one paradigmatic form, male ritual bragging narratives among American blacks (see Abrahams 1971 and Turner 1977), in fact uses the very term *signifying* for boasting of successes which involve not crude brute force, but a war of words. This is so much so that the *toasts*, or bragging contests, no longer involve personal exploits, but have become contests in pure narration, epic stories of the 'cat' who has style. The 'cat' who *signifies* is the one who wins by the manipulation of signs and not by physical force. He uses *style* to gain control, a style which becomes that of the narrative, and, like the Baudelairean dandy, elaborates a semiotic code of gesture and clothing. Like the dandy too he is 'cool' and he refuses other people's norms such as work and morality: as Baudelaire put it in 'The Painter of Modern Life', 'an indefinite credit will suffice him' (*Oeuvres complètes*, II: 710).[2]

The one thing such manipulators of signs must avoid is the transfer to action. If the distinction between play, as part of a ritual contest, and reality is not maintained, then problems arise (cf. Huizinga 1970). The results of such a breaking of the frame were admirably exploited in one of the oldest literary uses of the bragging contest, *Le Pèlerinage de Charlemagne* (Riquer 1957: 194–207). In this early send-up of the macho mystique, Charlemagne, to prove a point in an argument with his wife, goes off to Constantinople with his twelve peers. While there they follow the traditional pattern of licence, and, after a rather bibulous evening, indulge in a bragging contest, the famous *gabs*. Unfortunately a spy is listening to them, an *excluded* hearer breaking the frame of performance. To their dismay and horror, the spy reports back to the king of Constantinople, who demands that they make good their words. The speech acts of play are suddenly transferred to the context of reality. It is required that a lie become truth, fiction non-fiction. Needless to say, divine intervention is necessary to enable the embarrassed knights to make good their boasts, to make the transition between signifiers and signified. The last *gab*, that of Olivier, underlines the parallel between sexual potency and narrative potency. Olivier has told one story too many. He is as trapped by his promise to pleasure the king's daughter one hundred times in a night as is Scheherazade by her need to perform 1,001 nights in a row. In each case an act or acts of intercourse are involved: in each case control is equated with the capacity to renew production and with the deferral of satisfaction. The parallel between narrative potency and sexual potency is the same as that exploited by Baudelaire in his narrative contest. Peter Brooks mentions this 'specifically erotic nature of the tension of writing and its rehearsal in reading' and sees 'narrative desire [as an] arousal that creates the narratable as a condition of tumescence, appetency, ambition, quest' (1984: 103). In other words it is something which participates in the nature of both the aggressive and the sexual.

THE EROTIC MODEL: NARRATIVE AND SEXUALITY

The title chosen for the Baudelairean contest, the only true *authorial* speech act, as opposed to the different narrative voices, contains the maximum possibilities for both interpretation and irony. This title, 'Portraits of Mistresses', announces a relationship of artist to subject which is also that of the teller to the tale; it involves the ambiguity of both the narrative relationship and the sexual relationship. The teller or writer or drawer of a portrait exposes the subject to the public view. In a portrait the subject is posed, exposed, and framed. But, by the double bind so characteristic of the *Little Prose Poems*, the very act of portraying, the production of a certain image for consumption, also exhibits the producer. The portrait exemplifies the problems of focalization, because the focalizers of narrated portraits also portray themselves. Indeed the metaphor chosen by narratologists, *focalizer*, reminiscent of theatrical lighting, is particularly apt because it reminds us that the light focused goes back to a source as well as illuminating a chosen object or scene. Thus a portrait is in itself a double revelation.

This doubleness is intensified by the present subjects of the portraits, the mistresses. The word 'mistress' is one of the most ambiguous of all, with its almost equal connotations of power and powerlessness, of being a possessor and of being possessed. The very name implies the ambivalence of proprietorial claims. No one can possess another without being themselves possessed (I: 649–50). Rather than being theft, the ownership of another is enslavement in Baudelaire's eyes. The man who buys a woman acquires a mistress in the most literal sense of the term.

Indeed Baudelaire said of the sexual contract: 'The irritating thing about love is that it is a crime in which an accomplice is indispensable' (I: 689). It is clear that this also applies to the narrative contract, which is also a crime where an accomplice is indispensable. The author is in the thrall of the reader. As Louis Marin puts it: 'The *cogito* of the writer is "You are, therefore I exist"' (verbal communication). No text is produced without a receiver, actual or implied, no narrator exists without a narratee. This becomes particularly clear in cases like the present where role reversal comes into play, where the active partner becomes in turn the passive partner, where the receiver becomes the performer, and the performer the receiver, as in all narrative contests.

Portraits of Mistresses(XLII)[3]
In a men's boudoir, that is to say, in a smoking room adjoining an elegant gambling den, four men were smoking and drinking. They

were neither exactly young nor old, neither handsome nor ugly; but old or young, they bore the unmistakable distinction of veterans of joy, the indescribable *je ne sais quoi*, the cold and mocking sadness which says clearly: 'We have lived to the full, and we seek what we could love and esteem.'

One of them turned the chat to the subject of women. It would have been more philosophical not to speak of them at all; but there are intelligent people who, after drinking, do not disdain banal conversations. Then one listens to the person speaking as one would listen to dance music.

'All men,' said the speaker, 'have been Cherubino's age: it is the time when, for want of dryads, one kisses, without disgust, the trunks of oak trees. It is the first degree of love. In the second degree one begins to choose. To be able to deliberate is already a form of decadence. That is when one decidedly seeks beauty. As for me, gentlemen, I pride myself on having arrived, long ago, at the culminating period of the third degree where beauty itself no longer suffices, if it is not seasoned by perfume, adornment, et cetera. I will even admit that I sometimes aspire, as to an unknown happiness, to a certain fourth degree which should be marked by absolute calm. But during my whole life, except at Cherubino's age, I have been more sensitive than any other to the enervating stupidity, to the irritating mediocrity, of women. What I particularly like in animals is their candour. Judge then how much I must have suffered because of my last mistress.

'She was the bastard of a prince. Beautiful, it goes without saying; without that, why would I have taken her? But she spoilt this great quality by an unbecoming and deformed ambition. She was a woman who always wanted to act the man. "You are not a man! Ah, if I were a man! Of us two, it is I who am the man!" Such were the unbearable refrains that emerged from this mouth from which I would only have wished to see songs flutter. Discussing a book, a poem, an opera, for which I allowed my admiration to escape: "Perhaps you find that very strong," she would say immediately; "what do you know about strength?" and she would start arguing.

'One fine day she took up chemistry; with the result that between my mouth and hers I found henceforward a mask of glass. And into the bargain, very prudish. If sometimes I inflicted on her a gesture that was a little too amorous, she would writhe as though her delicacy had been raped . . .'

'How did it end?' asked one of the three others. 'I did not know you were so patient.'

'God,' he replied, 'provided the remedy with the sickness. One day I found this Minerva, so hungry for ideal strength, intimate with my servant and in a position which obliged me to withdraw discreetly so as not to make them blush. That evening I dismissed the two of them, paying them their back wages.'

'As for me,' went on the one who had interrupted, 'I have no one to complain about but myself. Happiness came to dwell with me, and I did not recognize it. Destiny had granted me, not long ago, the enjoyment of a woman who was certainly the most gentle, the most submissive, and the most devoted of creatures, and always ready! and without enthusiam! "I am quite willing, since it gives you pleasure." That was her usual reply. You could give a beating to this wall or this sofa, and you would draw from it more sighs than were drawn from the bosom of my mistress by the transports of the most ardent love. After one year of life together, she admitted to me that she had never known pleasure. I grew tired of this unequal duel, and this incomparable girl got married. Later I had the fancy to see her again, and she said to me, showing me six fine children: "Well! my dear friend, the wife is still as *virgin* as was your mistress." Nothing had changed in this person. Sometimes I regret her: I should have married her.'

The others started to laugh, and a third said in his turn: 'Gentlemen, I have known enjoyment which you have perhaps neglected. I mean the comic side of love, and comic in a way which does not exclude admiration. I admired my last mistress more, I believe, than you can have hated or loved yours. And everyone admired her as much as I did. When we entered a restaurant, at the end of a few minutes everyone would forget to eat in order to watch her. The waiters themselves and the lady at the till would be so caught up in this contagious rapture that they would forget their duties. In short, I lived intimately for a while with a living *phenomenon*. She would eat, chew, crunch, devour, swallow up, but with the lightest and most carefree expression in the world. Thus for a long while she kept me in raptures. She had such a sweet, dreamy, English, romantic way of saying: "I am hungry!" And she would repeat these words day and night showing the prettiest teeth in the world, which would have touched and at the same time amused you. I could have made my fortune showing her in fairs as a *polyphagous monster*. – I used to feed her well; and yet she left me. . .'

'For a supplier of provisions probably?'

'Something like it, a sort of employee in the supply corps who, by some knack of waving his wand, is now perhaps supplying the poor child with the rations of several soldiers. At least that is what I have supposed.'

'I,' said the fourth, 'endured atrocious suffering through the opposite of what we usually hold against female egoism. Too fortunate mortals, you have picked the wrong recipient for complaints about the imperfections of your mistresses!'

This was said in a very serious tone, by a man of gentle composed appearance, with almost clerical features, unfortunately lit up by light grey eyes, the sort of eyes with a look which says: 'I want' or: 'I must!' or: 'I never forgive!'

'If, nervous as I know you, G . . . , to be, cowardly and frivolous as you two, K . . . and J . . . , are, you had been coupled with a certain woman of my acquaintance, either you would have fled, or you would be dead. As for me, I survived, as you see. Imagine a person incapable of committing a mistake of feeling or reasoning; imagine an unnerving serenity of character; a devotion without play-acting and without exaggeration; a sweetness without weakness; an energy without violence. The story of my love resembles an endless trip on a surface as pure and polished as a mirror, dizzyingly monotonous, which would reflect all my feelings and gestures with the ironic precision of my own conscience, so much so that I could not allow myself an unreasonable gesture or feeling without immediately perceiving the mute reproach of my inseparable spectre. Love appeared to me like a guardianship. How many stupidities she prevented me performing, which I regret not having committed! How many debts paid in spite of myself! She deprived me of all the benefits which could have resulted from my personal madness. With cold incontrovertible decision, she put a stop to all my whims. To add insult to injury, she demanded no gratitude once the danger was passed. How many times did I not restrain my impulse to strangle her, crying: "Be imperfect, you wretch! so that I can love you without uneasiness and without anger!" For several years I admired her, my heart full of hate. Well, after all that, I am not the one who died.'

'Ah!' said the others, 'so she died?'

'Yes! It could not go on like that. Love had become for me an overwhelming nightmare. Victory or death, as Politics says, such was the alternative which destiny imposed on me! One evening, in a wood . . . beside a pond . . . after a melancholy stroll during which *her* eyes reflected the softness of the sky, and during which *my* heart was clenched as is hell. . . .'

'What!'

'What on earth!'

'What do you mean?'

'It was inevitable. I had too much feeling for justice to beat, outrage, or dismiss an irreproachable servant. But I had to reconcile that feeling with the horror which this being inspired in me; to get rid of this being without failing in respect for her. What would you expect me to do with her, *since she was perfect?*'

The three other friends looked at the speaker with a vague, slightly stunned expression, as if pretending not to understand and as if admitting implicitly that, as far as they were concerned, they did not feel capable of so rigorous an action, although they had to admit it was adequately explained.

Afterwards new bottles were ordered, to kill Time which has so tough a life, and to speed up Life which flows so slowly.

This particular contest, as announced by the frame narrator, is one which implies rigorous exclusion. Everything which follows is explicitly stated to be for men's ears only.[4] As we have seen, Baudelaire four times defined his work as not being intended for wives, daughters, or sisters, and yet we find an inherent contradiction: the only way to limit smoking-room stories to the smoking-room is *not* to publish them. They belong, as we have seen, to an age-old ritual which implies oral performance to a strictly limited audience. We find all the markers of a private masculine territory here, as well as wine and tobacco, those ritual signs of verbal licence. One of the things which adds to the attraction of this verbal licence is precisely the code of silence which surrounds it. In the same way all-female groups have always allowed themselves great freedom in both physical discussion and in derogation of the opposite sex, confident that *their* rituals were for women's ears only. Open performance, especially publication, admits the hitherto excluded audience, widens the possibilities of interpretation, and invites the satiric gaze. Such satiric possibilities are indicated by the very first words of the text, by that unexpected equation of the smoking-room with the *boudoir* or withdrawing-room, the room often derided as the space for narratives of spite, derogation, sexual fantasy, and dubious confidences. The men present are united by their low opinion of women which makes this first parallel *with* women the more demeaning.

The frame narrator's initial emphasis on gender,[5] on the masculine mystique, is setting up a very highly controlled stage on which the performance will take place. This narrative space is clearly framed by the emphasis on drinking at the beginning and end of the text. The performers are dandies, like the signifying 'cats' of Harlem, men whose life is predicated on the power of signs. Their gestures and expressions are part of a code and speak as clearly as words. This is their territory, a territory which is itself the signifier of the contract of inclusion/ exclusion. Inevitably too, their words, at first casual, 'a chat', stimulate aggression as they turn to the subject of women. What was at first a mere entertainment, words to be listened to as if they were 'dance music', turns into something else again. The game becomes a contest, enactment becomes *agon* as well as *mimicry*, and the space becomes an arena.

THE FRAME AND THE QUOTATION

The particular role of the hidden spectator in the Baudelairean re-enactment cannot be over-emphasized: the ultimate frame is perhaps the keyhole or the camera's aperture. We have seen the function of the spy behind the arras in the *Pèlerinage de Charlemagne*. Here that role is taken by the frame narrator, who, although he does not break the frame as does the hidden spy, does expose the secret territory. He establishes the parameters of the performance and its space. When he has not only set the scene, but, as it were, persuaded the reader to join him as voyeur, as eavesdropper on the conversation, then the actual performance can begin.

The frame of the contest and the frame of the four portraits are clearly indicated by quotation marks, just as further quotations will indicate a progressive embedding of discourse. This text is polyphonic in Bakhtin's sense of the word (1973: 151–68). Multiple resonance is added to the narrative by embedded quotation as each voice is heard filtered and modified by the plural speaking subjects. The first contestant, the second speaking subject, opens with a structural *mise-en-abyme* which emphasizes again the narrative/sexual parallel. There are four stages of love just as there will be four narratives, the stages like the narratives are cumulative in effect, and both end in the highly ambiguous goal of absolute calm. This opening segment, characterized syntagmatically by its structural relationship to the whole, is characterized paradigmatically by the insistent reification of the feminine, and of course by almost caricatured misogyny (cf. p. 103). From the point of view of this study the last sentence of this preamble is the most important: 'Judge then how much I must have suffered because of my last mistress.' This direct command, 'Judge', is the speech act which sets the contest in motion: the other three men are now not just narratees, they are constituted as judges, and the implication is the one characteristic of such rituals: 'See if you can beat this one!'

The agonistic, aggressive, nature of the narrative sequence is echoed in the subject matter of each performance. The theme is in each case an 'unequal contest'. Four different experiences of mistresses are presented. What remains constant is the battle of the sexes, and the fact that each woman remains mistress in the second sense of the word, because she is unsatisfied or unsatisfiable. A mistress may be dismissed or disposed of, she may not be disregarded, once the sexual contract has been embarked upon. The same may be said of entering into a narrative contract.

The first woman is presented as one who wishes to tamper with signs, to change the most basic code of all, that of gender. Two important narrative techniques are used here. One is the double voice inherent in quotation (Stewart 1978: 122–3). The problem in the use of quotation is that while it is a means of asserting textual power (one only quotes what one wants to), it involves the loss of textual control as the voice of the original speaker can still be heard even when its values are being questioned. The utterance of the woman is filtered, its values are reassigned when quoted by the man just as *his* values are reassigned when quoted by the narrator. The irony of this becomes stronger given her stated desire to *be* a man. The other nice point is that the topics of the argument are themselves performances: a book, a song, an opera. All this makes clear that what she has been criticizing is *his performance*.

CONTROL AND SATISFACTION

The last section from 'One fine day' to 'their back wages' is a classic example of narrative feedback. One of the beauties of sexual innuendo to the analyst of narrative is that it makes abundantly clear the function of reader response, of textual consumption as well as textual production. Here we are deliberately led to make the conventional assumptions about prudishness and then are left with an artful blank in the text marked by the ellipsis. At this moment we are reminded of the function of the narratee; one friend breaks in with the demand for satisfaction, 'How did it end?' plus a dash of scepticism. Finally, the ancient pornographic device of the master witnessing the coupling of mistress and man-servant forces the reader to reassess and reinterpret the whole of the preceding utterance. Because of the almost universal liveliness of sexual fantasy and because of its immense variations each narratee and each reader will no doubt come up with a different version of what the narrator's sexual tastes actually were. Thus it is clear that we have, each in our own way, participated in the production of the text by our very consumption of it. This is one form of feedback where we *always* complete the loop. The incompetence of the first narrator is finally made clear by the fact that the only way he could reassert the power he had lost was to reduce the sexual contract to a monetary contract, to use only that code over which he had control. He is forced to revert from the worth or gift value of sex to its exchange value in order to maintain his authority.

The second contestant then picks up the narrative gauntlet. He has various possibilities open to him and chooses that of inversion. His problem, that of the submissive 'virgin' mistress,[6] appears the exact opposite of the first, and yet this too is an unequal contest. The frigid woman exercises control *because* she is unsatisfied. Similarly no teller wants to be told that the reception of his or her narrative is a matter of total indifference to the hearer. A parting of the ways is inevitable, although again a switch in contract, from that of 'enjoyment' to that of legal marriage, is envisaged as a solution. It is already clear that the second narrator has beaten the first hands down precisely because he has the advantage of coming second, of already having been a narratee. So he can substitute self-depreciation for boasting, humour for outrage: he knows not to protest too much. He still, however, makes the mistake of using the double-edged, double-voiced weapon of direct quotation, although of only twenty-five words as opposed to the first speaker's thirty-nine.

Now yet another spectator takes on the role as performer. The effect again is cumulative, he has the advantage of having consumed two previous narratives and the topic of his entry in the competition, 'his turn', is in fact consumption.[7] He chooses not only to invert the previous narrative but to surpass it in the comic vein. This is achieved by an extraordinary exercise in sustained metonymy, everything in it is a *double entendre*. It plays on that most enduring of masculine fantasies (perhaps because it is also one of the great masculine fears), the woman who is never satisfied. What is more, this performer underlines his *tour de force* by picking up and recycling keywords from the previous narratives: 'enjoyment' from the second and 'intimate' and 'hungry' from the first. He is in fact using his reception of texts as a spring-board for his production of a text.

The unequal combat of the second narrator with total passivity gives way to the third narrator's impossible struggle to keep up with those pretty teeth in that charming mouth which incessantly, day and night, ate, chewed, devoured, and swallowed up. The account is hilariously funny, perhaps because comedy is close to cruelty, but like the two others, the choice of vocabulary reveals the sadism close to the surface: the sadism of 'delicacy . . . raped' in the first, 'you could give a beating' in the second, and now 'polyphagous monster' in the third (cf. Blin 1948; Mehlman 1974). The analogy between hunger for food and sexual appetite is an example of engaging the narratees in a double reading of parallel isotopies, an example of *coupling*, yet another term shared by the narrative and sexual codes. This remarkable piece of textual prestidigitation, not the least of which is the wide range of meanings of *tour de bâton* (which I can only approximate in 'waving his wand'), shows yet another means of extending control, the limitation of quotation. This time the lady is allowed exactly three words of direct speech: 'I'm hungry!'

So the progression continues. Again we must award the palm for successful narrative aggression and for the combination of tale-telling with hearer response to the most recent performer! So how is the fourth and last competitor to assert his narrative dominance?

CHANNELLING THE DESIRE OF THE OTHER

He chooses the path of negation. He picks up the covert sadism of his predecessors and makes it overt. He takes the unequal combat of the battle of the sexes and turns it into a war to the death, 'victory or death'. He deliberately changes the usual value of signs. Woman, instead of being the *object* of man's desire, becomes the *impediment* to desire. Whereas the previous mistress embodied the transgressive power of the libido (though one with teeth!), this one has the full castrating power of the super-ego. The description of this woman is a stream of negations, in fact it *is* only negation. Her actions are all recounted as ones of negation and prevention, except for the significant fact, that when she forces him to pay his debts, she forces him to live up to his contracts.[8] The woman disappears completely behind the negative reflection,[9] a 'mask of glass' like that which hid the first mistress. However, this woman is never directly quoted, even her utterances are abolished. Instead the embedded quotation here is the narrator quoting his former self. Love here is not a coupling with another (although the expression 'coupled' is used) but a vertiginous reflection in the mirror of self: 'The dreadful marriage of man with himself',[10] such as that which Baudelaire observed in drug-taking.

Here the sexual contract becomes a *tutelle*, a guardianship (one of the most emotionally[11] charged of all words for Baudelaire). This woman, who is the only one who is *never* called 'mistress', is so completely the mistress that the only solution is to eliminate her.[12] In other words this final narrative suggests, but *only* suggests, the most complete example of narrative reversal, just as it suggests the violence of narrative closure.

But this is not the reason why the final contestant is the victor. The reason lies in the fact that this performance directly harnesses the desires and fears of the earlier performers.[13] All have shown how threatened they felt by the sexual contract, all have used language showing a repressed aggression and desire for violence. This desire is now used to produce direct audience participation. The return of the repressed is triggered by performer/spectator aggression too, since the audience, composed of the first three narrators, have been directly insulted. Their stories have been adversely assessed, they have been given derogatory labels. They are challenged to aggression by the first words of the final story: 'If . . . you had been coupled with a certain woman . . . either you would have fled, or you would be dead.' Then their co-operation is solicited in the work of *portrayal*: 'Imagine . . . imagine'. After all, the whole point of a narrated portrait is that it is most effective when it can be imagined differently by each narratee, and their vulnerability will heighten their imagination.

The threat to potency is built up by the implacable repetition of words paradigmatic of calculation and negation.[14] The last sentence of this paragraph is deliberately phrased to provoke immediate narratee response and to remind the reader of the collective nature of the audience. Here the response comes not just from one hearer, as occurred previously, but from all three together: '"Well, after all that, I'm not the one who died!" "Ah!" *said the others*, "so she died?"' (my emphasis).

What follows is a remarkable exploitation of the absent signifier. In the dramatized scenario three times key verbs are missing and are replaced by ellipses. Absolutely no ending is given and no explanation. The other contestants are trapped into supplying the ending to the story themselves, they are forced to become performers in another's narrative, and what *they* imagine is left to *our* imagination. '"What!" "What on earth!" "What do you mean?"' The progress made in manipulating the audience is clear. The first narrator gave his hearers power to fill in the gaps, a power which they could use against him. This one averts the threat by involving them in a dramatization of their own covert sadism. Similarly, in the reading of any text, the reader must 'fill in the blanks' (Iser 1982: 111), and this confers immense power on readers which writers must control as best they can.

The ending of the story is a masterly reminder that 'they do but jest, poison in jest, no offence i' the world' (Hamlet). The sadistic fantasy is contingent on the existence of perfection, *which is impossible*: you cannot beat, outrage, or dismiss a nightmare, but you can wish it out of existence. Better, you can persuade others that your story is true and get them to commit *your* murder in *their* imagination.[15] The giveaway of course is the final answer in question form with the subtle italicization of the last words: 'What would you expect me to do with her, *since she was perfect?*' This reminder that the whole contest has been a game of signifiers without real signified, an exercise in pure fiction, leads to the last quotation mark and the closing of the frame on the last portrait.

The fourth contestant claims the narrative victory, the other narrators are dazed by the trap[16] into which they have been led, and admit that they are incapable of imagining such a performance, let alone of performing such an action. The narrators are ritually united by their common desire to assert their masculine identity by the exclusion of the feminine, but they are exposed to the cruel illumination of both the sexual contest and the narrative contest. In this arena, time is the only thing which has been killed, and time is unkillable (Johnson 1983). Instead, narrative succession is used here as a form of symbolic execution.

VOYEURISM AND INTERPRETATION

Now, I have been following the fortunes of the *competing* narrators which are complicated enough, but we may say that the *frame* narrator exercises the true power because he gives away the game. He tells us the story.[17] He has enabled us, the readers, to remain hidden in the wings throughout the performance. At another level, an even more important form of exposure is the fact that the narrative has also been *published*, with its ambiguous and satiric title to remind us of the authorial presence. By this, the final illumination within this particular textual space of *Little Prose Poems*, those excluded from the narrative are included in the audience. The bragging contest becomes even more ambivalent when it is no longer for men's ears only.

As in the story itself, we find that reader desires and fears are mobilized in the service of the work of art. Which is the greater, the voyeuristic pleasure of the text or the omnipresent threat of symbolic sacrifice? The reader who can identify as a member of the male club may feel a stirring of encapsulated prejudice against the invasion of territory, or may be torn between horror at seeing the code of silence broken and the awful desire to break it and revel in the consequences of outrage, either male or female. The excluded *lectrice* (the female reader)[18] may enjoy the satiric light thrown on the 'men's boudoir', or, like some of the men involved, she may find that fantasies of violence beget violent reactions. The fiction of woman as the figuration of lack, as the ultimate representation of otherness, begets a parallel fantasy. Men too can be a representation of otherness. Love, like interpretation, is a crime which needs a victim and an executioner, as Baudelaire said (*Oeuvres complètes*, I: 651). A text needs a reader. Indeed, as the role of the reader in the construction of narrative (see Ruthrof 1981) emerges from the power fantasy of authorial intention, it is clear that it parallels the role of the partner in other contracts, be they monetary or sexual. As Baudelaire very nearly said,[19] when we put our story-telling between covers, we expose ourselves to close reading, and are judged on performance.

7 · *Listening ear and whispering voice: analysis and desire*

Desire takes many forms, and its representations are as ubiquitous in narrative as in life. Certain narratives of desire, however, are symptomatic. They endeavour to relate and to textualize moments such as hallucination, obsession, dream, or fantasy when unconscious desire seeks to break through the barrier of repression. Such attempts at representation fall into two main categories. In the first, the text is *directly* presented to the hearer/reader with the narrator/performer conveying an existential experience of desire, as in the oneiric or fantasmic narrative. Sometimes, on the other hand, in what I shall call the analytic narrative, the experience of desire is *mediated*. It is first conveyed to a listener, an analyst who elicits and interprets the primary text. It is then reformulated in a second stage, which involves the production of a new text by the analyst. This text is the one presented to the hearer/reader.

THE NARRATIVE BEFORE ANALYSIS

The desiring text is characterized by a basic fragmentation. Its attempt to speak the experience of lack is constantly frustrated by the effects of repression. It is a text studded with pauses and gaps, as the speaking voice endeavours to formulate the unspeakable. The story of desire is the story of the Other, an Other which can be attained only in the partial form of the representative object, the image made concrete. The process of visual representation characteristic of the dream work (Freud 1982: 204–19) is a form of concretization. The desiring text must use words to similar effect, and often shows a progression from abstraction towards ever greater concretization, as the speaker seems to come closer to the elusive object of desire. Concrete representation, however, allows for only a partial realization, a displacement or condensation of the object. In the spoken or written text, these partial representations take the form of metonymies, constantly representing, by the displacement of synecdoche or the collusion of contiguity, the unachievable whole.

The text itself is a web of repetitions, of over-determinations, which mark the effect of the unconscious drives. Its performance is a display of symptoms, of images, of phantasms, a fragmented and at the same time redundant display for the benefit of an audience (Wright 1984: 113). It is this audience whose presence is supposed to elicit the coherent narrative which will give sense to the whole. The network of over-determination must be read as the threads, the clues, the 'traces' of the unconscious drives which are the wellspring of desire (Leclaire 1968: 53). The narrative of desire, because of its sources in the unconscious, speaks and yet does not know what its own voice is saying. It follows a spiral movement, one which constantly returns to similar orbits while tending ever closer to a centre. The centre itself, however, must ultimately prove empty, as desire remains essentially a manifestation of lack, an emptiness which our drives can only attempt to fill. This attempt is ultimately doomed to failure. The structure of desire is such that its story must for ever remain unfinished and open-ended. The very wish-fulfilment detected by Freud in both dreams and fantasies is in fact a contradiction in terms. The visual representation of the partial realization of desire merely emphasizes its own status as illusion and its ephemerality compared to the ever-present lack which underlies it.

CONSCIOUS AND UNCONSCIOUS NARRATIVE

Direct narratives of desire, those in which the narrator endeavours to communicate his or her own text, tend to divide between the oneiric and the fictive or fantastic. The difference (in so far as one can evaluate it at all) appears to lie in the proportional relations of the conscious and the unconscious in the elaboration of the text. In the dream narrative, the ingredients and their visual representation have been produced by the unconscious. Of course, in order for them to become text, they must undergo the process of secondary revision or, in Lacanian phraseology, must be formulated in terms of the *symbolic*. A dream narrative such as 'The Double Bedroom' (V) (see p. 60), with its portrayal of events and impressions completely beyond the narrator's control, is a very different form of wish fulfilment from the consciously elaborated fantasy of 'The Gallant Marksman' (XLVI) (see pp. 61–2). In the latter, the kernel of unconscious compulsion, of morbid desire, is buried deep under a highly structured fiction, just as the word play and verbal condensation are no longer reported as beyond control and comprehension, but as symbolically devised to meet the needs of the text.

THE ANALYTIC TEXT

Rather different is the analytic text, of which we are about to study an example. The analytic text involves not only the story of desire itself, but the relationship between that text and its hearer, a hearer who in turn endeavours to interpret the first text (cf. Brooks 1984: 164–285). There is a performance relationship between the *énonciation* of the analysand and the reception/response of the analyst. The monologue of the original narrative of desire now alternates with dialogue with the listener, and this alternation corresponds to the long bouts of attentive silence punctuated by brief periods of questioning which characterize the analytic relationship. The 'dialogue' is typically a *dialogue de sourds*, a speaking *past* rather than *to* each other. The psychoanalytic narrative as such, D. H. Thomas's *The White Hotel*, for instance, is of course a twentieth-century invention. In a more general sense, the confessional story, such as Constant's *Adolphe* or Fromentin's *Dominique*, is also analytic in its structural relationship between narrator-listener and narrator-performer. What makes a story more properly analytic, however, is again perhaps the balance between conscious and unconscious in the unwinding of the story. In the confessional story, guilt is conscious because an impulse or act is socially or morally reproved; in other words a problem is identified and a social 'solution' is provided. In the analytic story, on the other hand, guilt is often unconscious because repressed, and the problem to be analysed is often not even acknowledged. The analysand feels 'innocent', a prey to feelings beyond his or her own control, as in Maupassant's stories of madness. The feeling may not even be that of being a victim to unconscious drives, but merely of not understanding why behaviour that seems 'natural' to oneself is not universal.

The analytic narrative is close to the detective story. It is the function of the analyst to follow the clues provided by the primary narrative of desire, to fill in the multiple gaps left by its fragmentation and incompleteness, and to provide or endeavour to provide an interpretation. It is no accident that the Baudelairean text owes much to Edgar Allan Poe, the pioneer both of the story of psychosis and the detective story. The analyst could also provide to some extent the model of the audience of the *énonciation* or that 'implied reader', as Iser puts it, whose interpretative function is stimulated by the gaps in the text. Here again it is a question of degree; whereas we automatically fill in the gaps in an everyday communication, the narrative of desire tends to leave larger noticeable gaps, elliptical 'black holes', in its fabric. Of course the analyst's interpretation is *only* an interpretation; there is none of the material certainty accorded to the detective. Indeed, the analyst, in reproducing the narrative of desire, cannot even accurately represent the original text, any more than we can actually reproduce a dream. The original text, that of the analysand, is in the first instance filtered through the attention of the listener, subject to all the factors of redundancy and noise. Then it is filtered by the ideological presumptions of the analyst, who chooses and discards even while remaining apparently objective (Leclaire 1968: 18–27).

THE ANALYST AS NARRATOR

When the analyst produces his or her own text, which 'reproduces' and 'interprets' the primary material, what is in fact appearing is a new text. Like the analysand, the analyst is controlled by his or her own language and own discourse, as well as by the relation between the conscious and the unconscious, between 'what can be said' and 'what cannot be said'. The framing and presentation of an analytic text is totally dependent on the speaking subject, the analyst, and the speaker–hearer relationship posited in the analytic discourse.[1]

The text presents a 'translation' of the narrative of the analysand, but it is also the *mise-en-scène* of a double performance, the monologue of desire and the 'dialogue' between analysand and analyst:

> in the analyst's consulting room, a play is enacted between the couch and the armchair. But let us not imagine that the performance in this space is monotonous, for the simplicity of the set carries no implications for the peripeteia of the plot or the allocation of the parts.
>
> (Leclaire 1968: 174)

The analyst transforms and translates the narrative of the analysand and incorporates it into a narrative of his or her own, in a kind of redoubled secondary revision (Spence 1982; cit. Suleiman 1986). Thus *another text* is created, which is in itself both the account of an analysis, or a failed analysis, and a *self-analysis*, since the repressed of the analyst is itself a factor in the final *énonciation*. The performance of an analytic text thus becomes an interplay of multiple voices, both conscious and unconscious. The traces of the analysand are everywhere overlaid by those of the analyst, like different sets of footprints walking the same path (cf. Suleiman 1986: 465–7).

ANALYSIS AND FICTION

This happens even in the case books of scientific analysis, as theorists are becoming increasingly aware. François Roustang (1980) titled one study suggestively 'The analyst, a novelist?', which is at least as valid as the more usual 'The novelist, an analyst?'. Even psychoanalysts succumb to the conditions inherent in producing a display text, and create a narrative in which the speech acts of the analysand already function on the second level, that of the alternative or transformed world. The experiential power of such writings is not lessened by their dubious position in the old fact–fiction division and debate. How does one answer the question, 'Is this true, or is it a story?', in the case of the analytic narrative? It indicates rather that the debate should be couched in other terms and that 'Representative discourses, fictional or non-fictional, must be treated as simultaneously world-creating, world-describing, and world-changing undertakings' (Pratt 1986: 71).

The analytic text bears a double relationship to fictional narrative. In so far as it is a creation whereby the voices of desire are filtered and retransformed in the discourse of the narrator, it is related to the production of the fictional text. In so far as it shows the action of the discerning ear, it reflects the process of reception. The analyst, like the reader, *elicits* a narrative simply by being an ear, a listener to whom a story can be told; *filters* the text by what is heard and what is left unheard; *interprets* the text by filling in the gaps and following up the clues; and finally uses the reading as a means of *self-analysis*, whether wittingly or not. This double relationship of creation and reception becomes unified if the analytic reader puts the experience into writing, thus creating a further text.

I want to elucidate these hypotheses about the narrative of desire generally and the analytic text in particular by examining a specific example from *Little Prose Poems*. It has frequently been pointed out[2] that Baudelaire seems a Freudian *avant la lettre*, and certainly this story involves a quite conscious analysis. The narrator functions as both producer of a text of his own and as audience to the text of another. He becomes reader and interpreter of a very specific text, the enigma of desire.

Mademoiselle Bistouri [Miss Lancet] (XLVII)[3]

As I was reaching the very end of the district, under the flicker of the gas lights, I felt an arm slipping softly under mine, and I heard a voice saying in my ear: 'You're a doctor, sir?'

I looked around; it was a tall girl, solidly built, eyes very wide open, lightly made-up, her hair blowing in the wind with the strings of her bonnet.

' – No; I'm not a doctor. Let me past.' 'Oh! yes! You're a doctor. I'm sure of it. Come home with me. You'll be very pleased with me, go on.' 'I'll probably come and see you, but later, *after the doctor*, damn it!' . . . 'Ah! Ah!' she let out, still hanging on my arm, and bursting out laughing 'you're a wag of a doctor, I've known several of that sort. Come on.'

I love mystery passionately, because I always hope to get to the bottom of it. So I let myself be carried off by this companion, or rather by this unhoped-for enigma.

I omit the description of the hovel; it may be found in several old, well-known, French poets. Only, a detail not perceived by Régnier, two or three portraits of famous doctors were hanging on the walls.

How I was coddled! Blazing fire, hot wine, cigars; and, as she presented me with these good things and lit a cigar herself, the comical creature said: 'Make yourself at home, my friend, make yourself comfortable. It'll remind you of the hospital and the good days of your youth. – By the way! where did you get that white hair from? You didn't look like that, not very long ago, when you were L.'s intern. – I remember that it was you who assisted him with serious operations. Now there's a man who loves to cut and hack and clip! It was you who handed him the instruments, the sutures and the sponges. – And, when the operation was over, how proudly he would say, looking at his watch: "Five minutes, gentlemen!" – Oh! I go everywhere, I do. I know the gentlemen well.'

A few moments later, on familiar terms now,[4] she was starting on her litany again, and saying to me: 'You're a doctor, aren't you, my pet?'

This meaningless refrain made me leap to my feet. 'No!' I yelled angrily.

'A surgeon, then?'

'No! no! unless it's to cut off your head! G . . . d . . . and blast it to h . . . !'[5]

'Wait,' she replied, 'you'll see.'

And she pulled from a cupboard a bundle of papers, which were none other than the collection of portraits of the famous doctors of the period, lithographs by Maurin, which could be seen displayed for several years on the quai Voltaire.

'Look! do you recognize this one?'

'Yes! it's X. The name's on the bottom anyway: but I know him personally.'

'I was sure of it! Look! Here's Z., the one who used to say in his lectures, speaking of X., "The monster whose face bears the marks of the blackness of his soul!" And all because the other didn't agree with him on some matter! How they laughed about that at the

School, in the old days! Do you remember? – Look, here's K., the one who denounced to the government the insurgents he was looking after in his hospital. It was the time of the riots. How could such a handsome man have so little heart? – Now here's W., a famous English doctor; I caught him on his trip to Paris. He looks like a young lady, doesn't he?'

And as I touched a packet tied with string, also placed on the little round table: 'Wait a bit,' she said; 'that's the residents, and this packet is the non-residents.'

And she fanned out a mass of photographs, representing much younger physiognomies.

'When we meet again, you'll give me your picture, won't you, darling?'

'But,' I said to her, pursuing, in my turn, my own fixed idea, 'why do you think I'm a doctor?'

'It's because you're so nice and so kind to women.'

'A queer kind of logic!' I said to myself.

'Oh! I don't often make mistakes in that way; I've known a fair number. I like the gentlemen so much that, even when I'm not sick, I sometimes go and see them, just to see them. There are some who say coldly to me: "You are not sick at all!" But there are others who understand me because I make eyes at them.'

'And when they don't understand you . . .?'

'Lord, since I've bothered them *for nothing*, I leave ten francs on the mantelpiece. – They're so kind and so gentle, those men! – I discovered at La Pitié a little resident, pretty as an angel and polite into the bargain! and hard-working, poor boy! His pals told me he hadn't a penny, because his parents are poor and can't send him anything. That gave me confidence. After all, I'm a pretty good-looking woman, even though I'm not too young. I told him: "Come and see me, come and see me often. And with me, no need to worry; I don't need money." But, you understand that I got it over to him in roundabout ways; I didn't just come right out with it; I was so afraid of humiliating him, the dear child! – Well! would you believe that I've a funny kind of fancy that I don't dare to mention to him? – I'd like him to come and see me with his instrument bag and his gown, even with a bit of blood on it!'

She said this with a very candid expression, just as a dis-criminating man might say to an actress he loved: 'I want to see you dressed in the costume you wore in that famous role you created.'

Persevering, I tried again: 'Can you remember the period and the occasion when this very special passion was born in you?'

I had difficulty in making myself understood; finally, I succeeded. But then she replied with a very sad look, even, as far as I can remember, averting her eyes: 'I don't know . . . I don't remember.'

What oddities does one not find in a city, when one knows how to walk around and look? Life swarms with innocent monsters. – Lord God! you, the Creator, you, the Master; you who have made Law and Liberty; you, the sovereign who permits everything, you, the judge who pardons; you who abound in motives and causes, and who have perhaps given my mind the taste for horror to convert my heart, like healing at the tip of a blade; Lord, have pity, have pity on mad men and mad women! O Creator, can monsters exist in the eyes of Him who alone knows why they exist, how they *came into being* and how they might *not have come into being*?

THE VOICE OF THE OTHER

'Mademoiselle Bistouri' operates under the sign of doubleness, doubleness within the discourse and doubleness *of* the discourses. The seeming paradox of the title leads into a narrative in which the narrator acts principally as audience and transmitter to another story, the story of lack. It is also almost the only prose poem which foregrounds the voice of the other, and the only text in the series in which the female voice in direct speech predominates.

A text which appears thoroughly contextualized, set in a Paris *faubourg* in a period defined by such indices as the gas lighting and street riots, it still leads to an extremity, and the story's 'very end', like that of the street, is strangely empty. As Prévost (1953: 121–2) remarks, it is a text full of dark emptinesses and lit only by scattered gleams. The narrator himself is physically a shadowy figure, though emotionally a powerful one. He is first present as a receiver, one who feels and hears. The constant incompleteness of the text is already present in the opening metonymies. The woman is at first only an insinuating arm and murmuring voice, just as the narrator is mainly a hearing ear, the intellectual organ *par excellence*. Indeed, this is the way they will remain for some time, a shadowy hearer attentive to a discourse of lack (cf. Leclaire 1971: 32).

The first paragraph suggests this relationship, and also immediately establishes the direct speech of the woman, whose voice is the most striking feature of the text. This first sentence in direct speech contains already the two over-determined paradigms of the text, those of medicine and of masculinity. It is also important that this should take the form of a question. Indeed (like most French questions these days but not so commonly in educated language in the nineteenth century), 'You're a doctor, sir?' contains the basic ambivalence of being both a statement and a question simultaneously. It at the same time demands an answer and is unanswerable.

The second paragraph finally adds to hearing and touch the more characteristically Baudelairean element of the look, the observation on which the narrator prides himself – he is one who 'knows how to walk around and look'. However, at this stage the observation is both accurate and ultimately misleading, since the words 'girl' (*fille* also means prostitute) and 'made-up' suggest a casual encounter with a street-walker. The interchange which follows not only sets the obsessive pattern of her whole discourse, with the repetition of 'You're a doctor', but continues to suggest prostitution. However, an element of doubleness is already present to intrigue both narrator and reader. To the narrator's crude joke, 'after the doctor', which suggests a visit only after she has been checked for venereal disease, her reaction is not that of the kind of woman suggested (shrill vituperation, for instance), but that of a certain kind of man – a burst of hearty laughter at a male joke. This is followed by the suggestion of an 'all-boys-together' note which gets stronger as the story proceeds.

THE ENIGMATIC TEXT

The narrator has his own obsession, indicated by the verbal tense, 'I love mystery . . . '. This is the passion for analysis. In other words, he represents both the hearer/questioner who *elicits* the text and the reader/interpreter who hopes to solve its mysteries. He is in fact a detective, like every analyst. This 'enigma', in the best tradition of detective stories, begins with a deliberate misleading of the reader by its suggestion of an encounter with a prostitute. The tale will in fact contain a form of prostitution, but in the guise one least expects. The narrator, as narratee of the woman's story, is led into a maze where many seeming paths are dead ends. He must be prepared as analyst to follow the clues but also to discard invalidated hypotheses. The woman, as 'enigma', also represents the seductive text, one which carries off its reader as the narrator himself is 'carried off' by his mysterious companion. Her voice proposes a female text, provocative not through its femininity, but because there speaks through it another voice, another gender, as yet unexplained.

The narrator seeks in an unexpected, 'unhoped-for', context the means to satisfy his passion, just as the woman seeks in a chance encounter the means to satisfy hers:

the law of the destiny of the drive is to seize craftily, but violently, on everything it *can* in a given context, and, if it can, to pass from one context to another. There is no end to this exploration and exhaustion of contexts. Each time the drive helps itself in a given context, and yet it does not help itself, it takes what the context offers it anyway, but remains free to move on thereafter.

(Deleuze 1983: 181)

Neither passion is that suggested by the intertextuality of paragraph five, the tradition of satirical poetry about the squalors of the brothel. Once again the narrator's text, like the woman's text, both leads and misleads. The false clue of the allusion to Régnier (*Satires*, XI and XII) is combined with the vital clue of the medical portraits.

The analytic narrative always presents a performance, the relationship of a teller to an audience. The performance here, characteristically for an analysis, involves an alternation of dialogue and monologue. Fragmentary dialogue between the woman and the man is interspersed with the three major speeches in which the woman gradually reveals the extent of her obsession.

FEMININE AS MASCULINE

These speeches are very subtle examples of what Bakhtin calls double voice or bivocalism and Deleuze (1980, 1983) calls 'indirect speech', which produces in language different forms of hybridization, as different voices speak in and through each *énoncé*, even the most banal. Through this female discourse there constantly emerges the *male* discourse of the medical student or teaching hospital circles which fascinate her. This mixing of voices is filtered in its turn through the *énonciation* of the narrator whose final choice it is how to present, edit, and stress the discursive performance he has witnessed. Thus, we are presented with a female voice in which two genders vie for supremacy and constantly overlay each other, a voice which has been itself chosen and framed by the analytic consciousness of the male observer.

The symptomatic opposition of voices is stressed by the clash of signs. The visitor is first 'coddled' (*dorloté*), a word redolent of maternity and femininity; however, his hostess not only presents him with wine and cigars but lights a cigar *herself*, in an assumption of masculinity which already strikes her visitor as comical, in other words as incongruous. A similar clash ends the paragraph. The first 'gentlemen' belongs to masculine discourse, the second to feminine, as in

'Time, gentlemen, please' and 'Gentlemen prefer blondes'. The force of the obsession becomes clear as she fits her guest, despite himself, into the context which compulsively recurs to her. From the evocation of this hospital context there emerges the concrete image which is at the root of her obsession and which is represented by the word 'lancet' (*bistouri*) in the title. The narrative structure is not a coherent sequence but a series of random fragments, separated by the pauses and gaps represented by the dashes interspersed in the text. In this discursive collage the over-determination of verbal redundancy suddenly brings out a vital sequence: 'operations'; then three verbs, 'cut', 'hack', 'clip'; three nouns, 'instruments', 'sutures', 'sponges'; and, closing the chiasmic grouping, 'operation' again. This fragmented *énonciation*, with the violent, almost volcanic, emergence of the obsessive detail, characterizes the language of desire, and particularly that of the unconscious drives, as Gilles Deleuze points out:

> For, if they are 'elementary' or 'primal' in the sense that they refer back to originating [unconscious] worlds, they can assume very complex, strange and incongruous forms in relation to the derived [conscious] contexts in which they appear. . . . The second aspect is the object of the drive, that is to say the fragment which, simultaneously, belongs to the originating world and is torn from the real object in the derived context. The object of the drive is always the 'partial object' or the fetish, joint of meat, raw piece, scrap thrown away, woman's pants, shoe. . . . The drive is an act which snatches, tears, disjoints.
>
> (1983: 179–80)

The drive depicted in 'Mademoiselle Bistouri' is strong enough to change the woman's whole pattern of behaviour and to produce a scandalous inversion of the expected narrative development. Instead of being a seller in the sexual market-place (at least within the framework of this story), she has assumed the usual masculine role of buyer. Her guest has accepted the gift contract, he owes her for the fire, the wine, the cigar. Her hospitality (which may also have included her sexual favours, a question discreetly left unresolved) gives her certain intimate rights. She can now treat her visitor familiarly and possessively, call him *tu* and 'my pet' (*mon chat*), and expect him to co-operate in her private fantasies. It is this assumption, recognizable to any woman who has been treated to an expensive dinner and invited back to a man's flat for coffee, which seems to provoke the outburst of rage from her guest, as much as does the 'meaningless refrain' of her medical obsession.

THE DISPLAY AND THE COLLECTION

The second part of her performance as analysand consists in a *display* which begins with 'Wait . . . you'll see' and ends with 'you'll give me your picture, won't you, darling?' Another aspect of the drive is *accumulation*. When the drive *possesses* you, exposes you to the force of unsatisfiable desire, one possible reply is to endeavour to possess in your turn those material objects on to which you can *displace* the obsession. Her passion for doctors (or for the exercise of surgery?) is assuaged by the *collection of portraits*. Each bundle of portraits is a way of controlling the unattainable. They are her 'etchings', both literally and in the salacious sense of the term, the equivalent of the traditional masculine pin-ups. Through the portraits she *possesses* the medical profession, the pictures are metonymic, *fragments* which, as Deleuze says, belong both to the conscious derived world and, as symptoms, to the unconscious originating world. Each portrait, each photograph, both contains the face it displays and yet is totally empty, just as the packets and bundles which contain them, when released from their string, disintegrate into discrete entities. The 'physiognomies' displayed are in synecdochic relation to the medical profession, the parts stand for the whole, just as the letters, L., Z., X., K., W., stand for the complete names of the doctors they represent.

The narrative of an analysand is in many ways just that: the display of a collection. The repeated symptoms, the hidden images, the cherished or hated fantasies, the thoughts that one is neither allowed to enact nor to forget belong in the museum of desire. The analyst, or simply anyone who will listen to the story, is the person to whom the collection is displayed and the display itself one of the purposes of the narrative. The truth of this is finely demonstrated in an account by Baudelaire of a nightmare of his own (18 March 1856), analysed in its turn by Michel Butor (1961). This nightmare takes place in an imaginary museum where the displays are malformed foetuses and other monsters of the imagination. Each abortion[6] is presented as a work of art, as a framed picture, though frequently unfinished or distorted.

> In a mass of little frames, I see drawings, miniatures, photographic proofs. They represent coloured birds, with very brilliant plumage, whose eye is *living*. Sometimes there are only halves of birds. – They sometimes represent images of strange, monstrous, almost amorphous beings, like aeroliths. – In a corner of each drawing, there is a note: The girl (*la fille*) so and so, aged . . . , gave birth to this foetus, in such and such a year.
>
> (*Correspondance*, I: 375)

Baudelaire's letter is paradigmatic of both the analytic narrative of desire, with its fragmented structure, its frequent blanks or gaps, its compulsive display, here made to a close friend, and of the obsessional features of any collection. In the text of 'Mademoiselle Bistouri', the strings binding the packets of photos are physical signs of this drive, but so too is the choice of vocabulary, particularly 'a famous English doctor; *I caught him* on his trip to Paris.'

The drive of the analysand, revealed in the symptomatic narrative, runs parallel to and is complemented by the passion of the analyst. If *she* must 'collect' doctors, *he* must collect clues. He too must 'pursue' his 'own fixed idea', must ask the questions, elicit the text and follow the trace of the hidden desire he wishes to bring to light. His logic of the intellect is as dissective and all-absorbing as her strange fixation. 'In a certain way the analyst always carries a knife, always enacts the young Alexander and recognises no bonds' (Serres 1985: 81).

TRANSGRESSION AND SEXUALITY

It is in her last long revelation, the last act of her analytic performance, her emotional strip-tease, that the truly scandalous nature of her perversion-inversion appears. She does not give herself *to* doctors, or does not see it in these terms. Rather she gives herself doctors, she permits herself a doctor as a treat. In other words, she takes a masculine view of satisfying sexual fancy, a truly incomprehensible transgression for a woman in the context of nineteenth-century Paris. When she wants a doctor she pays for him either with her body or with money. The wonderfully revealing words 'I leave ten francs on the mantelpiece' complete the inversion of the 'normal' venal sexual contract. One can at last correctly interpret the clues suggesting prostitution which have been liberally present from the beginning of the text. They have been, as we have seen, both leading and misleading, preparing the way for this inversion which forms part of the female/male inversion constantly at work in her text. The doctor W., who was 'caught', looked like 'a young lady'; doctors generally are 'nice', 'good', and 'gentle'; the intern she snares, 'dear child', is as 'pretty as an angel'. Indeed, she speaks of seducing him with all the care of a man of the world anxious not to offend the susceptibilities of a débutante.

There is a *mise-en-abyme* of the whole narrative of desire, with its displacements and partial clues, in the words 'you understand that I got it over to him in roundabout ways; I didn't just come right out with it'. The particular scandal here (and the probable reason why the story was initially refused for publication) is of course the perverse light thrown on female desire and female sexuality. This, of all things, is something one just does not 'come right out with'. The second scandal is the overt fetishism of her final confession, the thing she has not 'dared to say'. The scandal is stressed by the punctuation: the dashes marking the blanks in the text, the question form and the exclamation mark after the climax in the ultimate expression of lack: 'I'd like him to come and see me with his instrument bag and his gown, even with a bit of blood on it!'

This is also a textbook demonstration of metonymic progression in the narrative of desire. At first the lack, the drive, was symptomatically represented in the collection of portraits, then in the collection of the doctors' professional services, whether medical or sexual. Now the part which stands for the missing whole is expressed most clearly and takes on physical and concrete form, in the instruments and the blood which stand for the right to 'cut and hack and clip', the power of *operation*. They may be read either as a fetish representing the power of gender in a masculine profession, or representing the power of sex in its masculine projection. Seen from another point of view (Bellemin-Noël 1986), they may be interpreted as a phantasm of the castrating mother, the masochistic inversion of a sadistic drive. Any solution to the enigma would be hypothetical, representing an intellectual satisfaction, a symbolic filling of a lack, which *ipso facto* remains unsatisfiable.

Although the narrator does not arrive at a solution to the mystery, he does quite clearly state the parallel and the paradox which have dominated the development of this narrative of desire. The woman's 'candid expression' as she reveals her 'funny kind of fancy' is a sign of that innocence which marks the discourse of one in the grip of unconscious drives. The narrator shows the 'discriminating man' as equally unaware of the unconscious implications, and equally a prey to fetishism. And yet, though Mademoiselle Bistouri assumes masculine discourse and masculine prerogatives, it is clear that her fetishism would not be seen in the same light as its masculine equivalents, such as the demand for costumes of particular sorts in brothels. The *discriminating man* would arouse surprise rather than social opprobrium if his desire were centred on the accoutrements rather than on the woman who wears them.[7]

The use of the extended simile here to establish a parallel: 'She said this . . . as a discriminating man would say' points to a double level in the text as a whole. The audience of the *énonciation* is encouraged to focus on the whole series of male/female parallels which run right through this analytic narrative. These begin indeed with the title, in which the feminine form of address, *Mademoiselle*, is allied to the sobriquet of *Bistouri*, the lancet whose connotations, both professional and symbolic, are exclusively masculine. As we have seen in other prose poems, there is a difference between the reaction of outraged prudery, obviously to be expected from the average nineteenth-century audience, and that hoped for from the few capable of appreciating the deeper subtleties of the text.

The last act of the analytic performance is the archetypal question of the analyst, 'Can you remember . . .?', as he perseveres in his determination to reach the heart of the mystery. He must make her go back, back to the 'originating world', the 'period and the occasion' hidden in the past when this 'very special passion', the fetishistic drive, was born. What we know now is that the birth of a drive is precisely what lies in the *unconscious* mind, inaccessible to conscious memory, able to be read only in the traces it leaves, like half-effaced inscriptions in a forgotten language. And so inevitably the narrator/analyst comes up against the two defences of analysands when confronted with a direct question about the compulsion they cannot even admit to themselves. The first reaction is not to understand the question, the second is to reveal the gap in the memory from which the origin of the obsession has been excised, the blank characteristic of repression. Repression, as Serge Leclaire remarks, is not forbidding; it is an *interdiction*, a removal of the power of speech, the impossibility of putting something into words. Mademoiselle Bistouri's story ends at that impasse, where psycho-analytic narratives usually end, since they, unlike detective or quest stories, must in the end revert from the physical world to the mental world and from the conscious to the unconscious.

The narrative as a whole makes a classic use of space in this progression, or *regression*, towards the unconscious. The text begins in the 'street', already distinguished by its isolation and its intermittence of light and darkness.

> The hazardous activities of the street – the people one encounters, the meetings one makes, the things one sees – are also remarkably and disturbingly characterized by the fact that they are discontinuous episodes . . . lived in the disorder of a random succession. Reader of the text of the city, the *flâneur* can only get to know it in the form of fragments divided from the context which would give them meaning. His experience would be that of a metonymy, or *pars pro toto*, but one which would lack not only the feeling of the whole but also any possibility of wholeness.
> (Chambers, 1987b: 170–1)

The narrative then moves into a 'room' of which only the symptomatic features are described. Then gradually any description of the room itself vanishes, the circle shrinks first to a 'cupboard' and then to the 'little round table' which holds the photographs, and finally only the deictic space (see pp. 110–11) between the interlocutors remains. The woman then vanishes from the scene, disappearing with the final revelation of the repression of the underlying drive, and in the end the only space which remains is a mental one, the thoughts in the man's mind. The deictic space has become the most mental and abstract of all: the field between man and God, seen at once as the universal audience and the ultimate analyst whose relation to space is that he is simultaneously everywhere and nowhere.

ANALYSIS AND SELF-ANALYSIS

The final paragraph shows the framing of the enigma of the self, as the question 'What oddities does one not find in a city . . . ?' is addressed in the first instance to the self as internalized narratee. However, as the question is at the same time part of a published text, it is also addressed to any reader using that text as a means of confirming and extending their experience. The word 'innocent' in 'Life swarms with innocent monsters', like the word 'candid' earlier, suggests the unconscious nature of compulsion, an unconscious not yet 'discovered' and yet suggested for centuries in the use of the word 'innocent' for the deranged. In conjunction with 'monsters' it acts as an oxymoron, a *coniunctio oppositorum* which extends to the meaning of the word monster itself (Maclean 1982). The monster is a creature which combines two natures or two beings in one, such as man and animal, man and god, god and animal. Mademoiselle Bistouri is a monster not so much because of her 'perversion', as because she combines two genders and two voices, male and female. But the narrator is also a monster, an 'innocent' victim of his own drives, and also one who combines the 'taste for horror' with the 'heart' which feels compassion.

The analyst, relating and applying the woman's story, has created a further text, which absorbs the narrative of the woman herself and which now needs a reader. More than that, in the final prayer, the *ear* which listened to the woman's voice has become a *voice*, in its turn in need of a hearer. Both voices are addressed simultaneously to the self and to the other. Thus Mademoiselle Bistouri addressed her account of her obsession to a phantasm created by her own mind, the *surgeon* she imagines, as much as to her actual male visitor. The narrator analyst in his turn addresses his text and his prayer to a construct of his own mind, the 'Creator . . . who abound[s] in motives and causes', in other words, both the undivided *same* who represents total awareness, and the eternally absent *other*. The Lord is the ultimate analyst, the presence which can always be presumed to be listening and yet can never reply. As 'God', 'Creator', 'Master', 'sovereign', and 'judge', he is the pure mental representation of the law of the Father. Yet this God is also strangely monstrous; having produced those seeming opposites, 'Law' and 'Liberty', he is also the paradoxical 'sovereign who permits everything, . . . the judge who pardons'. As Jean Prévost said:

> Does not the daring of this prayer contain a sense of vertigo? The poet feels himself too close to that taste for the horrible for which he implores divine clemency; and, demanding that God have pity, he is very close to demanding of divine Providence the reasons for crime and punishment. One step more, and this fervour would be doubt and almost blasphemy.
>
> (1953: 122)

Baudelaire's God is monstrous because always dual, both 'male' and 'female', both judge and that 'Supreme Prostitute' (*Oeuvres complètes*, I: 692), omnipresent and all-embracing, who, in his charity, couples with even his most imperfect creations. At the same time, however, this God is eternally absent and can never reply to prayers. As Jacques Lacan remarked (cit. Leclaire 1968: 178), the desire of the analyst is ultimately the desire to obtain absolute difference. The symbol of this difference could well be the absent God, the ultimate object of transference. The prayer and the text, both as analysis and as self-analysis, necessarily end in an unanswered question: 'O Creator, can monsters exist in the eyes of Him who alone knows why they exist, how they *came into being* and how they might *not have come into being*?'

This cry, which stresses human ignorance (and innocence?), echoes the end of the embedded text of the analysand, 'I don't know . . . I don't remember.' The narrative of lack and of obsession in each case returns compulsively and inevitably to the lack which underlies desire. Fulfilment is for ever deferred, the solution suggested by the analytic text 'never ceases, like bliss in the word of God, to be promised and refused, accorded only beyond death' (Leclaire 1968: 149–50).

The *énonciation* as well as the *énoncé* of the narrator show that the listener feels as much need as does the woman to display a deep unconscious lack by means of a fragmented narrative. The narrator is at once audience to the multiple voices seeking to be heard through the performance of desire and the performer of another personal drama. What appears to be one coherent voice, the analytic voice, is actually itself a discourse of lack, revealing the many traces of both the desire of the Other and the other's desire. By analysing in my turn the em-

bedded text, the fragments and half-heard messages, both conscious
and unconscious, I am merely repeating the process, and adding one
more layer to the archaeological deposits of the desiring and ever-
unfinished text.[8] As Jean Bellemin-Noël puts it, the reader is here
condemned:

> to take part and take sides, first, in a *projection*, in which, as in a film,
> the desire of the prostitute and the picture the teller draws of it are
> presented to us objectively; then, in an *identification* with this narrator
> so close to what he tells, who compromises and betrays himself as
> the narration unwinds; finally, in an original *phantasmization*, at once
> free and guided, in which we not only play the part of the analyser,
> but in which we move back to the place and then into the position of
> the analyst.
>
> (1986: 211)

APPENDIX: THE OTHER STORY

To show the depth of the archaeological deposits, I include one version
of the original story on which Baudelaire based the present text. It is so
akin, and yet so different, to the prose poem that it demonstrates the
processes of analysis, self-analysis, and transformation in exemplary
fashion. As Robert Kopp discovered (1969: 347–8), there appeared in
L'Epoque, 30 January 1866, a story called 'La Mère Bistouri', written by
Adrien Marx for a column called 'Chronique Parisienne'. This was
reprinted the next day by *L'Evènement*, in a column which used
attractive items from other papers.[9]

We do not know when Baudelaire wrote 'Mademoiselle Bistouri',
only that a stroke finished his writing career at the end of March 1866,
and he was in deep depression and producing little for some time before
that. The first record we have of 'Mademoiselle Bistouri' is that it was
announced for publication in *La Revue nationale*, on 28 September 1866,
but then apparently put aside as unpublishable. All in all, Baudelaire
almost certainly had the story from a source other than *L'Evènement*,
and his text is earlier in date, but the parallels in subject matter remain
striking and point to a common origin. Certainly the story of 'La Mère
Bistouri' is both similar, and yet very different, to the Baudelairean
version, and a comparison of the two texts reveals, in a particularly
accessible form, the workings of the process of self-analysis through the
rewriting of another's story.

Mother Bistouri   (*L'Evènement*, 31 January 1866)

She was a desiccated spinster, with a yellowish complexion, always
dressed in black. She dwelt in the hospital, waited for the doctor in

the wards, where she had arrived well before the interns, and was always in close attendance on the medical director.

The great surgeon thought a great deal of her and did not disdain to entrust to her certain tasks which she performed admirably. She had in particular a lightness of touch impossible to describe and opened a wound with a speed (I was going to say with a grace) which I have rarely encountered.

While she was operating, she would smile or address soft words to the patient. M. de Lamballe was very brutal; his friendship for this strange *doctoresse* had nothing surprising about it. Contrast in natures is almost a magnet which attracts them, and one can apply to this phenomenon the laws which governed the fulgurating material which I mentioned earlier: *electricities of contrary names attract one another - those of the same name repel one another*.

Mother Bistouri was, they said, of American origin. She had completed, in the other world, fairly extensive medical studies and had come to perfect her notions of surgery in Paris.

The science of the practitioner – who unfortunately has become mad – had seduced her. At first she haunted his clinics through admiration, the love of humanity grafted itself on to her love of study, and, having become necessary to the unfortunates lying in the beds of the public wards, she settled in at L'Hôtel Dieu [a large hospital] where she had been offered a room. She paid for her lodging by helping the sisters of charity in their dressings, the students in their research, and the professors in their operations.

After ten years of pathological involvement, she became as skilful at cutting off an arm or a leg as M. de Lamballe himself, and I heard her more than once whisper, during these pious butcheries, words of approval or advice which bore witness to her superiority in the field . . . I could not express my confidence in the worthy woman in a better way than by confessing that if ever the arm which pens these lines should have to be removed, I should wish the task to be performed by *Mother Bistouri* . . . if she is not dead, for I am speaking of ten years ago.

Whether the story reached Baudelaire in this form or another, it is fascinating to see its adaptation to the needs of the narrator of the prose poem. The obsession, which in the original took the form of the actual practice of surgery, has been translated into a physical and emotional obsession with doctors. The necessary sexual element in all obsession, already recognizable in the relationship with M. de Lamballe (the L. of our text), has been magnified and turned into full-scale fetishism. The withered old maid, *la mère Bistouri* (a derogatory title in French), has become the robust and still attractive *Mademoiselle Bistouri*, a form of address suggesting more an actress than a nurse. The element of great professional skill has been lost, thus turning the lancet into a much more symbolic attribute, and substituting something close to unconscious penis envy for the more conscious need to exercise a masculine profession. And yet, the deep scandal of the confusion of gender, of the woman who acts like a man, remains constant in both stories. It is for this reason that the madness which strikes the male doctor in the original story is attributed to the female in the prose poem. The coexistence of opposites, the confusion of gender, and the compulsion of fetishism are the elements chosen to be highlighted in the text we have studied. It is obvious that, if the anecdote were analysed by a woman in the twentieth century, for instance, the resulting text would be entirely different (cf. Suleiman 1986). The choice of the original analyst, the author, a choice which itself involved components of obsession and repression, is echoed in the 'choice' made by the narrator in pursuit of his 'passion' and his *idée fixe*. As Deleuze remarks:

> the neurotic character, or the man seeking an identity [portrayed in the text], will enter into a 'free, indirect' relationship with the poetic vision of the author which affirms itself in him, through him, even as it distinguishes itself from him. The pre-existent framework induces a curious detachment of the character who watches himself act. The images of the male or female neurotic thus become visions of the author who moves and reflects *through* the phantasms of his hero.
>
> (1983: 109)

8 · *Theory and practice: allegories of reception*

In examining the analytic narrative we looked at a textual performance which was concerned with a *problem*, one in which the narrator was involved in tracing the results of an event and the interposition of hazard in a given situation. Now we turn to a form of narrative more concerned with *theorem*, that is the development of logical consequences from a principle.[1]

THE ENERGETIC MODEL

The work of Deleuze and Guattari on the *agencement machinique*, the interlocking network or interplay of energies, is useful in approaching this theorematic text (see pp. 62–4). It provides us with a dynamic view of the changing relations within a text and its interrelated and super-imposed fields of content and expression, seeing them rather in terms of a game of three-dimensional chess. This is an approach clearly fitting to the particular narrative example chosen, which might be said to demonstrate that 'every action has its equal and opposite reaction'. The notion of the *agencement machinique* forces one to look at the variable relations of all the interlocking parts, whether syntactic or semantic, whether those of the *énonciation* or those of the *énoncé*, and at their infinite extensions, both backward into intertextuality and forward into inter-pretation. This text, for instance, can be seen to work on the mechanical principles of balance and proportion. Such a view of the energies at work in the whole network yields a very different reading from those which approach the text selectively, using only sections of it to support their interpretative exercises. Such exercises as these are justified by other theoretical criteria. However, I believe the Deleuze and Guattari approach is particularly valuable, as it allows for the investigation of not only intratextual but also intertextual networks, and sees a text as dynamic rather than static.

The second theory I hope to demonstrate is Serres's on 'the parasite' or 'noise' in the information network (see p. 59). This theory does not apply to the constitution of a single text, but throws light on certain processes in the evolution of texts. Textual evolution is seen by Serres as forming part of the adaptation and mutation of energy-using processes in general. In this particular case the relations of power and energy between the sender and receiver of a message, the function of 'noise' in the channel, and the transfer from entropy to negentropy when the receiver becomes in turn a sender, are the focus of attention.

Thirdly, the notion of Paul de Man (1979) that texts provide allegories of their own reading is particularly applicable to modernist texts and to such pre-modernism as the highly allegorical writing of Baudelaire. The extensions of meaning provided by the interplay between the concrete *actants* or literalized figures of the texts and the abstract equivalents summoned up by the reader are like those imaginary lines and curves traced in the sky by the ever-changing movement of a ship's spars, ropes, and masts: the geometry of motion which Baudelaire compared to the moving body of the text (see p. 63). De Man's view of the interplay and transformation of tropes as an integral part of such a textual process is demonstrated here by the fact that every metaphor has its equal and opposite metonymy and it is on the *agencement* between these two that much of our allegorical reading must depend.

The text we will use is '*Assommons les pauvres!*'

Let's Knock out the Poor! (XLIX)[2]

For a fortnight I had imprisoned myself in my room, and I had surrounded myself with books fashionable at that period (sixteen or seventeen years ago); I mean books which deal with the art of making nations happy, wise and rich in twenty-four hours. So I had digested, – swallowed, I should say, – all the elucubrations of all these purveyors of public happiness, – those who advise all the poor to make slaves of themselves, and those who persuade them that they are all dethroned kings. – You will not be surprised that I should then have been in a state of mind bordering on dizziness or stupidity.

Nevertheless, it had seemed to me that I felt, imprisoned in the depths of my intellect, the obscure seed of an idea superior to all the old wives' prescriptions of which I had recently perused the dictionary. But it was only the idea of an idea, something infinitely vague.

So I went out, very thirsty. For the passionate taste for second-rate reading matter engenders a proportionate need for fresh air and pick-me-ups.

As I was just about to go into a tavern, a beggar held out his hat to me, with one of those unforgettable looks which would topple thrones, if mind moved matter, and if the eye of a mesmerist made the grapes ripen.

At the same time I heard a voice whispering in my ear, a voice which I recognized very well; it was that of a good Angel, or of a good Demon, which accompanies me everywhere. Since Socrates had his good Demon, why should I not have my good Angel, and why should I not have the honour, like Socrates, of obtaining my certificate of madness, signed by the subtle Lelut and the knowledgeable Baillarger?

There exists this difference between Socrates' Demon and mine, that Socrates' only showed itself to him to forbid, warn, prevent, whereas mine deigns to advise, suggest, persuade. Poor Socrates only had a forbidding Demon; mine believes in affirmation, mine is a Demon of action, a Demon of combat.

Now, its voice was whispering this to me: 'He alone is the equal of another who proves it, and he alone is worthy of his liberty who knows how to conquer it.'

Immediately, I jumped on my beggar. With one punch I blackened his eye, which, in a second, swelled up like a ball. I broke one of my nails smashing two of his teeth, and as I did not feel myself strong enough, since I was born delicate and I had no experience in boxing, to knock the old man out quickly, I seized him by the collar of his coat with one hand, with the other I grabbed him by the throat, and I started to bash his head vigorously against a wall. I must admit that I had made a preliminary inspection of the surroundings with a glance and I had made sure that, in this deserted suburb, I was, for an appreciable time, out of reach of any policeman.

After that, having floored this weakened sixty-year-old by a kick in the back forceful enough to break his shoulder-blades, I seized a big tree branch which was lying on the ground, and I beat him with the obstinate energy of cooks who want to make a steak tender.

Suddenly, – oh miracle! oh bliss of the philosopher who verifies the excellence of his theory! – I saw this ancient carcass turn round, pick himself up with an energy which I would have never suspected in such an extraordinarily run-down machine, and, with a look of hate which seemed to me to *bode extremely well*, the decrepit rogue threw himself on me, blackened both my eyes, broke four of my teeth, and with the same tree branch beat me to a pulp. – By my forceful dosing, I had thus restored to him pride and life.

Then, by a number of gestures, I made him understand that I

ered the debate over, and getting up with the satisfaction of a
 of the Portal, I said to him: 'Sir, *you are my equal*! Please do me
  nour of sharing my purse with me; and remember, if you are
truly a philanthropist, that you must apply to all your colleagues,
when they ask you for alms, the theory which I have had the *pain* of
trying out on your back.'

He swore black and blue that he had understood my theory, and
that he would obey my advice.

CLOSED AND OPEN ALLEGORY

The allegorist has traditionally worked on two levels, the concrete and
the abstract, or the textual and the imaginary. The conventional
allegorist maintained a firm hold on the relationship between the two
levels of signification; the reader or spectator was guided towards a
revelation which was not only structured by the text but limited by the
isomorphism of the religious, historical, or perhaps sexual parallelism
clearly signposted by the author, such as that found in *The Pilgrim's
Progress* or *The Garden of Love*. Once the intended doubleness, the
coherent alternative set of paradigmatic choices, was revealed to the
reader and his or her perspective was consequently enlarged, the
allegorist's work was done.

> In allegory the vision of the reader is larger than the vision of the
> text; the reader dreams to an excess, to an overabundance. To read
> an allegorical narration is to see beyond the relations of narration,
> character, desire. To read allegory is to live in the future, the
> anticipation of a closure beyond the closure of narrative . . . . The
> locus of action is not in the text but in the transformation of the
> reader.
>
> (Stewart 1984: 3)

Modern allegory, however, by problematizing the closure of the text
also problematizes the closure of the reading. The reader is to be
transformed, but the transformation depends on the reading and on the
network of possibilities created as a result of this activity to parallel the
network of the text. Open allegory makes each reader the creator of a
new interpretative reflection of the original sequence of possibilities.
The text must contain not individual symbols but an interrelated series
which initiates the reader's performance, which announces that
parallel paradigmatic choices are possible whereby the reader can
enlarge and at the same time appropriate the message.

'CONIUNCTIO OPPOSITORUM'

In the case of 'Let's Knock out the Poor!' (*'Assommons les pauvres!'*) the series is set under way by signals immediately present in the title. We have already seen that the title functions as a direct speech act between author and reader. This is particularly marked in the present case as the reader is actually addressed. The use of the first-person plural imperative ('Let's Knock out') not only involves the reader directly but sets up a particular form of complicity, even more so than, for instance, the title of another prose poem 'Intoxicate Yourselves' (or, more simply, 'Get drunk' (XXXIII)). This other form of direct address also reaches the reader as immediately as it shocks, but the second-person imperative is only a command whereas the first-person plural imperative is a conspiracy. The prose poems are notable for the extent of their reader involvement by the use of commands, rhetorical questions, and exclamations (Nies 1976: 369), but this is the most striking example. (I let the adjective stand to show signs at work.)

The shock effect of the totally inexplicable command – only a very naïve reader is going to believe that he or she is really expected to beat up or knock out the poor – sets up a suspicious and therefore active participation in the text which follows. It should be explained here that the title contains a deliberate ambiguity, a potential trope. The French *assommer* is used as often figuratively as literally – or more often. It means not only 'to knock out' or 'to put to sleep', but 'to bore to death' or 'to blind with science'. An *assommeur* is not a mugger but one of the world's great bores.

This is the second-to-last text in the series of prose poems and, if read after many of the others, would display a marked incongruity with the compassion displayed towards the unfortunate, such as we have seen in 'The Eyes of the Poor'. However, as has been observed, the texts may be read in any number or order, and a command of Baudelairean intertextuality is not necessary to perceive the shock effect here. The sign 'poor' has the whole history of Christianity to add to its connotations and to signal the convention, if not always the practice, of charity and sympathy. So this title is linked in form and action to the oxymoron, the union of opposites, which always provokes the set-forming and decoding activities of the human brain.

The text proper immediately establishes two parallel reading relationships, the one in the past tense ('I had imprisoned myself . . . sixteen or seventeen years ago') between the narrator as receiver, shut up in his room to read the works of Utopian political scientists, and the one in the present tense ('I mean', 'I should say') between the narrator and narratee or implied reader (perhaps shut up in his or her room to read the story). Not only this but the writers of the books and treatises, the theories which should be so easy to put into practice ('the art of making nations happy, wise and rich in twenty-four hours'), have themselves sat up all night in their rooms (the original meaning of elucubrations) to produce these weighty tomes. Didactic literature is an active literature, characterized by the use of performatives, which in themselves imply a certain textual violence. These books do not just state facts: they 'advise' the poor of excessive duties and they also 'persuade' them of delusory rights. Thus the text sets in place its keywords, paradigmatic of books and theories but also of their would-be applications. Here too it establishes another key metaphor or trope: didactic literature is barely digestible, sententious advice must be swallowed like a medicine. The last sentence in the paragraph then appeals once again to the narratee ('you will not be surprised'), thus reaffirming a double reader/receiver relationship, that of the narrator reading his books and that of the narratee reading his story. The culmination of this first grouping of interlocking parts is the first of a series of ingenious allusions to the title. If the narrator ended his literary investigations dizzy or stunned (stupidity comes from *stupor*, the loss of the faculties) it was because he had been knocked silly or bored stiff by the weight of these pedantic and impracticable theories. So in the first paragraph, the initial form of the interplay of the *énonciation*, as well as the main paradigms and the tropes, is already established.

THE FUNCTION OF THE 'PARASITE'

In examining what follows, a new dimension is added to our reading of the text in terms of narrator–narratee or sender–receiver relationships by the information-based approach of Serres. For, when boredom or incredulity produces stupidity, it also produces 'noise'. It knocks out the reader, interferes in the reception of the original message, in this case the Utopian message, and distorts the channel. Noise means that the receiver will not receive the original message, the one intended by the sender; it also frequently means a mutation in that message. Try sending a joke or a poem by whisper around a line of people; usually the message emerges mutilated, but occasionally the mutilation becomes a mutation, and a new and exciting message takes the place of the original. This is a simple example of the positive function of noise, the function of evolution. Serres sees this function as not merely random, but necessary.

Here the noise (dizziness or stupidity) functions as the grit in the oyster; there grows, evolves, in the depths of the narrator's mind, the obscure 'seed' of an idea. The change in the message is stressed by its association with a repetition, the second use of the word 'imprisoned'. Just as the narrator was imprisoned to receive the first message, so the seed of a new message is imprisoned in his mind. Again signs belonging to the paradigm of theorization (prescriptions (French *formules*), dictionary, idea) accompany the noise-based transformation.

The turn-around in the mind, as the 'parasite' begins its work, is paralleled by the mutation of a trope. The absorption of all the theories which have been 'swallowed' is now transferred from metaphor to metonymy and appears simply as thirst. The narrator leaves his room as he leaves his literary Utopias and is equally transferred from the closed space of the dwelling to the open space of the street. Here we are given a strong clue as to the functioning of the mechanical interplay of the text with the appearance of what Dällenbach would call a *mise-en-abyme du code* (see pp. 82–3): 'the passionate taste for second-rate reading matter engenders a proportionate need for fresh air and pick-me-ups.' The keys here are the words 'engenders a proportionate need', since the whole text under consideration relies on parallelism and proportion to establish the allegorical framework.

The evolution of the narrator continues as, from having been up to this point the receiver of messages, messages subject to the effects of noise, however, he now becomes a potential sender. We have already examined at some length the parallelism between currency and verbal or textual signs and between reception and payment (see pp. 78 ff.), we have also seen how the beggar is paradigmatic of all receivers in the Baudelairean opus. As was made clear, the beggar sets up a contractual relationship in which he has to accept the payment/message even if it is not what he bargained for. The beggar is a parasite on society, excluded from its structures, just as the reader is a parasite on the text and excluded from its structures. Both are subject to violence, the pressures of society and the pressures of the text, but, like all parasites, both can respond with noise, which can take the form of either aggression or subversion.

THEORY AND PERFORMANCE

The other relationship established here by the interplay of the text is that between theory and practice. The beggar (a 'dethroned king' according to some of the theorists under consideration) could 'topple thrones, if mind moved matter'. Alas, however, it is otherwise in practice. The relationship between theory and performance is posited as that between abstract and concrete, between mind and matter. This will also be shown to be the relationship between the two halves of this prose poem.

Simultaneously with the beggar's demand for alms a transformation in the nature of 'noise', the parasite, takes place. The 'seed of an idea' has now engendered a concrete manifestation, an allegory within an allegory, the voice of the good Demon. This good Demon who accompanies the narrator everywhere is the physical manifestation of 'noise', the grit in the oyster, the uninvited guest at the wedding feast, the court jester at the banquet.

> Thus the satire is first a meal.[3] Interrupted and ridiculous. Nothing could be understood of the stable presence of the banquet in the midst of these cultural institutions of language if it were not a question of the speaking subject, of the transformation of vital material and living energy into verbal, disordered, or linguistic information. The parasite is the location and the subject of the transformation.
>
> (Serres 1982: 211)

Like the gadfly of Athens, Socrates, the exploiter of 'noise' and the harbourer of the parasite may be treated as mad by the bourgeois implied readers. After all, two nineteenth-century doctors had pompously certified the madness of Socrates (just as naïve readers of this text have been known to decide that Baudelaire must have been unhinged when he wrote it).

The elaborate network of the text is once again playing with a series of parallelisms, between the narrator and Socrates, between voice and Demon, and between those performatives paradigmatic of didactic aggression: 'forbid, warn, prevent' on the one hand, and 'advise, suggest, persuade' on the other. The words 'advise' and 'persuade' act as relay mechanisms in the text, occurring as they do (with 'persuade' once changed into 'understood') at the beginning, the middle, and the end of the text. The 'voice' (similarly at the third repetition) completes its work as parasite when it turns the narrator into an author, the reader into a writer. With the formulation of the mutated message the parasite's work is done and its voice becomes that of the narrator.

The message in direct speech is rigorously proportioned as is the whole text, and set out in exact syntactic and semantic parallelism. The precept of equality applies in the first place to the narrator who has produced a parallel theory, 'an equal and opposite reaction', and thus liberated himself from the imprisonment of the Utopian text, producing his own 'equal' text to replace it.

METAPHOR AND METONYMY

It is at this moment, exactly half-way through the text, and at its turning-point, that the metamorphosis of the main trope occurs. In a progress of displacement and visual representation, as characteristic of modern allegory as it is of Freudian 'dream work', the figural meaning of the word *assommer*, 'knock out', is literalized. The narrator, as receiver, has been knocked silly, bored witless, and blinded by the Utopian 'science'. Now the metaphor is to become metonymized, the abstract signs are to be made concrete, and the cliché is to be given new vitality by its enactment. Also of course the narrator is turning mind into matter and theory into practice in the most literal way. Dream work, says Freud, is a translation, a rendering into another script or language. However, he continues:

> a translation normally endeavours to preserve the distinctions made in the text and particularly to keep things that are similar separate. The dream-work, quite the contrary, tries to condense two different thoughts by seeking out (like a joke) an ambiguous word in which the two thoughts may come together.
>
> (1982: 207)

The ambiguous nature of the word *assommer* permits the process here, allowing the transformation of the trope from metaphor to metonymy.

The concrete representation of violence which follows is so extreme that it assumes the proportions of a literary Punch and Judy show. As Barbara Johnson points out (1983: 96), the figure is itself a form of violence against language, a violence here retranslated in the grotesque extremes of the text. The exchange is crude in all ways. We could translate it into fairground terms:

- What's that you've got there?
- A theory.
- Theories don't grow on trees.
- This one does.
- What's it good for?
- To bash brains out. (Whack, Whack, Whack!)

'PROSAIC ALLEGORIZATION'

The very enormity of this metonymic translation confronts the reader. Whether one finds it funny or shocking depends on the basic functioning of the comic, which, as Baudelaire remarked in *Concerning the Essence of Laughter* . . . , is a direct result of the always variable interaction between the text and the spectator, hearer or reader: 'for the comic to exist, that is to say an emanation, an explosion, a release of the comic, there must be two beings confronting each other . . . it is specially in the laugher, in the spectator, that the comic resides' (*Oeuvres complètes*, II: 543).

Reader reaction here has been extremely varied, as we will see. This is a direct result of the dynamics of the text, but also of the fact that, as Bakhtin remarked:

> there is real difficulty with the problem of *prosaic allegorization*, if you will, the problem of the prosaic metaphor (which of course has nothing in common with the poetic metaphor) that is introduced into literature by the rogue, the clown and the fool, and for which there is not even an adequate term ('parody', 'joke', 'humor', 'irony', 'grotesque', 'whimsy' are but narrowly restrictive labels for the heterogeneity and subtlety of the idea).
>
> (1981: 166)

The force of the textual representation of the knocking out is quite surprising. Indeed force and energy are the keywords in this section apart from the signs paradigmatic of assault and battery. However, the unreal quality of the episode is indicated by the improbable emptiness of the street in which it occurs. The stage of dreams contains only that décor and those props which form part of the machinery of condensation and displacement.

The knock-out, the persuasion (the tree branch functions as 'persuader' in the same way as a gun is supposed to), and the whole *force* of the argument certainly give the beggar food for thought. In fact he suddenly responds to his *assommeur* in the same way that the narrator had responded to the literature which left him 'dizzy and stupid'. He produces an energetic reaction. And so, there occurs the miracle: 'bliss of the philosopher who verifies the excellence of his theory'. Again a trope-like effect similar to that of the oxymoron is used here, an unlooked-for juxtaposition between logic and desire, mind and matter, proof and 'persuasion'. The word 'bliss' (*jouissance* which has strong sexual connotations) is set against the dry and abstract 'philosopher', just as the words 'verifies' and 'theory' are set against the grotesque violence of the physical action.

> Persuasion and proof should not, in principle, be distinct from each other, and it would not occur to a mathematician to call his proofs allegories. From a theoretical point of view, there ought to be no difficulty in moving from epistemology to persuasion. The very occurrence of allegory, however, indicates a possible complication.

> Why is it that the furthest reaching truths about ourselves and the
> world have to be stated in such a lopsided, referentially indirect
> mode?
>
> (de Man 1981: 2)

This text, by physically demonstrating the performative qualities of
persuasion, as opposed to the cognitive properties of proof or veri-
fication, demonstrates the efficacy of the referentially indirect mode.
The 'force' of persuasion always involves an inherent degree of
violence. The very need for expression in terms of performatives shows
that it works in terms of pressure and resistance to that pressure. In the
allegory of the beggar, the proportion between mind and matter is
preserved, the action provokes its equal and opposite reaction, and the
enforced message produces what it was supposed to produce, a
message of transgression.

FORCE OF SIGNS OR SIGNS OF FORCE

That 'run-down machine', the beggar/receiver, turns round, picks
itself up, and, impelled by this novel, *assommante*, version of philosophy,
a different form of the same 'noise' experienced by the narrator, pro-
ceeds to the performance of applied theory. The narrator is now
'knocked out' for a second time, getting, as is fit, *two* black eyes instead
of the beggar's one, and *four* broken teeth instead of the beggar's two,
not to mention being persuaded by the same persuader. Proportion
engenders proportion, equal means bring equal ends. The second
receiver, like the first, has taken his medicine, the 'forceful dosing' he
has had to swallow, just as the narrator had to swallow Utopian
didacticism. The narrator responded first by his rhetorical aggressive-
ness, using words as a cudgel against the bookish recipes for instant
popular kingdoms on earth. Now once again the worm has turned. The
beggar, like the narrator, has been changed from receiver of a
stupefying message to a sender in an equally stupefying code. He has
responded to aggression 'with a vengeance'.

The narrator now plays the role of parasite to the beggar, putting the
parasitical message into words just as the voice of the Demon had done
for him. The French text contains a nice clue here to the nature of the
transaction between the two. For 'by a number of gestures, I made him
understand' the original text reads *je lui fis force signes pour lui faire
comprendre* which means the same but, by an elegant process of con-
densation, also refers to the relationship between *signs* (words or
gestures) and *force*, a relationship which has characterized the whole

agencement machinique of the text. Force, as de Man (1981) has pointed out, is pure performance and here stands in direct relation to the dynamism of the allegorical text. This particular use of words, *force signes*, like the other double meanings we have noted:

> is what ancient rhetoric called a syllepsis – a word that is used once, within one context, yet carries two competing meanings . . . a word understood at one and the same time as meaning and significance . . . the syllepsis provides a model for an interpretation, since the syllepsis is an example, guaranteed by linguistic usage, of context and intertext with a point in common, the one phonetic or graphemic shape shared by two acceptations.
>
> (Riffaterre 1983a: 125–6)

All the signs in the text in this concluding segment now work to reverse the main trope yet again and to return the 'knock-out' to its original, metaphorical, acceptation.[4] The 'debate', that other form of combat, is over, and the 'proportionate' need engendered by second-rate reading is satisfied. The renewed reference to Socrates, that ear-basher *par excellence*, shows that the narrator is himself now in the position of the 'Demon' and playing the part of 'parasite' to the beggar. The philosophical narrator is shown by this parallelism to be *also* a social parasite, noise in the system, a subverter of both Utopian ideals *and* establishment values.

What remains in the interplay of the text is the apostrophe in direct speech which echoes and comments by feedback on the previous direct speech, the aphorism of the 'voice'. 'He alone is the equal of another who proves it' is picked up in 'Sir, *you are my equal*'. This is followed by the division of the contents of the purse, shared between the two receiver/senders, just as the text has been shared equally between the mental and the physical forms of reception. The imperative addressed to the beggar, 'remember', echoes the imperative of the title and thus associates the three levels of reception: the receiver of the *énoncé* (the beggar), the receiver of the *énonciation* (the narratee), and the receiver of the authorial illocution (the reader). The true philanthropist, as opposed to the Utopian socialist, should apply his theories and *enact* his verbal constructs.

ENTROPY AND NEGENTROPY

It must be remembered that *passivity of reception* is the target. The beggarly colleagues will no longer merely ask for alms, hold out their hats, and take what they are given in an entropic dissipation of the money or the message. They too will undergo the effects of 'noise' and react negentropically, using energy to produce *theories* of their own which will of course not necessarily coincide with those of the narrator. The openness of this possible outcome of the process of communication, a progressive repetition, but a repetition of mutations induced by the *liberty* of the receiver's reaction, works against the minute parallelism of the allegorical structure. Thus Bersani's view (1977: 148) of the text as embodying an 'absolute power', 'an ideal freedom', and 'a triumphant narcissism', in which the narrator merely produces a replica of himself in the beggar, takes account of the sado-masochistic structure of the second half of the poem. It does not, however, take into account the progressive relationship to theory, that relationship of advice to performance which underlies the whole text. It is very true, however (Bersani 1977: 147), that the sado-masochistic nature of the 'dream work', the metonymic construct, is admirably summed up in the word *pain* which, by its very position in a syntagm which is also a cliché, contains within itself its opposite, pleasure.

The final sentence contains both the promise for the future – the beggar's performative ('he swore black and blue . . . that he would obey') – and the feedback to the past, in that theory has for the third time done its work of persuasion and advice. The promise for the future links in with the future implicit in the command of the title. It is interesting that the author–reader relationship of the title was originally reinforced by a complementary final line in the manuscript which spelt out the inverse reader–author or receiver–sender relationship. The prose poem originally ended with the words: 'What do you have to say to that, citizen Proudhon?'

Here the direct address to the most famous contemporary Utopian socialist (recently, but safely, dead) dramatizes the allegory while at the same time reminding us that the beggar's relationship to the narrator is also that of the narrator to such theorists as Proudhon and *his* colleagues. The narrator in fact has delivered a counterblow to the very elucubrations which had originally left him groggy and on the ropes.

INTERPRETATIVE ENERGY AND ALLEGORICAL VIOLENCE

The intensive machinery of signals, tropes, and parallelisms necessary to allegorical writing, the interplay of parts which we have just been witnessing, is best seen as that fusion of energy and organization, that multi-level and polysemic action and reaction which Deleuze and Guattari call the *agencement machinique* of the text. Such a machinery calls for a corresponding interpretative elaboration, an allegory of reading, which, as Joel Fineman has noted, links the desire to apprehend the structurality of literature with the desire *for* allegory 'implicit in the idea of structure itself'. He continues:

> the movement of allegory, like the dreamwork, enacts a wish that determines its progress – and, of course, the dream-vision is a characteristic framing and opening device of allegory, a way of situating allegory in the *mise en abyme* opened up by the variety of cognate accusatives that dream a dream, or see a sight, or tell a tale . . . analysis itself, the critical response to allegory, rehearses the same wish and therefore embarks on the same pilgrimage.
>
> (1981: 26–7)

Certainly the interpretative elaboration called forth by this particular text has been considerable.

The readings of 'Let's Knock out the Poor!', as befits an open-ended allegory, are many and varied, ranging from seeing it as a direct call to active intervention in the real world (Fairlie 1976: 404), as an expression of latent sado-masochism with all its Freudian implications (Bersani 1977: 145–9), or as a revelation of the self-destructive tendencies of Baudelaire's 'social self' (Mauron 1966: 113–14). Any one reading alone would be insufficient because it would ignore:

> the manifestly allegorical intention of a text that explicitly directs its structure, such as it is or as we have idealized it, to correspond to other structures of experience – psychological, physical, metaphysical, and literary – from which the text derives its own authority. . .
>
> (Fineman 1981: 40)

Bersani, for instance, admits that the 'concreteness of the lesson is somewhat dissipated in the emblematic nature of the tale' (1977: 149), which seems to me an understatement. The interpretation which is both the least pre-emptive and comes closest to the 'force' of this allegory of reading is that of Jeffrey Mehlman who takes up Mauron's suggestion of the 'Zarathustrian' nature of the text, and who sees 'Let's Knock out the Poor!' as a study of the essence of force in relation to other forces and an affirmation of an energetic differential which finds its outcome in 'a certain violence of metaphoricity, as it *exceeds* and decenters individual consciousness' (1974: 9). Mehlman, reading the passage with Freud and Nietzsche in mind, selects the exchange of beatings for his focus, 'perhaps less an exchange of *douleurs* than the *douleur* of a certain kind of exchange' (1974: 8), as he perciently puts it. However, he too omits to take account of the unfolding and interplay of the text as a whole, although he realizes its lack of closure:

> The way beyond Art then is a different kind of art: an art of repetition-in-difference, such as the interpretative art which, after Nietzsche, we are here attempting to practice. . . . It is not a question of negating other interpretations but of affirming the differences between them.
>
> (Mehlman 1974: 11)

So we have here an allegory of a relationship of power, power which could take many forms: that of master–slave or lover–mistress just as much as that of donor–beggar or of writer–reader. The basic evolution of the relationship is that, from being originally active-passive in nature, it becomes active-active, an interplay of forces, 'an exchange of pain', rather than a one-way street. The writer–reader relationship is particularly susceptible to such a shift in forces; indeed many writers would maintain that textual violence, rather than being a function of *énonciation*, is that exercised *on* the text by the reader who can always produce noise by misreading, by non-reading, or by 'dizziness and stupidity'.

Let us take the case, however, of the enforced reader. Is not the child in school, the student at the university, the penitent in church, the plaintiff in court, rather in the position of the Baudelairean beggar who goes cap in hand to ask for alms? On these receivers descends a text or texts which they are expected to accept passively and, indeed, gratefully. They are knocked silly by moralizing, blinded by science, and stupefied by theory which is notable rather for precept than for practice.

However, one fine day it may all become too much. The passive receiver may suddenly pick himself up and, with a look of hate, realize that two can play at the text game. The realization comes in two stages: first the transgressive *reading* of the authoritarian text and then the *production* of a new text, either mentally as active reader or eventually as reader turned writer. Beat certain readers over the head long enough and, to the consternation of many, they will produce *A Season in Hell*, *Ulysses*, *Notes from the Underground*, or *Little Prose Poems*. For these readers repetition-in-difference has moved through yet another stage. In their case the donor and recipient of the message have established recipro-city of power. However, the recipient-become-donor is about to knock out the next set of readers. The fate of the great transgressive texts is eventually to join the canon, to acquire their own enforced readers, so that in true Darwinian or Nietzschean fashion the whole exchange of forces, which is one aspect of the reading process, may be repeated. This is one further interpretation of the Baudelairean allegory of reading.

Finally, when I meet you in the encounter of theoretical performance and critical practice, the force of the allegory still applies. The reading of theory should not consist of supine or passive acceptance but of reaction and interaction. My readers should take matters into their own hands and respond, like the beggar, by fighting back.

Notes

All translations, unless specified in the bibliography, are my own.

1 THE DYNAMICS OF NARRATIVE

1. See Elam (1980: 46–9) for a definition of performance text.
2. These are assumed to be narrative universals by van Dijk (1977) and Brémond (1973), among·others. For another view of narrative universals see Labov (1972: 369).
3. Peter Brook (1972:74) gives an excellent example of this fruitful function of noise, in the interplay between the stage and electronic music.
4. The parallel between performance and the performative which is explored in Chapter 3 is marked in this distinction. Cf. Austin (1975: 99–100).
5. I regret the slight awkwardness in keeping these terms in the French form throughout this study, but so much confusion has arisen through varying English translations that it seems safer. Greimas and Courtés (1982) give 'enunciation' for *énonciation* and 'utterance' for *énoncé*, but this fails to convey the relationship between the two.
6. Language includes that 'indirect discourse' (Bakhtin 1981: 41–51) whereby the different 'dialects' of society, of history, and of the psychoanalytic forces within the individual performer are moulded into a single voice.
7. This is an idiosyncratic use of the term 'dramatis personae' adapted by Propp for the seven major narrative 'actants' he identified in wonder-tales: the dispatcher, the hero, the villain, the helper, the donor, the princess, the false hero.
8. Elam's account of dramatic *énonciation* (1980:144) suffers from a confusion about the basically double notion of *all* discourse, which must necessarily include both the speaking, the *énonciation*, and what is spoken, the *énoncé*. As will be seen, speech-act theory offers a multiple approach to the actor-actor and actor-audience enunciatory situation (Ubersfeld 1981) and can also be used to show similar effects in written narrative.
9. An even more far-reaching recognition of the relation between the narrative and the dramatic is Brecht's demand that actors in all drama should play their parts as though they were speaking in the third person, in other words as though they were narrating the dialogue of the character they represent rather than 'identifying' with the role.
10. I am adopting with Jakobson (for a clear, short statement of his position see Hawkes 1972:77) the view that a single basic figure, metonymy, subsumes

other tropes of contiguity such as synecdoche, just as metaphor subsumes simile.

11. Barbara Herrnstein Smith's trenchant essay 'The ethics of interpretation' (1978: 133–54) should be read as a corrective to the proprietorial critical stance.

12. An interesting variation is provided by film, which is a public performance and allows for audience *interaction*, and which at the same time denies immediate audience feedback. It is thus in an intermediate category between the dramatic performance and the printed text which provokes *individual* interpretation.

13. Whereas the authority of the narrator is no longer taken for granted and is seen as a matter for interaction, this contrasts with the extra-narrative authority exercised by censors, educators, and, indeed, publishers.

14. See Lanser (1981: 122–5) on the role of extra-fictional elements in narration. She identifies, as well as the title, the dedications, preface, chapter headings, and notes. I would contend that the title has a special role among these various elements.

15. It is certainly true that, within the world of the text, there may be more than one narrative world, in fact there may be a hierarchy of narrative worlds, one embedded within the other (see Lanser 1981: 144). However, the status of the illocutionary acts involved remains the same.

16. See Picard (1986) for an examination of identification and of the sublimation of the oral, visual, and anal drives in the reading process.

17. I originally used the word *ideology* here. I owe to Ross Chambers the observation that ideology often subsumes desire, and that the reason for this bourgeois reaction is that guilt has been a component of bourgeois ideology since at least 1848, when it became clear that its universalist, progressive tendencies were self-delusory and that self-interest was the real name of the game.

18. Some of the problems of reader desire in its relation to the text are tackled in *Problèmes actuels de la lecture* (Dällenbach and Ricardou 1982), and particularly in the contributions of Michel de Certeau and Ross Chambers.

2 THE WRITER AS PERFORMER

1. The details of this scattered and controversial publication may be found in the critical edition of Robert Kopp (1969).

2. His productive work ended in March 1866, when a stroke left him unable to speak or write.

3. All translations of Baudelaire's texts are my own, and all page numbers for his work refer to the *Oeuvres complètes* (1975/1976 Pleiade edition, ed. C. Pichois). The original French text will be given in the notes throughout.

Mon cher ami, je vous envoie un petit ouvrage dont on ne pourrait pas dire, sans injustice, qu'il n'a ni queue ni tête, puisque tout, au contraire, y est à la fois tête et queue, alternativement et réciproquement. Considérez, je vous prie, quelles admirables commodités cette combinaison nous offre à tous, à vous, à moi et au lecteur. Nous pouvons couper où nous voulons, moi ma rêverie, vous le manuscrit, le lecteur sa lecture, car je ne suspends pas la volonté rétive de celui-ci au fil interminable d'une intrigue superflue. Enlevez une vertèbre, et les deux morceaux de cette tortueuse fantaisie se rejoindront sans peine. Hachez-la en nombreux fragments, et vous verrez que chacun peut exister à part. Dans l'espérance que quelques-uns de ces tronçons seront assez vivants pour vous plaire et vous amuser, j'ose vous dédier le serpent tout entier. . . .

Quel est celui de nous qui n'a pas, dans ses jours d'ambition, rêvé le miracle d'une prose poétique, musicale sans rythme et sans rime, assez souple et assez heurtée pour s'adapter aux mouvements lyriques de l'âme, aux ondulations de la rêverie, aux soubresauts de la conscience?

C'est surtout de la fréquentation des villes énormes, c'est du croisement de leurs innombrables rapports que naît cet idéal obsédant.

4. Barbara Johnson (1979) makes the excellent point that the work is both headless, *décapitée*, and capital in both senses of the word. It is constantly elusive and the more capital for being ungraspable (cf. Blin 1948: 164–7).

5. For a definition of these terms, taken from the German, for the basic forms of oral narrative, see Dundes (1965).

6. I use the term oppositional in the way described by Michel de Certeau (1980). See also Maclean (1987).

7. In references to *Little Prose Poems* I will use the accepted numbering, from one to fifty, rather than page references, so that they may be found in any edition.

8. 'The term "subject of the enunciation", which is often used as a synonym for the enunciator, in fact covers both actantial positions of the enunciator and enunciatee' (Greimas and Courtés 1982: 105).

9. Fancioulle, secoué, réveillé dans son rêve, ferma d'abord les yeux, puis les rouvrit presque aussitôt, démesurément agrandis, ouvrit ensuite la bouche comme pour respirer convulsivement, chancela un peu en avant, un peu en arrière, et puis tomba roide mort sur les planches.

10. Ce que les hommes nomment amour est bien petit, bien restreint et bien faible, comparé à cette ineffable orgie, à cette sainte prostitution de l'âme qui se donne tout entière, poésie et charité, à l'imprévu qui se montre, à l'inconnu qui passe.

11. **Les Fenêtres** (XXXV)
Celui qui regarde du dehors à travers une fenêtre ouverte, ne voit jamais autant de choses que celui qui regarde une fenêtre fermée. Il n'est pas d'objet plus profond, plus mystérieux, plus fécond, plus ténébreux, plus éblouissant qu'une fenêtre éclairée d'une chandelle. Ce qu'on peut voir au soleil est toujours moins intéressant que ce qui se passe derrière une vitre. Dans ce trou noir ou lumineux vit la vie, rêve la vie, souffre la vie.

Par delà des vagues de toits, j'aperçois une femme mûre, ridée déjà, pauvre, toujours penchée sur quelque chose, et qui ne sort jamais. Avec son visage, avec son vêtement, avec son geste, avec presque rien, j'ai refait l'histoire de cette femme, ou plutôt sa légende, et quelquefois je me la raconte à moi-même en pleurant.

Si c'eût été un pauvre vieux homme, j'aurais refait la sienne tout aussi aisément.

Et je me couche, fier d'avoir vécu et souffert dans d'autres que moi-même.

Peut-être me direz-vous: 'Es-tu sûr que cette légende soit la vraie?' Qu'importe ce que peut être la réalité placée hors de moi, si elle m'a aidé à vivre, à sentir que je suis et ce que je suis?

12. **Le Miroir** (XL)

Un homme épouvantable entre et se regarde dans la glace.

' – Pourquoi vous regardez-vous au miroir, puisque vous ne pouvez vous y voir qu'avec déplaisir?'

L'homme épouvantable me répond: ' – Monsieur, d'après les immortels principes de 89, tous les hommes sont égaux en droits; donc je possède le droit de me mirer; avec plaisir ou déplaisir, cela ne regarde que ma conscience.'

Au nom du bon sens, j'avais sans doute raison; mais, au point de vue de la loi, il n'avait pas tort.

13. See Note 3.

14. Jacques Plessen has admirably described this parallel in his *Promenade et poésie* (1967), dealing with a similar phenomenon in the work of Rimbaud.

15. Both the use of the city streets as text, and the almost infinite combinative possibilities, are modernist features which will be even more developed in twentieth-century texts such as Joyce's *Ulysses* or Cabrera Infante's *Three Trapped Tigers*.

16. Il n'est pas donné à chacun de prendre un bain de multitude: jouir de la foule est un art; et celui-là seul peut faire, aux dépens du genre humain, une ribote de vitalité, à qui une fée a insufflé dans son berceau le goût du travestissement et du masque, la haine du domicile et la passion du voyage.

Multitude, solitude: termes égaux et convertibles pour le poëte actif et fécond. Qui ne sait pas peupler sa solitude, ne sait pas non plus être seul dans une foule affairée.

Le poëte jouit de cet incomparable privilège, qu'il peut à sa guise être lui-même et autrui. Comme ces âmes errantes qui cherchent un corps, il entre, quand il veut, dans le personnage de chacun.

17. Au bout, à l'extrême bout de la rangée de baraques, comme si, honteux, il s'était exilé lui-même de toutes ces splendeurs, je vis un pauvre saltimbanque, voûté, caduc, décrépit, une ruine d'homme, adossé contre un des poteaux de sa cahute; une cahute plus misérable que celle du sauvage le plus abruti, et dont deux bouts de chandelles, coulants et fumants, éclairaient trop bien encore la détresse.

Partout la joie, le gain, la débauche; partout la certitude du pain pour les lendemains; partout l'explosion frénétique de la vitalité. Ici la misère absolue, la misère affublée, pour comble d'horreur, de haillons comiques, où la nécessité, bien plus que l'art, avait introduit le contraste. . . .

Et, m'en retournant, obsédé par cette vision, je cherchai à analyser ma soudaine douleur, et je me dis: Je viens de voir l'image du vieil homme de lettres qui a survécu à la génération dont il fut le brillant amuseur; du vieux poëte sans amis, sans famille, sans enfants, dégradé par sa misère et par l'ingratitude publique, et dans la baraque de qui le monde oublieux ne veut plus entrer!

18. Il a posé plus d'une fois pour moi, et je l'ai transformé tantôt en petit bohémien, tantôt en ange, tantôt en Amour mythologique. Je lui ai fait

porter le violon du vagabond, la Couronne d'Epines et les Clous de la Passion, et la Torche d'Eros.

19. Baudelaire got many of his ideas from small items of daily news and from reports from the police courts. He was also, of course, intimately acquainted with court procedure because of the notorious trial involving *Les Fleurs du mal*, which resulted in the censoring of a number of poems, a fine, and the loss of almost the whole of the first edition.

20. *Une tour-labyrinthe. Je n'ai jamais pu sortir. J'habite pour toujours un bâtiment qui va crouler, un bâtiment travaillé par une maladie secrète.* – Je calcule, en moi-même, pour m'amuser, si une si prodigieuse masse de pierres, de marbres, de statues, de murs, qui vont se choquer réciproquement seront très souillés par cette multitude de cervelles, de chairs humaines et d'ossements concassés.

21. Baudelaire's mother was brought up in England, and he read English fluently from an early age. Some of his most famous works are his extraordinary translations of Poe and De Quincey.

22. et le choc le renversant, il acheva de briser sous son dos toute sa pauvre fortune ambulatoire qui rendit le bruit éclatant d'un palais de cristal crevé par la foudre.

Et, ivre de ma folie, je lui criai furieusement: 'La vie en beau! la vie en beau!'

23. Un homme va au tir au pistolet, accompagné de sa femme. – Il ajuste une poupée, et dit à sa femme: Je me figure que c'est toi. – Il ferme les yeux et abat la poupée. – Puis il dit en baisant la main de sa compagne: Cher ange, que je te remercie de mon adresse!

24. Deleuze draws this distinction from Leibnitz. The 'vital machine' or the 'divine machine' is *machinique*, that is to say that all its parts, to infinity, are further machines. On the other hand, the 'mechanical machine', made by the hand and mind of man, is composed of inert parts which are final in themselves and finite (verbal communication).

25. Je crois que le charme infini et mystérieux qui gît dans la contemplation d'un navire, et surtout d'un navire en mouvement, tient, dans le premier cas, à la régularité et à la symétrie qui sont un des besoins primordiaux de l'esprit humain, au même degré que la complication et l'harmonie, – et, dans le second cas, à la multiplication successive et à la génération de toutes les courbes et figures imaginaires opérées dans l'espace par les éléments réels de l'objet.

L'idée poétique qui se dégage de cette opération du mouvement dans les lignes est l'hypothèse d'un être vaste, immense, compliqué, mais eurythmique, d'un animal plein de génie, souffrant et soupirant tous les soupirs et toutes les ambitions humaines.

26. This notion of the *thyrsus* or *caduceus* was taken by Baudelaire from De Quincey.

27. Le bâton, c'est votre volonté, droite, ferme et inébranlable; les fleurs, c'est la promenade de votre fantaisie autour de votre volonté; c'est l'élément féminin exécutant autour du mâle ses prestigieuses pirouettes. Ligne droite et ligne arabesque, intention et expression, roideur de la volonté, sinuosité du verbe, unité du but, variété des moyens, amalgame tout-puissant et

indivisible du génie, quel analyste aura le détestable courage de vous diviser et de vous séparer?

28. Both Barbara Johnson (1980) and Toril Moi (1985) have used this satisfying formulation before me.

29. ceux-là qui aiment la mer, la mer immense, tumultueuse et verte, l'eau informe et multiforme, le lieu où ils ne sont pas, la femme qu'ils ne connaissent pas, les fleurs sinistres qui ressemblent aux encensoirs d'une religion inconnue, les parfums qui troublent la volonté, et les animaux sauvages et voluptueux qui sont les emblèmes de leur folie.

30. C'est alors que la couleur parle, comme une voix profonde et vibrante; que les monuments se dressent et font saillie sur l'espace profond; que les animaux et les plantes, représentants du laid et du mal, articulent leur grimace non équivoque; que le parfum provoque la pensée et le souvenir correspondants; que la passion murmure ou rugit son langage éternellement semblable.

31. Goût invincible de la prostitution dans le coeur de l'homme, d'où naît son horreur de la solitude. – Il veut être *deux*. L'homme de génie veut être *un*, donc solitaire.

   La gloire, c'est rester *un*, et se prostituer d'une manière particulière.

   C'est cette horreur de la solitude, le besoin d'oublier son *moi* dans la chair extérieure, que l'homme appelle noblement *besoin* d'aimer.

32. Des rêves! toujours des rêves! et plus l'âme est ambitieuse et délicate, plus les rêves l'éloignent du possible. Chaque homme porte en lui sa dose d'opium naturel, incessamment sécrétée et renouvelée, et, de la naissance à la mort, combien comptons-nous d'heures remplies par la jouissance positive, par l'action réussie et décidée? Vivrons-nous jamais, passerons-nous jamais dans ce tableau qu'a peint mon esprit, ce tableau qui te ressemble?

33. Baudelaire had, from earliest childhood, dreamt of being an actor and proposed to write about the state, reputation, and situation in society of the actor (*Oeuvres complètes*, I: 702–3). He had always seen himself as acting a part and glorified in the ironical stance which deceived even his friends. Only into his poems did he put his whole self, his whole heart, love, and hate and even then he would swear, he says, 'that it is a book of *pure art*, of *antics*, of *juggling*, and I will be lying in my teeth' (Letter to Ancelle, 18 February 1866). But if you expose your whole heart in poems, it is still at several removes from reality.

34. Jean Mitry sees in the cinema a similar 'metaphoric expression founded on metonymy' (cit. Deleuze 1985: 208).

35. Aspect général; fraîcheur, clarté, blancheur, vivacité de couleur d'un parterre.

   Rubans, fanfreluches, tulles, gazes, mousselines, plumes, etc. . . .

   Les chapeaux font penser aux têtes, et ont l'air d'une galerie de têtes. Car chaque chapeau, par son caractère, appelle une tête et la fait voir aux yeux de l'esprit. Têtes coupées.

   Quelle tristesse dans la frivolité solitaire! Sentiment navrant de la ruine folâtre. Un monument de gaîté dans le désert. La frivolité dans l'abandon.

36. XLII will be discussed in Chapter 6 and XLVII in Chapter 7, although from perspectives other than the purely feminist.

3 TRUE COIN AND FALSE COIN: NARRATIVE ACTS AND NARRATIVE CONTRACTS

1. In equating a convention with a contract I am assuming that contracts can be implicit as well as explicit and that precedent can set up not only a convention, but a contractual obligation. The legal obligation of right of way would be an example in a different sphere. Thomas Pavel (1986: 119–23) quotes David Lewis's account of convention as modelled on co-ordination behaviour and on games. He quotes Hume:

   a common sense of interest ... produces a suitable resolution and behaviour. And this may properly enough be called a convention or agreement betwixt us, though without the interposition of a promise; since the actions of each of us have a reference to those of the other, and are performed upon the supposition that something is to be performed on the other part.

   (*A Treatise of Human Nature*, III.ii.2)

   This is roughly my view of the performer–audience relation.

2. Shoshana Felman (1983) rightly points out that these theoreticians have largely ignored the subversive effects of Austin's humour and the emphasis he places on satisfaction rather than truth.

3. Ubersfeld does not actually define this as a second illocutionary level, though she comes close to this position in *L'Ecole du spectateur* (1981). This concept of negativity complements but differs from Wolfgang Iser's (1978) notion of negativity which involves the exploitation of blanks, gaps, and the non-fulfilment of desires in the text for the purpose of co-opting the reader. See also Holub (1984: 94–5), Warning (1979: 337). This is an equally basic form of negation but involves textual lack rather than change in textual status. Ubersfeld's notion of a negative level is closer to Ingarden's 'quasi-judgement' (1973: 170–6).

4. For multiple examples, see Thompson, Stith, *Motif Index to the Folktale*, under section headings F342, F348, N558.

5. An interesting parallel is in Calvino (1957) *Il Barone Rampante*, where texts revert to dead leaves.

6. André Gide (1964) *Les Faux-Monnayeurs*, Paris: Livre de poche. The text of the false coin, for those who wish to compare, occurs on pp. 238–40.

7. Barbara Johnson (1979) uses the homology with reference to 'Invitation to the Voyage' (XVIII), comparing poetry to capital, which both produce plus value.

8. **La Fausse Monnaie** (XXVIII)
   Comme nous nous éloignions du bureau de tabac, mon ami fit un soigneux triage de sa monnaie; dans la poche gauche de son gilet il glissa de petites pièces d'or; dans la droite, de petites pièces d'argent; dans la poche gauche

de sa culotte, une masse de gros sols, et enfin, dans la droite, une pièce d'argent de deux francs qu'il avait particulièrement examinée.

'Singulière et minutieuse répartition!' me dis-je en moi-même.

Nous fîmes la rencontre d'un pauvre qui nous tendit sa casquette en tremblant. – Je ne connais rien de plus inquiétant que l'éloquence muette de ces yeux suppliants, qui contiennent à la fois, pour l'homme sensible qui sait y lire, tant d'humilité, tant de reproches. Il trouve quelque chose approchant cette profondeur de sentiment compliqué, dans les yeux larmoyants des chiens qu'on fouette.

L'offrande de mon ami fut beaucoup plus considérable que la mienne, et je lui dis: 'Vouz avez raison; après le plaisir d'être étonné, il n'en est pas de plus grand que celui de causer une surprise. – C'était la pièce fausse', me répondit-il tranquillement, comme pour se justifier de sa prodigalité.

Mais dans mon misérable cerveau, toujours occupé à chercher midi à quatorze heures (de quelle fatigante faculté la nature m'a fait cadeau!) entra soudainement cette idée qu'une pareille conduite, de la part de mon ami, n'était excusable que par le désir de créer un événement dans la vie de ce pauvre diable, peut-être même de connaître les conséquences diverses, funestes ou autres, que peut engendrer une pièce fausse dans la main d'un mendiant. Ne pouvait-elle pas se multiplier en pièces vraies? ne pouvait-elle pas aussi le conduire en prison? Un cabaretier, un boulanger, par exemple, allait peut-être le faire arrêter comme faux monnayeur ou comme propagateur de fausse monnaie. Tout aussi bien la pièce fausse serait peut-être, pour un pauvre petit spéculateur, le germe d'une richesse de quelques jours. Et ainsi ma fantaisie allait son train, prêtant des ailes à l'esprit de mon ami et tirant toutes les déductions possibles de toutes les hypothèses possibles.

Mais celui-ci rompit brusquement ma rêverie en reprenant mes propres paroles: 'Oui, vous avez raison; il n'est pas de plaisir plus doux que de surprendre un homme en lui donnant plus qu'il n'espère.'

Je le regardais dans le blanc des yeux, et je fus épouvanté de voir que ses yeux brillaient d'une incontestable candeur. Je vis alors clairement qu'il avait voulu faire à la fois la charité et une bonne affaire; gagner quarante sols et le coeur de Dieu; emporter le paradis économiquement; enfin attraper gratis un brevet d'homme charitable. Je lui aurais presque pardonné le désir de la criminelle jouissance dont je le supposais tout à l'heure capable; j'aurais trouvé curieux, singulier, qu'il s'amusât à compromettre les pauvres; mais je ne lui pardonnerai jamais l'ineptie de son calcul. On n'est jamais excusable d'être méchant, mais il y a quelque mérite à savoir qu'on l'est; et le plus irréparable des vices est de faire le mal par bêtise.

9. While inadequately discussed in Propp's *Morphology of the Folktale* (1968), and virtually omitted in his various charts, for reasons of space, it may be seen from the detailed analyses which constitute Appendix II, pp. 128–34, just how important the notion of the *negative* function is in the Proppian analysis.

10. cf. Smith (1979: 101–2):

A natural utterance constitutes, for the listener, not only an invitation and a provocation, but ultimately an *obligation*, to respond to the speaker.

When we 'listen' to someone, as distinguished from merely noticing or overhearing what he says – in other words, when we identify ourselves as his audience – we implicitly agree to make ourselves available to the speaker as the instrument of his interests. We agree not only to hear but to *heed* his promises, excuses, questions and commands – and also, of course, his assertions. . . . We are commonly conscious of the social risks that the *speaker* incurs when he speaks (or writes, or publishes). . . . But there is also a risk involved for anyone who identifies himself as a *listener*, a fact apparently well-appreciated by children, servants, Army recruits, and others who, having been exploited as 'captive audiences' in the past, either learn to avoid verbal encounters or develop functional deafness.

11. Smith (1979: 112–14) gives very acute examples of authorial misuse of fictive discourse.
12. See Mannoni (1969: 96–8) for further discussion of negation (*la dénégation*).
13. An earlier version of part of this chapter appeared in Gunew and Reid (1984).

4 SCENE AND OSCENE: THE CONSTITUTION OF NARRATIVE AUDIENCES AND
GENDERED READING

1. Pratt claims that

   a description of display texts, and indeed a basic typology of assertions may have to wait for a theory of perlocutions. Jerry Sadock's hypothesis, Sadock, 1974, that all speech acts are perlocutions and that illocutions are only one subset of perlocutions, seems to suggest a possible way out for the display text.

   (1977: 151n.)

2. Picard (1986) detects three elements in the actual reader: a) *liseur*, the part which remains anchored in reality; b) *lu*, the part which identifies with the text; c) *lectant*, the part which uses education and intertextuality to produce an interpretation.
3. This implied audience is closer to Rabinowitz's narrative audience than to Iser's implied reader. See also Booth (1961: 138), and, for a rather different approach, Genette (1983: 183).
4. Twice in *projets de préface* (*Oeuvres complètes*, I: 181–2) and twice in *Journaux intimes* (I: 660).
5. **La Femme Sauvage et La Petite-Maîtresse** (XI)
   'Vraiment, ma chère, vous me fatiguez sans mesure et sans pitié; on dirait, à vous entendre soupirer, que vous souffrez plus que les glaneuses sex-agénaires et que les vieilles mendiantes qui ramassent des croûtes de pain à la porte des cabarets.
   'Si, au moins vos soupirs exprimaient le remords, ils vous feraient quelque honneur; mais ils ne traduisent que la satiété du bien-être et l'accablement du repos. Et puis, vous ne cessez de vous répandre en paroles inutiles: "Aimez-moi bien! j'en ai tant besoin! Consolez-moi par-ci, caressez-moi par-là!" Tenez, je veux essayer de vous guérir; nous en

trouverons peut-être le moyen, pour deux sols, au milieu d'une fête, et sans aller bien loin.

'Considérons bien, je vous prie, cette solide cage de fer derrière laquelle s'agite, hurlant comme un damné, secouant les barreaux comme un orang-outang exaspéré par l'exil, imitant, dans la perfection, tantôt les bonds circulaires du tigre, tantôt les dandinements stupides de l'ours blanc, ce monstre poilu dont la forme imite assez vaguement la vôtre.

'Ce monstre est un de ces animaux qu'on appelle généralement "mon ange!", c'est-à-dire une femme. L'autre monstre, celui qui crie à tue-tête, un bâton à la main, est un mari. Il a enchaîné sa femme légitime comme une bête, et il la montre dans les faubourgs, les jours de foire, avec permission des magistrats, cela va sans dire.

'Faites bien attention! Voyez avec quelle voracité (non simulée peut-être!) elle déchire des lapins vivants et des volailles piaillantes que lui jette son cornac. "Allons," dit-il, "il ne faut pas manger tout son bien en un jour", et, sur cette sage parole, il lui arrache cruellement la proie, dont les boyaux dévidés restent un instant accrochés aux dents de la bête féroce, de la femme, veux-je dire.

'Allons! un bon coup de bâton pour la calmer! car elle darde des yeux terribles de convoitise sur la nourriture enlevée. Grand Dieu! le bâton n'est pas un bâton de comédie, avez-vous entendu résonner la chair, malgré le poil postiche? Aussi les yeux lui sortent maintenant de la tête, elle hurle *plus naturellement*. Dans sa rage, elle étincelle tout entière, comme le fer qu'on bat.

'Telles sont les moeurs conjugales de ces deux descendants d'Eve et d'Adam, ces oeuvres de vos mains, ô mon Dieu! Cette femme est incontestablement malheureuse, quoique après tout, peut-être, les jouissances titillantes de la gloire ne lui soient pas inconnues. Il y a des malheurs plus irrémédiables, et sans compensation. Mais dans le monde où elle a été jetée, elle n'a jamais pu croire que la femme méritât une autre destinée.

'Maintenant, à nous deux, chère précieuse! A voir les enfers dont le monde est peuplé, que voulez-vous que je pense de votre joli enfer, vous qui ne reposez que sur des étoffes aussi douces que votre peau, qui ne mangez que de la viande cuite, et pour qui un domestique habile prend soin de découper les morceaux?

'Et que peuvent signifier pour moi tous ces petits soupirs qui gonflent votre poitrine parfumée, robuste coquette? Et toutes ces affectations apprises dans les livres, et cette infatigable mélancolie, faite pour inspirer au spectateur un tout autre sentiment que la pitié? En vérité, il me prend quelquefois envie de vous apprendre ce que c'est que le vrai malheur.

'A vous voir ainsi, ma belle délicate, les pieds dans la fange et les yeux tournés vaporeusement vers le ciel, comme pour lui demander un roi, on dirait vraisemblablement une jeune grenouille qui invoquerait l'idéal. Si vous méprisez le soliveau (ce que je suis maintenant, comme vous savez bien), gare la grue *qui vous croquera, vous gobera et vous tuera à son plaisir!*

'Tant poëte que je sois, je ne suis pas aussi dupe que vous voudriez le croire, et si vous me fatiguez trop souvent de vos *précieuses* pleurnicheries, je vous traiterai en *femme sauvage*, ou je vous jetterai par la fenêtre, comme une bouteille vide.'

6. Lanser (1981: 184) notes the importance of ideology in the textual *stance*.

7. I keep *entreteneur* in French because English appears to have no single term for the man who keeps a mistress. Another prose poem 'Le vieil entreteneur' was also planned (*Oeuvres complètes*, I: 367) and a drama 'La femme entretenue sans le savoir' (I: 645). 'L'Entreteneur' also features in 'Titres et canevas' (I: 591) as does 'Vieil entreteneur' (I: 594).

8. 'Les voluptés de l'entreteneur tiennent à la fois de l'ange et du propriétaire. Charité et férocité. Elles sont même indépendantes du sexe, de la beauté et du genre animal.'

9. e.g. 'Moi-même, dans un coin de l'antre taciturne,
Je me vis accoudé, froid, muet, enviant' (*Oeuvres complètes*, I: 96).

10. cf. Ubersfeld (1981: 112), who postulates that the spectator of the play within the play receives twice negated, that is, positive signs.

Thus is established for the spectator an uncertainty, a set question concerning the status of theatrical signs and their truth value. What is uncontestably said is 'We are at the theatre'; that is what the transmitted signs coming from the B zone, passing by A's gaze, say, while the signs coming directly from A or B and which have not passed 'through the relay' are suitably negative, in other words, their truth value is negated. The presence of actor-spectators on stage is a sort of materialisation of the premises: 'We are at the theatre, and signs have truth value only on stage.'

One understands how the theatre in the theatre says: (a) we are at the theatre, the theatre space inside the larger space being the display space of theatrality; (b) what we learn by this retransmitted channel is the truth.

11. Elle a faim et elle veut manger. Soif et elle veut boire.
Elle est en rut et elle veut être foutue.
Le beau mérite!
La femme est *naturelle*, c'est-à-dire abominable.

12. Quand même les deux amants seraient très-épris et très-pleins de désirs réciproques, l'un des deux sera toujours plus calme ou moins possédé que l'autre. Celui-là, ou celle-là, c'est l'opérateur, ou le bourreau; l'autre, c'est le sujet, la victime.

13. As Toril Moi remarks, feminist criticism should 'be aware of the politics of aesthetic categories as well as of the implied aesthetics of political approaches to art' (1985: 86).

5 IN THE EYES OF THE OTHER: THE CREATION OF NARRATIVE SPACE

1. As a corrective to this rather simplified version of connotation see Threadgold (1986: 28–31).

2. **Les Yeux des pauvres** (XXVI)
Ah! vous voulez savoir pourquoi je vous hais aujourd'hui. Il vous sera sans doute moins facile de le comprendre qu'à moi de vous l'expliquer; car vous êtes, je crois, le plus bel exemple d'imperméabilité féminine qui se puisse rencontrer.

Nous avions passé ensemble une longue journée qui m'avait paru courte. Nous nous étions bien promis que toutes nos pensées nous seraient communes à l'un et à l'autre, et que nos deux âmes désormais n'en feraient plus qu'une; – un rêve qui n'a rien d'original, après tout, si ce n'est que, rêvé par tous les hommes, il n'a été réalisé par aucun.

Le soir, un peu fatiguée, vous voulûtes vous asseoir devant un café neuf qui formait le coin d'un boulevard neuf, encore tout plein de gravois et montrant déjà glorieusement ses splendeurs inachevées. Le café étincelait. Le gaz lui-même y déployait toute l'ardeur d'un début, et éclairait de toutes ses forces les murs aveuglants de blancheur, les nappes éblouissantes des miroirs, les ors des baguettes et des corniches, les pages aux joues rebondies traînés par les chiens en laisse, les dames riant au faucon perché sur leur poing, les nymphes et les déesses portant sur leur tête des fruits, des pâtés et du gibier, les Hébés et les Ganymèdes présentant à bras tendu la petite amphore à bavaroises ou l'obélisque bicolore des glaces panachées; toute l'histoire et toute la mythologie mises au service de la goinfrerie.

Droit devant nous, sur la chaussée, était planté un brave homme d'une quarantaine d'années, au visage fatigué, à la barbe grisonnante, tenant d'une main un petit garçon et portant sur l'autre bras un petit être trop faible pour marcher. Il remplissait l'office de bonne et faisait prendre à ses enfants l'air du soir. Tous en guenilles. Ces trois visages étaient extraordinairement sérieux, et ces six yeux contemplaient fixement le café nouveau avec une admiration égale, mais nuancée diversement par l'âge.

Les yeux du père disaient: 'Que c'est beau! que c'est beau! on dirait que tout l'or du pauvre monde est venu se porter sur ces murs.' – Les yeux du petit garçon: 'Que c'est beau! que c'est beau! mais c'est une maison où peuvent seuls entrer les gens qui ne sont pas comme nous.' – Quant aux yeux du plus petit, ils étaient trop fascinés pour exprimer autre chose qu'une joie stupide et profonde.

Les chansonniers disent que le plaisir rend l'âme bonne et amollit le coeur. La chanson avait raison ce soir-là, relativement à moi. Non seulement j'étais attendri par cette famille d'yeux, mais je me sentais un peu honteux de nos verres et de nos carafes, plus grands que notre soif. Je tournais mes regards vers les vôtres, cher amour, pour y lire *ma* pensée; je plongeais dans vos yeux si beaux et si bizarrement doux, dans vos yeux verts, habités par le Caprice et inspirés par la Lune, quand vous me dîtes: 'Ces gens-là me sont insupportables avec leurs yeux ouverts comme des portes cochères! Ne pourriez-vous pas prier le maître du café de les éloigner d'ici?'

Tant il est difficile de s'entendre, mon cher ange, et tant la pensée est incommunicable, même entre gens qui s'aiment!

3. See Stanzel (1984: 189): 'The use of the personal pronoun facilitates the transfer of the reader to the consciousness of the character or the reader's empathy with the character's situation to a greater extent than does the mentioning of the name.'

4. Bakhtin (1981: 97–8) points out the great importance of the motif of the *meeting* in the definition of the represented space.

5. The street is the result of social processes (of house construction, traffic, trade, living in a place). Its signifiers are also signifiers of these processes. To the signifiers of the real street (signifiers of specific social processes) we are at liberty in our stage representations to add signifiers of social pro-

cesses which do not *show* the real street but which are signifiers of social processes which *produce* it (maybe price tags for houses or mortality statistics).

They now become signifiers of specific places (of factory yards, of rooms), and thus they are at the same time signifiers of specific social processes (of the production of goods, of living in a place).

(Brecht 1967: 15, 461; tr. H. Maclean)

6. See Barthes (1974: 35) on the structural role of the intermediate.

7. Baudelaire's private notebooks stress the importance of condensation and centralization, the centripetal movement of the subject or the text, as opposed to the centrifugal movement of vaporization.

8. Sur une route, derrière la grille d'un vaste jardin, au bout duquel apparaissait la blancheur d'un joli château frappé par le soleil, se tenait un enfant beau et frais, habillé de ces vêtements de campagne si pleins de coquetterie.

Le luxe, l'insouciance et le spectacle habituel de la richesse rendent ces enfants-là si jolis, qu'on les croirait faits d'une autre pâte que les enfants de la médiocrité ou de la pauvreté.

A côté de lui, gisait sur l'herbe un joujou splendide, aussi frais que son maître, verni, doré, vêtu d'une robe pourpre, et couvert de plumets et de verroteries. Mais l'enfant ne s'occupait pas de son joujou préféré, et voici ce qu'il regardait:

De l'autre côté de la grille, sur la route, entre les chardons et les orties, il y avait un autre enfant, sale, chétif, fuligineux, un de ces marmots-parias dont un oeil impartial découvrirait la beauté, si, comme l'oeil du connaisseur devine une peinture idéale sous un vernis de carrossier, il le nettoyait de la répugnante patine de la misère.

A travers ces barreaux symboliques séparant deux mondes, la grande route et le château, l'enfant pauvre montrait à l'enfant riche son propre joujou, que celui-ci examinait avidement comme un objet rare et inconnu. Or, ce joujou, que le petit souillon agaçait, agitait et secouait dans une boîte grillée, c'était un rat vivant! Les parents, par économie sans doute, avaient tiré le joujou de la vie elle-même.

Et les deux enfants se riaient l'un à l'autre fraternellement, avec des dents d'une *égale* blancheur.

6 FOR MEN'S EARS ONLY: NARRATIVE POWER PLAY AND THE SEXUAL/TEXTUAL NEXUS

1. See Picard (1986) for a critique of Caillois and an exposition of the relationship between game theory and reading.

2. Baudelaire on the dandy: 'un crédit indéfini pourrait lui suffire' ('Le Peintre de la vie moderne', *Oeuvres complètes*, II: 710).

3. **Portraits de maîtresses** (XLII)

Dans un boudoir d'hommes, c'est-à-dire dans un fumoir attenant à un élégant tripot, quatre hommes fumaient et buvaient. Ils n'étaient précisément ni jeunes ni vieux, ni beaux ni laids; mais, vieux ou jeunes, ils portaient cette distinction non méconnaissable de vétérans de la joie, cet indescriptible je ne sais quoi, cette tristesse froide et railleuse qui dit clairement: 'Nous avons fortement vécu, et nous cherchons ce que nous pourrions aimer et estimer.'

L'un d'eux jeta la causerie sur le sujet des femmes. Il eût été plus philosophique de n'en pas parler du tout; mais il y a des gens d'esprit qui, après boire, ne méprisent pas les conversations banales. On écoute alors celui qui parle, comme on écouterait de la musique de danse.

'Tous les hommes, disait celui-ci, ont eu l'âge de Chérubin: c'est l'époque où, faute de dryades, on embrasse, sans dégoût, le tronc des chênes. C'est le premier degré de l'amour. Au second degré, on commence à choisir. Pouvoir délibérer, c'est déjà une décadence. C'est alors qu'on recherche décidément la beauté. Pour moi, messieurs, je me fais gloire d'être arrivé, depuis longtemps, à l'époque climatérique du troisième degré où la beauté elle-même ne suffit plus, si elle n'est assaisonnée par le parfum, la parure, et caetera. J'avouerai même que j'aspire quelquefois, comme à un bonheur inconnu, à un certain quatrième degré qui doit marquer le calme absolu. Mais, durant toute ma vie, excepté à l'âge de Chérubin, j'ai été plus sensible que tout autre à l'énervante sottise, à l'irritante médiocrité des femmes. Ce que j'aime surtout dans les animaux, c'est leur candeur. Jugez donc combien j'ai dû souffrir par ma dernière maîtresse.

'C'était la bâtarde d'un prince. Belle, cela va sans dire; sans cela, pourquoi l'aurais-je prise? Mais elle gâtait cette grande qualité par une ambition malséante et difforme. C'était une femme qui voulait toujours faire l'homme. "Vous n'êtes pas un homme! Ah! si j'étais un homme! De nous deux, c'est moi qui suis l'homme!" Tels étaient les insupportables refrains qui sortaient de cette bouche d'où je n'aurais voulu voir s'envoler que des chansons. A propos d'un livre, d'un poème, d'un opéra pour lequel je laissais échapper mon admiration: "Vous croyez peut-être que cela est très fort? disait-elle aussitôt; est-ce que vous vous connaissez en force?" et elle argumentait.

'Un beau jour elle s'est mise à la chimie; de sorte qu'entre ma bouche et la sienne je trouvais désormais un masque de verre. Avec tout cela, fort bégueule. Si parfois je la bousculais par un geste un peu trop amoureux, elle se convulsait comme une sensitive violée...

— Comment cela a-t-il fini? dit l'un des trois autres. Je ne vous savais pas si patient.

— Dieu, reprit-il, mit le remède dans le mal. Un jour je trouvai cette Minerve, affamée de force idéale, en tête à tête avec mon domestique, et dans une situation qui m'obligea à me retirer discrètement pour ne pas les faire rougir. Le soir je les congédiai tous les deux, en leur payant les arrérages de leurs gages.

— Pour moi, reprit l'interrupteur, je n'ai à me plaindre que de moi-même. Le bonheur est venu habiter chez moi, et je ne l'ai pas reconnu. La destinée m'avait, en ces derniers temps, octroyé la jouissance d'une femme qui était bien la plus douce, la plus soumise et la plus dévouée des créatures, et toujours prête! et sans enthousiasme! "Je le veux bien, puisque cela vous est agréable." C'était sa réponse ordinaire. Vous donneriez la bastonnade à ce mur ou à ce canapé, que vous en tireriez plus de soupirs que n'en tiraient du sein de ma maîtresse les élans de l'amour le plus forcené. Après un an de vie commune, elle m'avoua qu'elle n'avait jamais connu le plaisir. Je me dégoûtai de ce duel inégal, et cette fille incomparable se maria. J'eus plus tard la fantaisie de la revoir, et elle me dit, en me montrant six beaux enfants: "Eh bien! mon cher ami, l'épouse est encore aussi *vierge* que l'était votre maîtresse." Rien n'était changé dans cette personne. Quelquefois je la regrette: j'aurais dû l'épouser.'

Les autres se mirent à rire, et un troisième dit à son tour:

'Messieurs, j'ai connu des jouissances que vous avez peut-être négligées. Je veux parler du comique dans l'amour, et d'un comique qui n'exclut pas l'admiration. J'ai plus admiré ma dernière maîtresse que vous n'avez pu, je crois, haïr ou aimer les vôtres. Et tout le monde l'admirait autant que moi. Quand nous entrions dans un restaurant, au bout de quelques minutes, chacun oubliait de manger pour la contempler. Les garçons eux-mêmes et la dame du comptoir ressentaient cette extase contagieuse jusqu'à oublier leurs devoirs. Bref, j'ai vécu quelque temps en tête à tête avec un *phénomène* vivant. Elle mangeait, mâchait, broyait, dévorait, engloutissait, mais avec l'air le plus léger et le plus insouciant du monde. Elle m'a tenu ainsi longtemps en extase. Elle avait une manière douce, rêveuse, anglaise et romanesque de dire: "J'ai faim!" Et elle répétait ces mots jour et nuit en montrant les plus jolies dents du monde, qui vous eussent attendris et égayés à la fois. – J'aurais pu faire ma fortune en la montrant dans les foires comme *monstre polyphage*. Je la nourrissais bien; et cependant elle m'a quitté . . . – Pour un fournisseur aux vivres, sans doute? – Quelque chose d'approchant, une espèce d'employé dans l'intendance qui, par quelque tour de bâton à lui connu, fournit peut-être à cette pauvre enfant la ration de plusieurs soldats. C'est du moins ce que j'ai supposé.

– Moi, dit le quatrième, j'ai enduré des souffrances atroces par le contraire de ce qu'on reproche en général à l'égoïste femelle. Je vous trouve mal venus, trop fortunés mortels, à vous plaindre des imperfections de vos maîtresses!'

Cela fut dit d'un ton fort sérieux, par un homme d'un aspect doux et posé, d'une physionomie presque cléricale, malheureusement illuminée par des yeux d'un gris clair, de ces yeux dont le regard dit: 'Je veux!' ou: 'Il faut!' ou bien: 'Je ne pardonne jamais!'

'Si, nerveux comme je vous connais, vous G . . ., lâches et légers comme vous êtes, vous deux K . . . et J . . ., vous aviez été accouplés à une certaine femme de ma connaissance, ou vous vous seriez enfuis, ou vous seriez morts. Moi, j'ai survécu, comme vous voyez. Figurez-vous une personne incapable de commettre une erreur de sentiment ou de calcul; figurez-vous une sérénité désolante de caractère; un dévouement sans comédie et sans emphase; une douceur sans faiblesse; une énergie sans violence. L'histoire de mon amour ressemble à un interminable voyage sur une surface pure et polie comme un miroir, vertigineusement monotone, qui aurait réfléchi tous mes sentiments et mes gestes avec l'exactitude ironique de ma propre conscience, de sorte que je ne pouvais pas me permettre un geste ou un sentiment déraisonnable sans apercevoir immédiatement le reproche muet de mon inséparable spectre. L'amour m'apparaissait comme une tutelle. Que de sottises elle m'a empêché de faire, que je regrette de n'avoir pas commises! Que de dettes payées malgré moi! Elle me privait de tous les bénéfices que j'aurais pu tirer de ma folie personnelle. Avec une froide et infranchissable règle, elle barrait tous mes caprices. Pour comble d'horreur, elle n'exigeait pas de reconnaissance, le danger passé. Combien de fois ne me suis-je pas retenu de lui sauter à la gorge, en lui criant: "Sois donc imparfaite, misérable! afin que je puisse t'aimer sans malaise et sans colère!" Pendant plusieurs années, je l'ai admirée, le coeur plein de haine. Enfin ce n'est pas moi qui en suis mort!

– Ah! firent les autres, elle est donc morte?

– Oui, cela ne pouvait continuer ainsi. L'amour était devenu pour moi un cauchemar accablant. Vaincre ou mourir, comme dit la Politique, telle était l'alternative que m'imposait la destinée! Un soir, dans un bois . . . au bord d'une mare . . . , après une mélancolique promenade où ses yeux, à elle, réfléchissaient la douceur du ciel, et où mon coeur, à moi, était crispé comme l'enfer. . .

– Quoi!

– Comment!

– Que voulez-vous dire?

– C'était inévitable. J'ai trop le sentiment de l'équité pour battre, outrager ou congédier un serviteur irréprochable. Mais il fallait accorder ce sentiment avec l'horreur que cet être m'inspirait; me débarrasser de cet être sans lui manquer de respect. Que vouliez-vous que je fisse d'elle, *puisqu'elle était parfaite*?'

Les trois autres compagnons regardèrent celui-ci avec un regard vague et légèrement hébété, comme feignant de ne pas comprendre et comme avouant implicitement qu'ils ne se sentaient pas, quant à eux, capables d'une action aussi rigoureuse, quoique suffisamment expliquée d'ailleurs.

Ensuite on fit apporter de nouvelles bouteilles, pour tuer le Temps qui a la vie si dure, et accélérer la Vie qui coule si lentement.

4. See Lanser (1981: 140) and Rousset (1982: 32) on the implications of the distinction between the public and the private narrator.

5. *Hommes* is used twice in the first two lines, and words paradigmatic of gender dominate throughout.

6. Baudelaire planned a complete work 'La Maîtresse vierge'.

7. cf. Brooks (1984: 143):

If plots seem frequently to be about investments of desire and the effort to bind and master intensive levels of energy, this corresponds on the one hand to narratives thematically oriented toward ambition, possession, mastery of the erotic object and of the world, and on the other hand to a certain experience of reading narrative, itself a process of reaching for possession and mastery. Speaking reductively, without nuance, one might say that on the one hand narrative tends toward a thematics of the desired, potentially possessable body, and on the other toward a readerly experience of consuming.

8. See especially the letter to Mme Aupick, 6 May 1861, in *Correspondance générale*, III. For a discussion of the biographical and psychoanalytical basis of this portrait see Mauron (1966).

9. For the idea of woman as the 'mystifying center' and the 'negative reflection', see Kristeva, 'Word, dialogue and novel' (1980).

10. 'L'épouvantable mariage de l'homme avec lui-même', *Les Paradis artificiels* (*Oeuvres complètes*, I: 426–41).

11. The profound emotional effect of being placed under the *tutelle* of a *conseil judiciaire* is documented at length in Baudelaire's *Correspondance*.

12. Given the present context and connotations we can read this also as *tue-t-elle*, with the implied message, kill or be killed. For an excellent discussion of figurative killing and the notion of killing time in conjunction with 'Le galant tireur' (XLIII), the text which follows 'Portraits de maîtresses', see Johnson (1979. 81–92).

13. See Ross Chambers, *Story and Situation: Narrative Seduction and the Power of Fiction* (1984) and 'Violence du récit: Boccace, Mérimée, Cortazar' (1986).

14. Ten in one paragraph. Note also that in the French text the constantly reiterated pronoun *elle* reverts in grammatical anaphora to *femme*, but in phonetic anaphora to the key word *tutelle*.

15. Baudelaire frequently experienced the confusion of fact and fiction induced by his own narratives in his hearers. See, *inter alia*, *Oeuvres complètes*, II: 854.

16. On narrative as trap see Louis Marin (1978: Chapter 1).

17. The frame narrator needs to speak in the third person to stress the difference between his aesthetic role and the existential roles of the first-person narrators (Stanzel 1984: 93).

18. Baudelaire was well aware of the *lectrice*. See particularly the ending of an early piece in a similar vein, *Choix de maximes consolantes sur l'amour*, *Oeuvres complètes*, I: 552.

19. cf. 'Moi qui vends ma pensée et veux être auteur' (*Oeuvres complètes*, I: 203).

7 LISTENING EAR AND WHISPERING VOICE: ANALYSIS AND DESIRE

1. Suleiman (1986) sums up the traditional Freudian position which attributes this to counter-transference, and the more radical Lacanian, which sees transference itself as a network of *two* desires.

2. See particularly Blin, *Le Sadisme de Baudelaire* (1948), Mauron, *Le dernier Baudelaire* (1966), Bersani, *Baudelaire and Freud* (1977). The best Lacanian approach is that of Barbara Johnson (1979).

3. **Mademoiselle Bistouri** (XLVII)
   Comme j'arrivais à l'extrémité du faubourg, sous les éclairs du gaz, je sentis un bras qui se coulait doucement sous le mien, et j'entendis une voix qui me disait à l'oreille: 'Vous êtes médecin, monsieur?'
   Je regardai; c'était une grande fille, robuste, aux yeux très ouverts, légèrement fardée, les cheveux flottant au vent avec les brides de son bonnet.
   ' – Non; je ne suis pas médecin. Laissez-moi passer. – Oh! si! vous êtes médecin. Je le vois bien. Venez chez moi. Vous serez bien content de moi, allez! – Sans doute, j'irai vous voir, mais plus tard, *après le médecin*, que diable! . . . – Ah! ah! – fit-elle, toujours suspendue à mon bras, et en éclatant de rire, – vous êtes un médecin farceur, j'en ai connu plusieurs dans ce genre-là. Venez.'

J'aime passionnément le mystère, parce que j'ai toujours l'espoir de le débrouiller. Je me laissai donc entraîner par cette compagne, ou plutôt par cette énigme inespérée.

J'omets la description du taudis; on peut la trouver dans plusieurs vieux poëtes français bien connus. Seulement, détail non aperçu par Régnier, deux ou trois portraits de docteurs célèbres étaient suspendus aux murs.

Comme je fus dorloté! Grand feu, vin chaud, cigares; et en m'offrant ces bonnes choses et en allumant elle-même un cigare, la bouffonne créature me disait: 'Faites comme chez vous, mon ami, mettez-vous à l'aise. Ça vous rappellera l'hôpital et le bon temps de la jeunesse. – Ah ça! où donc avez-vous gagné ces cheveux blancs? Vous n'étiez pas ainsi, il n'y a pas encore bien longtemps, quand vous étiez interne de L. . . . Je me souviens que c'était vous qui l'assistiez dans les opérations graves. En voilà un homme qui aime couper, tailler et rogner! C'était vous qui lui tendiez les instruments, les fils et les éponges. – Et comme, l'opération faite, il disait fièrement, en regardant sa montre: "Cinq minutes, messieurs!" – Oh! moi, je vais partout. Je connais bien ces Messieurs.'

Quelques instants plus tard, me tutoyant, elle reprenait son antienne, et me disait: 'Tu es médecin, n'est-ce pas, mon chat?'

Cet inintelligible refrain me fit sauter sur mes jambes. 'Non! criai-je furieux.

– Chirurgien, alors?

– Non! non! à moins que ce ne soit pour te couper la tête! S. . . s. . . c. . . de s. . . m. . . !

– Attends, reprit-elle, tu vas voir.'

Et elle tira de l'armoire une liasse de papiers, qui n'était autre chose que la collection des portraits des médecins illustres de ce temps, lithographiés par Maurin, qu'on a pu voir étalée pendant plusieurs années sur le quai Voltaire.

'Tiens! le reconnais-tu celui-ci?

– Oui! c'est X. Le nom est au bas d'ailleurs; mais je le connais personnellement.

– Je savais bien! Tiens! voilà Z., celui qui disait à son cours, en parlant de X.: "Ce monstre qui porte sur son visage la noirceur de son âme!" Tout cela, parce que l'autre n'était pas de son avis dans la même affaire! Comme on riait de ça à l'école, dans le temps! Tu t'en souviens? – Tiens, voilà K., celui qui dénonçait au gouvernement les insurgés qu'il soignait à son hôpital. C'était le temps des émeutes. Comment est-ce possible qu'un si bel homme ait si peu de coeur? – Voici maintenant W., un fameux médecin anglais; je l'ai attrapé à son voyage à Paris. Il a l'air d'une demoiselle, n'est-ce pas?'

Et comme je touchais à un paquet ficelé, posé aussi sur le guéridon: 'Attends un peu, dit-elle; – ça, c'est les internes, et ce paquet-ci, c'est les externes.'

Et elle déploya en éventail une masse d'images photographiques, représentant des physionomies beaucoup plus jeunes.

'Quand nous nous reverrons, tu me donneras ton portrait, n'est-ce pas, chéri?

– Mais, lui dis-je, suivant à mon tour, moi aussi, mon idée fixe, – pourquoi me crois-tu médecin?

– C'est que tu es si gentil et si bon pour les femmes!

– Singulière logique! me dis-je à moi-même.

– Oh! je ne m'y trompe guère; j'en ai connu un bon nombre. J'aime tant ces messieurs, que, bien que je ne sois pas malade, je vais quelquefois les voir, rien que pour les voir. Il y en a qui me disent froidement: "Vous n'êtes pas malade du tout!" Mais il y en a d'autres qui me comprennent, parce que je leur fais des mines.

– Et quand ils ne te comprennent pas . . . ?

– Dame! comme je les ai dérangés *inutilement*, je laisse dix francs sur la cheminée. – C'est si bon et si doux, ces hommes-là! – J'ai découvert à la Pitié un petit interne, qui est joli comme un ange, et qui est poli! et qui travaille, le pauvre garçon! Ses camarades m'ont dit qu'il n'avait pas le sou, parce que ses parents sont des pauvres qui ne peuvent rien lui envoyer. Cela m'a donné confiance. Après tout, je suis assez belle femme, quoique pas trop jeune. Je lui ai dit: "Viens me voir, viens me voir souvent. Et avec moi, ne te gêne pas; je n'ai pas besoin d'argent." Mais tu comprends que je lui ai fait entendre ça par une foule de façons; je ne le lui ai pas dit tout crûment; j'avais si peur de l'humilier, ce cher enfant! – Eh bien! croirais-tu que j'ai une drôle d'envie que je n'ose pas lui dire? – Je voudrais qu'il vînt me voir avec sa trousse et son tablier, même avec un peu de sang dessus!'

Elle dit cela d'un air fort candide, comme un homme sensible dirait à une comédienne qu'il aimerait: 'Je veux vous voir vêtue du costume que vous portiez dans ce fameux rôle que vous avez créé.'

Moi, m'obstinant, je repris: 'Peux-tu te souvenir de l'époque et de l'occasion où est née en toi cette passion si particulière?'

Difficilement je me fis comprendre; enfin j'y parvins. Mais alors elle me répondit d'un air très triste, et même, autant que je peux me souvenir, en détournant les yeux: 'Je ne sais pas . . . je ne me souviens pas.'

Quelles bizarreries ne trouve-t-on pas dans une grande ville, quand on sait se promener et regarder? La vie fourmille de monstres innocents. – Seigneur, mon Dieu! vous, le Créateur, vous, le Maître; vous qui avez fait la Loi et la Liberté; vous, le souverain qui laissez faire, vous, le juge, qui pardonnez; vous qui êtes plein de motifs et de causes, et qui avez peut-être mis dans mon esprit le goût de l'horreur pour convertir mon coeur, comme la guérison au bout d'une lame; Seigneur, ayez pitié, ayez pitié des fous et des folles! O Créateur! peut-il exister des monstres aux yeux de Celui-là seul qui sait pourquoi ils existent, comment ils *se sont faits* et comment ils auraient pu *ne pas se faire*?

4. At this point the woman switches to the *tu* form of the second-person pronoun. This implies not only intimacy, but almost certainly that sexual intercourse has taken place, or that she expects it.

5. Bellemin-Noël (1986) has recently provided a more traditional (masculine) analysis of 'Mademoiselle Bistouri' as a picture of the phallic, castrating mother, the maternal prostitute who assuages her guilt by bloody incest fantasies. He sees the castration phantasm expressed in 'to cut off your head' and attaches great importance to the original swear words (in full in the

manuscript 'Sacré saint ciboire de sainte maquerelle!') which suggest female profanation and the assimilation of the Virgin to the Whore.

6. For an analysis of the Baudelairean preoccupation with abortion see Maclean (1982) 'Baudelaire and the paradox of procreation'.

7. The intertextual reference here is indeed to an early text of Baudelaire's own in which the hero, having finally succeeded in winning a night with the actress he desires, sees her advance towards him 'in the radiant and sacred splendour of her nudity' and cries: 'I want Columbine, give me back Columbine; give her back as she appeared to me the evening when she drove me mad with her fantastic costume and her fairground bodice' ('La Fanfarlo', *Oeuvres complètes*, I: 557).

8. The story, opening on the suggestion of prostitution and closing with a prayer, moves between the two extremes which characterize obsession, sexuality, and sanctity. The scandal which links these two extremes is similar to that which Deleuze sees in the work of Buñuel:

> the two poles of the fetish, fetishes of Good and fetishes of Evil, holy fetishes and fetishes of crime or sexuality, meet and change places. . . . One might call the first relics and the others, using the vocabulary of sorcery, *vults* or spell-binders, they are two aspects of the same symptom.
>
> (Deleuze 1983: 183)

9. The two other gleanings in this column would both have been of special interest to Baudelaire, since one was a slightly satirical piece about the doings of l'Abbé Listz (sic), the great pianist turned religious but *not* unworldly, according to *L'Avenir national*, and the other a touching story about the great animal tamer, Madame Leprince, giving the whole proceeds of her act with a tiger and two hyenas to rescue a fellow *saltimbanque* from destitution. The whole column, in fact, was so Baudelairean in tone that it is possible it was sent to him by a friend, although he was in Belgium at the time.

8 THEORY AND PRACTICE: ALLEGORIES OF RECEPTION

1. There are two mathematical instances which never cease referring back to one another, one embracing the other, the other shifting into the one, but both very different in spite of their union: they are the theorem and the problem. . . . Problematics is distinguished from theorematics (or constructivism from axiomatics) by the fact that the theorem develops internal relations from principle to consequences, whereas the problem introduces an event from outside, subtraction, addition, section, which constitutes its own conditions and determines the 'case' or the cases.

(Deleuze 1985: 227)

2. **Assommons les pauvres!** (XLIX)
Pendant quinze jours je m'étais confiné dans ma chambre, et je m'étais entouré des livres à la mode dans ce temps-là (il y a seize ou dix-sept ans); je veux parler des livres où il est traité de l'art de rendre les peuples heureux, sages et riches, en vingt-quatre heures. J'avais donc digéré, – avalé, veux-je dire, – toutes les élucubrations de tous ces entrepreneurs de bonheur public, – de ceux qui conseillent à tous les pauvres de se faire esclaves, et de

ceux qui leur persuadent qu'ils sont tous des rois détrônés. – On ne trouvera pas surprenant que je fusse alors dans un état d'esprit avoisinant le vertige ou la stupidité.

Il m'avait semblé seulement que je sentais, confiné au fond de mon intellect, le germe obscur d'une idée supérieure à toutes les formules de bonne femme dont j'avais récemment parcouru le dictionnaire. Mais ce n'était que l'idée d'une idée, quelque chose d'infiniment vague.

Et je sortis avec une grand soif. Car le goût passionné des mauvaises lectures engendre un besoin proportionnel du grand air et des rafraîchissants.

Comme j'allais entrer dans un cabaret, un mendiant me tendit son chapeau, avec un de ces regards inoubliables qui culbuteraient les trônes, si l'esprit remuait la matière, et si l'oeil d'un magnétiseur faisait mûrir les raisins.

En même temps, j'entendis une voix qui chuchotait à mon oreille, une voix que je reconnus bien; c'était celle d'un bon Ange, ou d'un bon Démon, qui m'accompagne partout. Puisque Socrate avait son bon Démon, pourquoi n'aurai-je pas mon bon Ange, et pourquoi n'aurais-je pas l'honneur, comme Socrate, d'obtenir mon brevet de folie, signé du subtil Lélut et du bien avisé Baillarger?

Il existe cette différence entre le Démon de Socrate et le mien, que celui de Socrate ne se manifestait à lui que pour défendre, avertir, empêcher, et que le mien daigne conseiller, suggérer, persuader. Ce pauvre Socrate n'avait qu'un Démon prohibiteur; le mien est un grand affirmateur, le mien est un Démon d'action, un Démon de combat.

Or, sa voix me chuchotait ceci: 'Celui-là seul est l'égal d'un autre, qui le prouve, et celui-là seul est digne de la liberté, qui sait la conquérir.'

Immédiatement, je sautai sur mon mendiant. D'un seul coup de poing, je lui bouchai un oeil, qui devint, en une seconde, gros comme une balle. Je cassai un de mes ongles à lui briser deux dents, et comme je ne me sentais pas assez fort, étant né délicat et m'étant peu exercé à la boxe, pour assommer rapidement ce vieillard, je le saisis d'une main par le collet de son habit, de l'autre, je l'empoignai à la gorge, et je me mis à lui secouer vigoureusement la tête contre un mur. Je dois avouer que j'avais préalablement inspecté les environs d'un coup d'oeil, et que j'avais vérifié que dans cette banlieue déserte je me trouvais, pour un assez long temps, hors de la portée de tout agent de police.

Ayant ensuite, par un coup de pied lancé dans le dos, assez énergique pour briser les omoplates, terrassé ce sexagénaire affaibli, je me saisis d'une grosse branche d'arbre qui traînait à terre, et je le battis avec l'énergie obstinée des cuisiniers qui veulent attendrir un beefteack.

Tout à coup, – ô miracle! ô jouissance du philosophe qui vérifie l'excellence de sa théorie! – je vis cette antique carcasse se retourner, se redresser avec une énergie que je n'aurais jamais soupçonnée dans une machine si singulièrement détraquée, et, avec un regard de haine qui me parut de *bon augure*, le malandrin décrépit se jeta sur moi, me pocha les deux yeux, me cassa quatre dents, et avec la même branche d'arbre, me battit dru comme plâtre. – Par mon énergique médication, je lui avais donc rendu l'orgueil et la vie.

Alors, je lui fis force signes pour lui faire comprendre que je considérais la discussion comme finie, et me relevant avec la satisfaction d'un sophiste du Portique, je lui dis: 'Monsieur, *vous êtes mon égal!* veuillez me faire l'honneur de partager avec moi ma bourse; et souvenez-vous, si vous êtes réellement philanthrope, qu'il faut appliquer à tous vos confrères, quand ils vous demanderont l'aumône, la théorie que j'ai eu la *douleur* d'essayer sur votre dos.'

Il m'a bien juré qu'il avait compris ma théorie, et qu'il obéirait à mes conseils.

3. Here Serres is playing on the Latin etymology of *satura* as a mixed salad. Baudelaire, an excellent latinist, also constantly revives and revises the original meanings of verbal signs, thus foreshadowing that semiotic extension which we now call deconstructive.

4. Peter Brooks's conclusions on metaphorical transactions in narrative are of interest here:

Narrative, I suggested, may work according to a model that begins with a blinded and collapsed, inactive metaphor, unpacks the givens of this initial figure through the enactments of metonymy, then reaches a terminal enlightened, transactive metaphor. I have been interested by how often the initial blinded metaphor seems to concern transmission blocked – not only in the brief narratives 'All-Kinds-of-Fur' and 'The Musgrave Ritual,' but also in *Heart of Darkness*, where Marlow seeks illumination of his life in another's death; in *Great Expectations*, where deciphering his parents' tomb-stones is Pip's impossible but necessary task; in *Le Rouge et le noir*, which entitles its fourth chapter 'Un Père et un fils'; and in *Absalom, Absalom!*, where Rosa Coldfield in the first pages calls attention to the relation of telling and transmission. The successfully transacted and transactive metaphor of the end ought to permit a passing-on.

(1984: 322–3)

Bibliography

Abrahams, Roger (1971) 'The negro stereotype', in A. Paredes and E. Stekert (eds) *The Urban Experience and Folk Tradition*, Austin and London: University of Texas Press.

Austin, J. L. (1975 [1962]) *How to Do Things with Words*, 2nd edn, London, Oxford, and New York: Oxford University Press.

Bakhtin, Mikhail (1968 [1965]) *Rabelais and his World*, trans. H. Iowolsky, Cambridge, Mass.: MIT Press.

—(1973 [1963]) *Problems of Dostoevsky's Poetics*, trans. R. W. Rotsel, Ann Arbor: Ardis.

—(1981 [1975]) *The Dialogic Imagination*, trans. L. Emerson and M. Holquist, ed. M. Holquist, Austin, Texas, and London: University of Texas Press.

Bal, Mieke (1977) *Narratologie: essais sur la signification narrative dans quatre romans modernes*, Paris: Klincksieck.

Barthes, Roland (1966) *Critique et vérité*, Paris: Seuil.

—(1972 [1964]) 'Baudelaire's theater', in *Critical Essays*, trans. R. Howard, Evanston, Ill.: Northwestern University Press.

—(1974 [1970]) *S/Z*, trans. R. Miller, New York: Hill & Wang.

—(1975a [1966]) 'An introduction to structural analysis of narrative', *New Literary History* 6: 237–72.

—(1975b [1973]) *The Pleasure of the Text*, trans. R. Miller, New York: Hill & Wang.

—(1977) *Image, Music, Text*, trans. S. Heath, New York: Hill & Wang.

—(1978a [1964]) *Elements of Semiology*, trans. A. Lavers and C. Smith, New York: Hill & Wang.

—(1978b) *Leçon*, Paris: Seuil.

—(1978c [1953]) *Writing Degree Zero*, trans. A. Lavers and C. Smith, New York: Hill & Wang.

—(1982 [1968]) 'The effect of reality', in T. Todorov (ed.) *French Literary Criticism Today*, Cambridge: Cambridge University Press.

Baudelaire, Charles (1947–63) *Correspondance générale* (6 vols), ed. Jacques Crépet, Paris: Conard.

—(1975–6) *Oeuvres complètes* (2 vols), ed. C. Pichois, Paris: Gallimard.

Beaujour, Michel (1983) 'Short epiphanies: two contextual approaches to the French prose poem', in M. Caws and H. Riffaterre (eds) *The Prose Poem in France*, New York: Columbia University Press.

Bellemin-Noël, Jean (1986) 'Baudelaire et la chronique des âmes', in J.-C. Mathieu (ed.) *Territoires de l'imaginaire*, Paris: Seuil.

Benjamin, Walter (1969 [1961]) 'On some motifs in Baudelaire', in *Illuminations*, trans. H. Zohn, New York: Schocken Books.

—(1973 [1969] *Charles Baudelaire: a Lyric Poet in the Era of High Capitalism*, trans. H. Zohn, London: New Left Books.

Benveniste, Emile (1971 [1966]) *Problems in General Linguistics*, trans. M. E. Meek, Coral Gables, Fla.: University of Miami Press.

—(1974) *Problèmes de linguistique générale II*, Paris: Gallimard.

Bernard, Suzanne (1959) *Le Poème en prose de Baudelaire jusqu'à nos jours*, Paris: Nizet.

Bersani, Leo (1977) *Baudelaire and Freud*, Berkeley: University of California Press.

Blin, Georges (1948) *Le Sadisme de Baudelaire*, Paris: Corti.

Booth, Wayne C. (1961) *The Rhetoric of Fiction*, Chicago: University of Chicago Press.

—(1974) *A Rhetoric of Irony*, Chicago: University of Chicago Press.

Brecht, Bertolt (1967) *Gesammelte Werke, Vols 15 and 17 (Schriften zum Theater,* 1 and 3), Frankfurt: Suhrkamp.

Brémond, Claude (1973) *Logique du récit*, Paris: Seuil.

Brémond, Claude and Verrier, J. (1984) 'Afanasiev and Propp', trans. T. Pavel and M. Randall, *Style* 18: 177–95.

Brook, Peter (1972 [1968]) *The Empty Stage*, Harmondsworth: Penguin.

Brooke-Rose, Christine (1980) 'The readerhood of man', in S. Suleiman and I. Crosman (eds) *The Reader in the Text*, Princeton, NJ: Princeton University Press.

Brooks, Peter (1984) *Reading for the Plot: Design and Intention in Narrative*, New York: Knopf.

Bruss, Elizabeth (1977) 'The game of literature and some literary games', *New Literary History* 9: 153–72.

Butor, Michel (1961) *Histoire extraordinaire, essai sur un rêve de Baudelaire*, Paris: Gallimard.

Caillois, Roger (1962 [1958]) *Man, Play and Games*, trans. M. Barash, London: Thames & Hudson.

Cargo, Robert T. (1971) *Concordance to Baudelaire's 'Petits poèmes en prose'*, Alabama: University of Alabama Press.

Carrard, Philippe (1984) 'From reflexivity to reading; the criticism of Lucien Dällenbach', *Poetics Today* 5(4): 839–56.

Caws, MaryAnn and Riffaterre, Hermine (1983) *The Prose Poem in France: Theory and Practice*, New York: Columbia University Press.

Certeau, Michel de (1980) 'On the oppositional practices of everyday life', *Social Text* 3 (Fall 1980): 3–43.

—(1982) 'La lecture absolue', in L. Dällenbach and J. Ricardou (eds) *Problèmes actuels de la lecture*, Paris: Clancier-Guénaud.

Chambers, Ross (1971a) *L'Ange et l'automate: Variations sur le mythe de l'actrice, de Nerval à Proust*, Paris: Minard.

—(1971b) '"L'art sublime du comédien" ou le regardant et le regardé', *Saggi e ricerche di letteratura francese* XI: 189–260.

—(1980) '"Je" dans les tableaux parisiens de Baudelaire', *Nineteenth Century French Studies* IX (1–2): 59–68.

—(1982a) 'Le secret est un oeuf: Lecture d'une fable de La Fontaine', *Versants* 2: 75–85.

—(1982b) 'Le texte "difficile" et son lecteur', in L. Dällenbach and J. Ricardou (eds) *Problèmes actuels de la lecture*, Paris: Clancier-Guénaud.

—(1984) *Story and Situation: Narrative Seduction and the Power of Fiction*, Minneapolis: University of Minnesota Press.

—(1985) 'Baudelaire et la pratique de la dédicace', *Saggi e ricerche di letteratura francese* XXIV: 121–40.

—(1986) 'Violence du récit: Mérimée, Bocacce, Cortazar', *Canadian Review of Comparative Literature/Revue canadienne de littérature comparée* XIII (2): 159–86.

—(1987a) 'Are Baudelaire's "Tableaux parisiens" about Paris?', in M. Issacharoff and A. Whiteside (eds) *On Referring in Literature*, Indiana: Indiana University Press.

—(1987b) *Mélancholie et opposition: les débuts du modernisme en France*, Paris: Corti.

Chatman, Seymour (1978) *Story and Discourse: Narrative Structure in Fiction and Film*, Ithaca, NY: Cornell University Press.

Cohn, Dorrit (1978) *Transparent Minds: Narrative Modes for Presenting Consciousness in Fiction*, Princeton, NJ: Princeton University Press.

Coquet, Jean-Claude (1973) *Sémiotique littéraire: contribution à l'analyse sémantique du discours*, Tours: Mame.

Coste, Didier (1980) 'Trois conceptions du lecteur', *Poétique* 43: 354–71.

Crago, Hugh (1981) 'The child as aidos: oral narrative and spontaneous narratives of pre-school children', Paper, Australian National University, Canberra.

Culler, Jonathon (1975) *Structuralist Poetics: Structuralism, Linguistics and the Study of Literature*, Ithaca, NY: Cornell University Press.

—(1976) 'Presupposition and intertextuality', *Modern Language Notes* 91: 1380–96.

—(1981) *The Pursuit of Signs: Semiotics, Literature, Deconstruction*, Ithaca, NY: Cornell University Press.

—(1982) *On Deconstruction: Theory and Criticism after Structuralism*, Ithaca, NY: Cornell University Press.

—(1984) 'Problems in the theory of fiction', *Diacritics* (Spring 1984): 2–11.

Dällenbach, Lucien (1976) 'Intertexte et autotexte', *Poétique* 27: 282–96.

—(1977) *Le récit spéculaire: essai sur la mise en abyme*, Paris: Seuil.

Dällenbach, Lucien and Ricardou, Jean (eds) (1982) *Problèmes actuels de la lècture*, Paris: Clancy-Guénaud.

Delas, D. and Filliolet, J. (1973) *Linguistique et poétique*, Paris: Larousse.

Delcroix, Maurice (1977) 'Un poème en prose de Baudelaire, "Les yeux des pauvres"', *Cahiers d'analyse textuelle* XIX: 47–65.

Deleuze, Gilles (1968) *Différence et répétition*, Paris: Presses Universitaires de France.

—(1983) *Cinéma I: L'Image – mouvement*, Paris: Minuit.

—(1985) *Cinéma II: L'Image – temps*, Paris: Minuit.

Deleuze, Gilles and Guattari, Felix (1975) *Kafka: pour une littérature mineure*, Paris, Minuit.

—(1980) *Mille plateaux*, Paris: Minuit.

Deloffre, F. (1955) Introduction to Marivaux, *Le Petit-maître corrigé*, Geneva: Droz.

de Man, Paul (1971) *Blindness and Insight: Essays in the Rhetoric of Contemporary Criticism*, New York: Oxford University Press.

—(1979) *Allegories of Reading: Figural Language in Rousseau, Nietzsche, Rilke and Proust*, New Haven: Yale University Press.

—(1981) 'Pascal's allegory of persuasion', in S. J. Greenblatt (ed.) *Allegory and Representation*, Baltimore and London: Johns Hopkins University Press.

Derrida, Jacques, (1977a [1972]) 'Signature, event, context', *Glyph* 1: 172–97.

—(1977b) 'Limited Inc.', *Glyph* 2: 162–254.

Douglas, Mary (1966) *Purity and Danger: an Analysis of Concepts of Pollution and Taboo*, London: Routledge & Kegan Paul.

Dundes, Alan (1965) *The Study of Folklore*, Englewood Cliffs, NJ: Prentice Hall.

Eco, Umberto (1975) 'Looking for a logic of culture', in T. Sebeok (ed.) *The Tell-Tale Sign: A Survey of Semiotics*, Lisse: Peter de Ridder Press.

—(1976) *A Theory of Semiotics*, Bloomington: Indiana University Press.

—(1979) *The Role of the Reader: Explorations in the Semiotics of Texts*, Bloomington: Indiana University Press.

—(1984) *Semiotics and the Philosophy of Language*, London: Macmillan.

Eichenbaum, Boris (1978 [1925 and 1929]) 'O. Henry and the theory of the short story' and 'Literary environment', in L. Matejka and K. Pomorska (eds) *Readings in Russian Poetics*, Ann Arbor, Mich.: University of Michigan Press.

Elam, Keir (1980) *The Semiotics of Theatre and Drama*, New York and London: Methuen.

Fairlie, Alison (1976 [1967]) 'Observations sur les "Petits poèmes en prose"', in A. Noyer-Weidner (ed.) *Baudelaire*, Darmstadt: Wissenschaftliche Buchgesellschaft.

Fanto, James (1978) 'Speech act theory and its applications to the study of literature', in R. W. Bailey, L. Matejka, and P. Steiner (eds) *The Sign: Semiotics Around the World*, Ann Arbor, Mich.: Michigan Slavic Publications.

Farcy, Gérard-Denis (1986) 'De l'obstination narratologique', *Poétique* 68: 491–506.

Felman, Shoshana (1983 [1980]) *The Literary Speech Act: Don Juan with J. L. Austin or Seduction in Two Languages*, trans. C. Porter, Ithaca, NY: Cornell University Press.

Fineman, Joel (1981) 'The structure of allegorical desire', in S. J. Greenblatt (ed.) *Allegory and Representation*, Baltimore and London: Johns Hopkins University Press.

Finnegan, Ruth (1977) *Oral Poetry: Its Nature, Significance and Social Context*, Cambridge: Cambridge University Press.

Fish, Stanley E. (1976) 'How to do things with Austin and Searle: speech act theory and literary criticism', *Modern Language Notes* 91: 983–1025.

Fiske, John (1982) *Introduction to Communication Studies*, London and New York: Methuen.

Flahault, François (1978) *La Parole intermédiaire*, Paris: Seuil.

—(1981) 'Sur *S/Z* et l'analyse des récits', *Poétique* 47: 303–14.

Fowler, Roger (1977) *Linguistics and the Novel*, London: Methuen.

Frank, Joseph (1945) 'Spatial form in modern literature', *Sewance Review* 53: 221–40, 433–56, 643–53; reprinted in Joseph Frank (1968) *The Widening Gyre: Crisis and Mastery in Modern Literature*, Bloomington: Indiana University Press.

Freud, Sigmund (1960 [1905]) *Jokes and their Relation to the Unconscious*, The Standard Edition, Vol. VIII, ed. J. Strachey, London: The Hogarth Press.

—(1982 [1915]) *Introductory Lectures on Psychoanalysis*, trans. J. Strachey, Harmondsworth: Penguin.

Genette, Gérard (1966) *Figures I*, Paris: Seuil.

—(1969) *Figures II*, Paris: Seuil.

—(1972) *Figures III*, Paris: Seuil.

—(1980 [1972]) *Narrative Discourse: an Essay in Method*, trans. J. Lewin, Ithaca, NY: Cornell University Press.

—(1982) *Figures of literary discourse*, trans. A. Sheridan, New York: Columbia University Press.

—(1983) *Nouveau discours du récit*, Paris: Seuil.

—(1987) *Seuils*, Paris: Seuil.

Girard, René (1965 [1961]) *Deceit, Desire, and the Novel; Self and Other in Literary Structure*, trans. Y. Freccero, Baltimore: Johns Hopkins University Press.

—(1977 [1972]) *Violence and the Sacred*, trans. P. Gregory, Baltimore: Johns Hopkins University Press.

Goffmann, Erving (1974) *Frame Analysis*, Harmondsworth: Penguin.

—(1981) *Forms of Talk*, Philadelphia: University of Pennsylvania Press.

Goldmann, Lucien (1975 [1965]) *Towards a Sociology of the Novel*, rev. edn, trans. A. Sheridan, London: Tavistock.

Goody, Jack and Watt, Ian (1968) 'The consequences of literacy', in J. Goody (ed.) *Literacy in Traditional Societies*, Cambridge: Cambridge University Press.

Greenblatt, S. J. (ed.) (1981) *Allegory and Representation*, Baltimore and London: Johns Hopkins University Press.

Greimas, A. J. (1970) *Du sens: Essais sémiotiques*, Paris: Seuil.

—(1976) 'The cognitive dimension of narrative discourse', *New Literary History* 7: 433–48.

—(1983 [1966]) *Structural Semantics: an Attempt at a Method*, Lincoln: University of Nebraska Press.

Greimas, A. J. and Courtés, J. (1982 [1979]) *Semiotics and Language: An Analytical Dictionary*, trans. L. Crist, D. Patte, *et al.*, Bloomington: Indiana University Press.

Grice, H. P. (1975) 'Logic and conversation', in P. Cole and J. L. Morgan (eds) *Speech Acts*, New York: Academic Press.

Gunew, Sneja and Reid, Ian (eds) (1984) *Not the Whole Story: Tellings and Tailings from the ASPACLS Conference on 'Narrative'*, Sydney: Local Consumption.

Hamburger, Käte (1973 [1957]) *The Logic of Literature*, 2nd rev. edn, trans. M. J. Rose, Bloomington: Indiana University Press.

Harari, Josué (ed.) (1979) *Textual Strategies. Perspectives in Post-Structuralist Criticism*, Ithaca, NY: Cornell University Press.

Hartman, Geoffrey (1980) *Criticism in the Wilderness: The Study of Literature Today*, New Haven: Yale University Press.

—(1981) *Saving the Text*, Baltimore: Johns Hopkins University Press.

Hawkes, Terence (1972) *Metaphor*, London: Methuen.

—(1977) *Structuralism and Semiotics*, London: Methuen.

Holland, Norman (1968) *The Dynamics of Literary Response*, New York: Oxford University Press.

Holub, Robert (1984) *Reception Theory: a Critical Introduction*, New York and London: Methuen.

Huizinga, Johan (1970 [1944]) *Homo Ludens: a Study of the Play Element in Culture*, London: Paladin.

Hutcheon, Linda (1984) *Narcissistic Narrative: The Metafictional Paradox*, New York and London: Methuen.

—(1985) *A Theory of Parody: The Teachings of Twentieth-Century Art Forms*, New York and London: Methuen.

Hyde, Lewis (1983) *The Gift: Imagination and the Erotic Life of Property*, New York: Random House.

Ingarden, Roman (1973 [1965]) *The Literary Work of Art*, trans. G. G. Grabowicz, Evanston, Ill.: Northwestern University Press.

Iser, Wolfgang (1974 [1972]) *The Implied Reader: Patterns of Communication in Prose Fiction from Bunyan to Beckett*, Baltimore: Johns Hopkins University Press.

—(1978 [1976]) *The Act of Reading: A Theory of Aesthetic Response*, Baltimore: Johns Hopkins University Press.

—(1982) 'Interaction between text and reader', in S. Suleiman and I. Crosman (eds) *The Reader in the Text*, Princeton, NJ: Princeton University Press.

Issacharoff, Michael (1976) *L'Espace et la nouvelle*, Paris: Corti.

—(1978) 'Qu'est-ce que l'espace littéraire?', *L'Information littéraire* 30: 117–22.

—(1985) *Le Spectacle du discours*, Paris: Corti.

Jackson, Rosemary (1981) *Fantasy: the Literature of Subversion*, New York and London: Methuen.

Jakobson, Roman (1960) 'Closing statement: linguistics and poetics', in T. A. Sebeok (ed.) *Style in Language*, Cambridge, Mass.: MIT Press.

—(1963) *Essais de linguistique générale*, trans. N. Ruwet, Paris: Minuit.

—(1973) *Questions de poétique*, Paris: Seuil.

Jauss, Hans (1982 [1977]) *Toward an Aesthetic of Reception*, trans. T. Bahti, Brighton: Harvester.

Johnson, Barbara (1979) *Défigurations du langage poétique: la seconde révolution baudelairienne*, Paris: Flammarion.

—(1980) *The Critical Difference: Essays in the Contemporary Rhetoric of Reading*, Baltimore: Johns Hopkins University Press.

—(1983) 'Reading constants: the practice of the prose poem', in M. Caws and H. Riffaterre (eds) *The Prose Poem in France*, New York: Columbia University Press.

Jones, Louisa E. (1984) *Sad Clowns and Pale Pierrots*, Lexington, Ky.: French Forum.

Kaufman, Vincent (1982) 'Le tiers-lecteur', in L. Dällenbach and J. Ricardou (eds) *Problèmes actuels de la lecture*, Paris: Clancier-Guénaud.

Kestner, Joseph (1981) 'Secondary illusion: the novel and the spatial arts', in J. R. Smitten and A. Daghistany (eds) *Spatial Form in Narrative*, Ithaca and London: Cornell University Press.

Kopp, Robert (ed.) (1969) *Charles Baudelaire: Petits poëmes en prose*, Paris: Corti.

Kristeva, Julia (1980) *Desire in Language: a Semiotic Approach to Literature and Art*, New York: Columbia University Press.

—(1982 [1969]) *Semeiotikè*, New York: Columbia University Press.

—(1984 [1974]) *Revolution in Poetic Language*, trans. M. Waller, New York: Columbia University Press.

Labov, William (1972) *Language in the Inner City: Studies in the Black English Vernacular*, Philadelphia: University of Pennsylvania Press.

La Fontaine (1981) *Selected Fables*, trans. J. Michie, Harmondsworth: Penguin.

Lanser, Susan S. (1981) *The Narrative Act: Point of View in Prose Fiction*, Princeton, NJ: Princeton University Press.

Leclaire, Serge (1968) *Psychanalyser*, Paris: Seuil.

—(1971) *Démasquer le réel*, Paris: Seuil.

Levin, Samuel (1959) *Linguistic Structures in Poetry*, La Haye: Mouton.

Lewis, David (1973) *Counterfactuals*, Cambridge, Mass.: Harvard University Press.

Lima, Luiz Costa (1985) 'Social representation and mimesis', *New Literary History* XVI (Spring 1985) 3: 447–66.

Maclean, Marie (1982) 'Baudelaire and the paradox of procreation', *Studi francesi* 76: 87–98.

—(1987) 'Oppositional practice in women's traditional narrative', *New Literary History* 19(1): 37–50.

Mannoni, O. (1969) *Clefs pour l'imaginaire ou l'autre scène*, Paris: Seuil.

Maranda, Pierre (1972) *Mythology*, London: Penguin.

—(1980) 'The dialectic of metaphor', in S. Suleiman and I. Crosman (eds) *The Reader in the Text*, Princeton, NJ: Princeton University Press.

Marin, Louis (1978) *Le Récit est un piège*, Paris: Minuit.

—(1980) 'Toward a theory of reading in the visual arts: Poussin's *The Arcadian Shepherds*', in S. Suleiman and I. Crosman (eds) *The Reader in the Text*, Princeton, NJ: Princeton University Press.

Martinez-Bonati, Felix (1981) *Fictive Discourse and the Structures of Literature*, Ithaca: Cornell University Press.

Matejka, Ladislav and Pomorska, Krystyna (eds) (1978) *Readings in Russian Poetics*, Ann Arbor, Mich.: University of Michigan Press.

Mathieu, Jean-Claude (ed.) (1986) *Territoires de l'imaginaire: pour Jean-Pierre Richard*, Paris: Seuil.

Mauron, Charles (1966) *Le dernier Baudelaire*, Paris: Corti.

Mehlman, Jeffrey (1974) 'Baudelaire with Freud: theory and pain', *Diacritics* (Spring 1974): 7–13.

Mitchell, W. J. T. (ed.) (1980) *On Narrative*, Chicago: University of Chicago Press.

Moi, Toril (1985) *Sexual/Textual Politics: Feminist Literary Theory*, London and New York: Methuen.

Mulvey, Laura (1975) 'Visual pleasure and narrative cinema', *Screen* 16 (3): 6–18.

Nies, Fritz (1964) *Poesie in prosaischer Welt. Untersuchungen zum Prosagedicht bei Aloysius Bertrand und Baudelaire*, Heidelberg: C. Winter.

—(1976 [1964–71]) 'Der Poet als Flâneur und der "zyklische" Charakter der "Petits poèmes en prose"', in A. Noyer-Weidner (ed.) *Baudelaire*, Darmstadt: Wissenschaftliche Buchgesellschaft.

Norris, Christopher (1982) *Deconstruction: Theory and Practice*, New York and London: Methuen.

—(1985) *Contest of Faculties: Philosophy and Theory after Deconstruction*, New York and London: Methuen.

Noyer-Weidner, A. (ed.) (1976) *Baudelaire*, Darmstadt: Wissenschaftliche Buchgesellschaft.

Ohmann, Richard (1973) 'Literature as act', in S. Chatman (ed.) *Approaches to*

Poetics, New York and London: Columbia University Press.

Ong, Walter (1975) 'The writer's audience is always a fiction', *Proceedings of the Modern Language Association* 90: 9–21.

—(1977) *Interfaces of the Word*, Ithaca and London: Cornell University Press.

—(1981) *Fighting for Life: Contest, Sexuality, and Consciousness*, Ithaca: Cornell University Press.

—(1982) *Orality and Literacy: The Technologizing of the Word*, London and New York: Methuen.

Pavel, Thomas G. (1986) *Fictional Worlds*, Cambridge, Mass.: Harvard University Press.

Pavis, Patrice (1982) *Languages of the Stage: Essays in the Semiology of the Theatre*, New York: Performing Arts Journal Publications.

Picard, Michel (1986) *La Lecture comme jeu*, Paris: Minuit.

Piwowarczyk, M. A. (1976) 'The narratee and the situation of enunciation', *Genre* 9 (2): 161–77.

Plessen, Jacques (1967) *Promenade et poésie*, Paris: Mouton.

Pratt, Mary Louise (1977) *Toward a Speech Act Theory of Literary Discourse*, Bloomington: Indiana University Press.

—(1986) 'Ideology and speech-act theory', *Poetics Today* 7 (1): 59–71.

Prendergast, Christopher (1986) *The Order of Mimesis: Balzac, Stendhal, Nerval, Flaubert*, Cambridge: Cambridge University Press.

Prévost, Jean (1953) *Baudelaire. Essai sur l'inspiration et la création poétiques*, Paris: Mercure de France.

Prince, Gerald (1973a) *A Grammar of Stories*, The Hague: Mouton.

—(1973b) 'Introduction à l'étude du narrataire', *Poétique* 14: 178–96.

—(1980a) 'Aspects of a grammar of narrative', *Poetics Today* 1 (3): 49–63.

—(1980b) 'Notes on the text as reader', in S. Suleiman and I. Crosman (eds) *The Reader in the Text*, Princeton, NJ: Princeton University Press.

—(1982) *Narratology: the Form and Functioning of Narrative*, The Hague: Mouton.

—(1983a) 'Narrative pragmatics, message, and point', *Poetics* 12: 527–36.

—(1983b) 'Worlds with style', *Philosophy and Literature* 7: 78–88.

Propp, Vladimir (1968 [1928]) *Morphology of the Folktale*, 2nd rev. edn, Austin and London: University of Texas Press.

—(1972) 'Transformations of the wondertale', in P. Maranda (ed.) *Mythology*, London: Penguin.

—(1984) *Theory and History of Folklore*, trans. A. Y. and R. P. Martin *et al.*, Minneapolis: University of Minnesota Press.

Rabinowitz, Peter (1977) 'Truth in fiction: a re-examination of audiences', *Critical Inquiry* 4: 121–42.

—(1980) '"What's Hecuba to us?": the audience's experience of literary borrowing', in S. Suleiman and I. Crosman (eds) *The Reader in the Text*, Princeton, NJ: Princeton University Press.

—(1985) 'The turn of the glass key: popular fiction as reading strategy', *Critical Inquiry* 11: 418–31.

Rabkin, Eric S. (1981) 'Spatial form and plot', in J. R. Smitten and A. Daghistany (eds) *Spatial Form in Narrative*, Ithaca: Cornell University Press.

'Readers and spectators: some views and reviews', *New Literary History* 8, Special Issue, 1976.

'Reading, interpretation, response', *Genre* 10: 363–453, Special Section, 1977.

Ricardou, Jean (1978) *Nouveaux problèmes du roman*, Paris: Seuil.

Riffaterre, Michel (1959) 'Criteria for style analysis', *Word* 15: 154–74.

—(1971) *Essais de stylistique structurale*, Paris: Flammarion.

—(1978) *Semiotics of Poetry*, Bloomington: Indiana University Press.

—(1983a) 'On the prose poem's formal features', in M. Caws and H. Riffaterre (eds) *The Prose Poem in France*, New York: Columbia University Press.

—(1983b [1979]) *Text Production*, New York: Columbia University Press.

Rimmon-Kenan, Shlomith (1983) *Narrative Fiction: Contemporary Poetics*, New York and London: Methuen.

Riquer, Martin de (1957 [1952]) *Les Chansons de geste françaises*, 2nd edn, trans. I. Cluzel, Paris: Nizet.

Rousset, Jean (1982) 'La question du narrataire', in L. Dällenbach and J. Ricardou (eds) *Problèmes actuels de la lecture*, Paris: Clancy-Guénaud.

Roustang, François (1983 [1980]) *Psychoanalysis Never Lets Go*, Baltimore: Johns Hopkins University Press.

Ruthrof, Horst G. (1981) *The Reader's Construction of Narrative*, London: Routledge & Kegan Paul.

Ryan, Marie-Laure (1984) 'Fiction as a logical, ontological, and illocutionary issue', *Style* 18: 121–39.

Sadock, Jerrold (1974) *Toward a Linguistic Theory of Speech Acts*, New York: Academic Press.

Scheub, Harold (1975) 'Oral narrative process and the use of models', *New Literary History* 6(2): 353–77.

Scholes, Robert (1980) 'Language, narrative and anti-narrative', *Critical Inquiry* 7(1): 204–12.

—(1984) *Structuralism in Literature*, New Haven: Yale University Press.

Scholes, Robert and Kellog, R. (1968) *The Nature of Narrative*, New York: Oxford University Press.

Schor, Naomi (1980) 'Fiction as interpretation, interpretation as fiction', in S. Suleiman and I. Crosman (eds) *The Reader in the Text*, Princeton, NJ: Princeton University Press.

Searle, John R. (1969) *Speech Acts: An Essay in the Philosophy of Language*, Cambridge: Cambridge University Press.

—(1975) 'The logical status of fictional discourse', *New Literary History* 6 (2): 319–32.

—(1977) 'Reiterating the differences: a reply to Derrida', *Glyph* 1: 198–208.

Sebeok, T. (ed.) (1975) *The Tell-Tale Sign: A Survey of Semiotics*, Lisse: Peter de Ridder Press.

Serres, Michel (1977) *Hermes, IV: La distribution*, Paris: Minuit.

—(1982 [1980]) *The Parasite*, trans. L. R. Schehr, Baltimore: Johns Hopkins University Press.

—(1985) *Les cinq sens*, Paris: Grasset.

Smith, Barbara Herrnstein (1979 [1978]) *On the Margins of Discourse: The Relation of Literature to Language*, Chicago: University of Chicago Press.

—(1980) 'Narrative versions, narrative theories', *Critical Inquiry* 7(1): 213–36.

Smitten, Jeffrey R. and Daghistany, Ann (eds) (1981) *Spatial Form in Narrative*, Ithaca: Cornell University Press.

Souriau, Etienne (1970 [1950]) *Les deux cent mille situations dramatiques*, Paris: Flammarion.

Spence, Donald (1982) *Narrative Truth and Historical Truth: Meaning and Inter-pretation in Psychoanalysis*, New York: W. W. Norton.

Stanzel, Franz K. (1984 [1979]) *A Theory of Narrative*, trans. C. Goedsche, Cambridge and New York: Cambridge University Press.

Starobinski, Jean (1967) 'Sur quelques répondants allégoriques de l'artiste', *Revue de l'histoire littéraire de la France* 67: 402–12.

—(1970) *Portrait de l'artiste en saltimbanque*, Geneva: Skira.

Stewart, Susan (1978) *Nonsense: Aspects of Intertextuality in Folklore and Literature*, Baltimore and London: Johns Hopkins University Press.

—(1984) *On Longing: Narratives of the Miniature, the Gigantic, the Souvenir, the Collection*, Baltimore and London: Johns Hopkins University Press.

Suleiman, Susan (1977) 'Le récit exemplaire: parabole, fable, roman à thèse', *Poétique* 32: 468–89.

—(1986) 'La maîtrise et le transfert', *Poétique* 68: 463–73.

Suleiman, Susan and Crosman, Inge (eds) (1980) *The Reader in the Text: Essays on Audience and Interpretation*, Princeton, NJ: Princeton University Press.

Thompson, Stith (1955–8) *Motif Index to the Folktale*, Copenhagen: Rosen, Kilde, & Bagger.

Threadgold, Terry (1986) 'Semiotics – ideology – language', in T. Threadgold *et al.* (eds) *Semiotics Ideology Language*, Sydney: Sydney Association for Studies in Society and Culture.

Todorov, Tzvetan (1969) *Grammaire du Décaméron*, The Hague: Mouton.

—(1973 [1970]) *The Fantastic: A Structural Approach to a Literary Genre*, trans. R. Howard, Cleveland: Case Western Reserve.

—(1977 [1971]) *The Poetics of Prose*, trans. R. Howard, Ithaca: Cornell University Press.

Tompkins, Jane (1980) *Reader-Response Criticism: from Formalism to Post-Structuralism*, Baltimore: Johns Hopkins University Press.

Turner, John A. (1977) *The Signifying Monkey: a Bit of American Folklore*, Compton, Calif.: J. A. Turner.

Ubersfeld, Anne (1974) *Le Roi et le bouffon*, Paris: Corti.

—(1977) *Lire le théâtre*, Paris: Ed. Sociales.

—(1981) *L'Ecole du spectateur: Lire le théâtre II*, Paris: Ed. Sociales.

Valdes, Mario J. and Miller, Owen J. (eds) (1978) *Interpretation of Narrative*, Toronto: University of Toronto Press.

Van Dijk, Teun (1977) *Text and Context: Explorations in the Semantics and Pragmatics of Discourse*, London and New York: Longman.

Warning, Rainer (1979) 'Pour une pragmatique du discours fictionnel', *Poétique* 39: 321–37.

Waugh, Patricia (1984) *Metafiction: The Theory and Practice of Self-Conscious Fiction*, London and New York: Methuen.

Wright, Elizabeth (1984) *Psychoanalytic Criticism: Theory in Practice*, London and New York: Methuen.

Index